# The Trout
## A Fisherman's Natural History

# The Trout
## A Fisherman's Natural History

Rupert Watson

SWAN·HILL
PRESS

First published in the UK in 1993
by Swan Hill Press
an imprint of Airlife Publishing Ltd

**British Library Cataloguing in Publication Data**
A catalogue record for this book
is available from the British Library

ISBN 1 85310 235 0

Printed by Livesey Ltd, Shrewsbury.

# Swan Hill Press
an imprint of Airlife Publishing Ltd
101 Longden Road, Shrewsbury SY3 9EB

# Contents

# Acknowledgements

Despite the ascendancy of the computer, every word of this book was first inscribed in longhand. My handwriting is appalling — a luxury apparently allowed, if not expected, of the legal profession — and Melanie Mott can read it better than I can. Having transcribed my hieroglyphics onto her word processor, she was then cajoled into seemingly innumerable revisions of each chapter, until the book seemed to read as easily as its contents and my abilities allowed. No thanks are enough for her efforts.

To Tom Heaton, I am indebted for his skills as a BBC editor which he used with incredible patience on each page of this book. If any sentences lack clarity, it is because I have obstinately ignored his suggestions for their amendment. He is also a writer and gave freely of that most precious of all resources — time.

Colin McKelvie showed enough confidence in my first chapter to recommend the publishers give me a contract to write the other ten. That was an act of faith on his part which is something that, as a first-time author, I will never forget and hope he will never regret. Since then he has taken me fishing with his family in Lough Melvin and helped me over many of the hurdles that precede publication.

In Kenya, Charles Dewhurst checked my first chapter and Peter Walker read several subsequent ones; being a master of legal brevity, he taught me to dispense with so much verbiage. Ros Aveling read part of the book too, and as a zoologist, fielded an almost ceaseless succession of questions on basic biology.

Over in England, one 'Old Trout' helped me with the collection of research material as well as with much else. Nick Giles and Niall Graham both read the manuscript at different stages in its evolution and their comments on its errors and omissions were as invaluable as their encouragement. The staff at the libraries of the Institute of Freshwater Ecology at Windermere and the Freshwater Fisheries Laboratory at Pitlochry gave me more help than I dared ask for. My brother Julian drew the vignettes which head and tail each chapter and if Clare Oldridge had never introduced me to her brother Andrew Johnston, who is a director of the publishers of this book, it might never have been written at all. Many others gave of their time and knowledge or showed me kindness and hospitality in the course of my researches — thank you all.

Writing a book is a lonely, tedious and often agonisingly painful journey up a mountain whose peak appears permanently hidden from view. Sometimes it seemed that only those who had travelled the same path were really able to help and encourage: then Tom was always there and so was Carmen when she could be.

# Introduction

There are few greater gifts that a parent can give a child, than an interest which endures through life. My father gave me two, trout fishing and natural history, and this book is the product of their union.

Today, trout fishing is more popular than it has ever been and there seem to be no signs that such popularity has yet reached its zenith. Fishermen travel further and further afield in search of their sport and hatcheries have sprung up all over Britain to satisfy the demand for trout with which to stock still and running waters. Now neither the absence of natural breeding facilities nor sustained fishing pressure is any bar to the continued maintenance of stocks of catchable fish.

Historically, those that hunt or shoot for sport have set out to present themselves as the custodians of their quarry, maintaining that through its pursuit, they derive an unparalleled understanding of its life and habits. Much of this public image is fostered in an attempt to delude both sportsmen and their critics. Many hunters are disturbed by a crisis of conscience that besets every sensitive person who kills what he loves, which is conveniently eased by the reassurance that they are naturalists first and killers second. Some, but not many, critics are also assuaged by such an argument. However, knowledge of the habits of prey obviously enhances any predator's prospects of catching it and there is no denying that many of those who hunt foxes or shoot birds or mammals know a great deal about the animals they kill.

Yet, perhaps because trout and fishermen inhabit different elements, the latter seem to have a remoter affinity for their quarry than do other field sports enthusiasts. Somehow this remoteness creates either reason or excuse for ignoring the patterns of life below the great divide of the water's surfaces. If some knowledge helps catch more fish, then it may be worth absorbing, but to gain an understanding of how trout live, for its own sake, remains sadly low on the list of most fishermen's priorities. 'Environmental awareness' is a catch phrase to which more than lip service is now paid, and increased access to and enjoyment of the countryside has stimulated a far more genuine enthusiasm for the preservation of its plants and animals. Nevertheless, for most fishermen and many naturalists, under water is out of sight and thus remains out of mind, and fish lead their lives unremarked.

I believe and hope that at least one of the reasons for so many fishermen's disinterest in the ways of trout is the lack of any freely available text on the subject, since the publication of *The Trout* in the New Naturalist series nearly twenty-five years ago. I have persevered in this belief in the course of my writing despite occasional doubts which threatened to metamorphose hope into despair. One of the first letters I received from a publisher rejected my idea of a natural history book on the grounds that 'What anglers want to know is how to catch the creature.' How I hope to prove him wrong and that not only will the contents of this book create a better understanding in the minds of fishermen of the ways and wiles of trout, but also that such understanding will add a new dimension to every visit to river bank or lake shore.

I did not even pass biology 'O' level, which I like to think may be an advantage in writing for others whose education was similarly deficient. To remedy any defects from this shortcoming, the text has been checked by two eminent Salmonid biologists. I do have a legal qualification which appears to be slipping into gradual redundancy but has served me well, I think, in cultivating a logical and sequential approach to the subject of the trout's natural history. Above all I love trout, in all their myriad colours, sizes and habitats. At present I am still at ease with my conscience in catching lots of them to eat but I have a feeling that the scales may one day begin to tip in favour of their preservation.

This book is about the species *Salmo trutta*, called 'brown trout' throughout unless I need to contrast non-migratory and migratory trout. Then 'brown trout' sometimes specifically means 'non-migratory trout' in contrast to migratory 'sea trout' but I think where it does, this is apparent.

In all but the last chapter, except where it is stated otherwise, the trout's environment should be taken as in its pristine natural state, quite unaffected by human interference. This is a Utopian condition which, with the ever-present danger of far-reaching airborne pollution, exists almost nowhere in the British Isles. Nevertheless, it is a state of affairs that at least provides an environmental yardstick against which to consider all aspects of the trout's biology and of the aquatic community to which it belongs.

I live in Kenya and in Chapter 10 have indulged myself by using the introduction of trout into East Africa as an example of the impact on indigenous fauna of such introductions. If by so doing, the book appears unbalanced, I can only say that an example was needed from somewhere and I know more about trout in Kenya than in any other country where Nature never dispersed them.

Quotations are included from time to time but only if they add an historical perspective to the text, which perhaps they also serve to lighten. There are many other contemporary writers with a more sensitive, poetic touch than mine — fishing is renowned for the quantity of literature on the subject and the quality of some of it — but there is a need to draw a line.

In 1879, the Reverend W. Houghton published a magnificently illustrated book entitled, like so many others, *British Freshwater Fishes*. In the last paragraph of his introduction he wrote that

'This book treats of the natural history . . .; it is not intended to supply information as to the various modes of angling, whether trolling, spinning, bottom-fishing, fly-fishing, etc., adopted in this country. For such information the reader will find all, and perhaps even more than he wants, in the various numerous handbooks which have been published on this subject.'

This book too, treats of natural history.

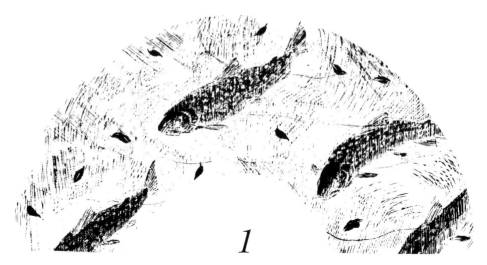

# 1
# *What, Where and Why?*

All Earth's creatures are on an evolutionary journey through time. Some seem continually coerced by environmental pressures into constant change in order to survive; for them the journey is an unremitting rush to avoid vanishing into oblivion. Others travel at a more leisurely pace, responding with only minimal modifications to barely perceptible pressures. Coelacanths *(Latimeria chalumnae)* from Indian Ocean depths have altered little in 350 million years; there has been little need for them to do so, but perhaps the price of their evolutionary indolence will be extinction. However, the forebears of today's trout were seldom granted the luxury of resting immutable for any length of time. Theirs was a turbulent world of massive climatic and topographical upheavals which forced them to adapt or face extinction. In the wider span of time, land masses shifted, islands were chipped off continents and barriers rose up to bar the free spread of fish through the sea. More recently, Ice Ages have ebbed and flowed, wreaking geological havoc in the process. And it was in response to these pressures that the trout's ancestors became trout and that trout themselves now seem to be diverging in so many different directions.

A study of trout, or of any other animal, must freeze its subject for an instant in the course of its evolvement, to see it as it is now, as a contemporary trout but it must never be forgotten that the trout is on a journey. Fossil records and some informed speculation may tell us where it has been, but we can only guess where it is going.

Zoologists call today's brown trout *Salmo trutta*, indicating that the fish is a member of the genus *Salmo* with its own distinctive species name of *trutta*. Sometimes an 'L.' or 'Linn.' follows the Latin name to denote that it was the Swedish naturalist Carl Linnaeus who first ascribed *trutta* to the genus *Salmo* in his great catalogue of the natural world, *Systema Naturae*.

Linnaeus classified species using a binomial Latin description for each and grouped genera into families, several of which made up an order. The tenth and definitive edition of his magnum opus was published in 1758 and since then genus *Salmo*, and species *trutta* in particular, has provided taxonomists with an almost unrivalled source of argument over its precise composition. For over two hundred years scientists have debated as to what extent variations of *trutta* may differ from the original type specimen before edging over the borders of that species into the confines of another, and have still reached no real consensus.

There is no certain definition of a species. If Darwin's theories of evolution are correct and species are the products of gradual change, any attempt to isolate a species is likely to run into difficulties as its frontiers become blurred by the continuation of such change. However, for general purposes most biologists accept that the principal characteristic of a species is that members of a species group are able to interbreed to produce fertile offspring, but cannot breed successfully with members of another species group. In addition, all members of the group usually resemble each other in their appearance, behaviour and metabolism. On a more practical level, a species may also be defined as a group of actually or potentially interbreeding populations isolated by reproductive, but not necessarily geographical, barriers from other such groups.

Being so widely farmed for food or to stock rivers and lakes for sporting purposes, brown trout and other related species have been subjected to more experimental breeding than any other family of fish. From such researches it is apparent that many of these species mock the accepted definition of such by successfully breeding with each other and, in many cases of hybridization, also producing fertile progeny. To confuse the issue further, experimental breeders have succeeded in crossing species from different genera although the resulting offspring are usually infertile. Nevertheless, for most of the twentieth century there was general agreement as to the specific components of the genus *Salmo* until, in 1988 its composition was radically amended. Now the results of recent researches have fuelled arguments for still further changes.

That the precise taxonomical classification of brown trout has caused such particular difficulties, is due simply to the extraordinary diversity of appearance and habit which has prompted the description of so many different sub-species, races, forms and varieties within the species itself. Izaak Walton was first to comment on this in his *Compleat Angler*, published in 1653. On the Third Day, Piscator observes

'. . . that there are several kinds of Trouts; but these several kinds are not considered but by very few men, for they go under the general name of Trouts: just as pigeons do in most places; . . . nay, the Royal Society have found and published lately that there be thirty and three kinds of Spiders: and yet all, for aught I know, go under that one general name of Spider. And t'is so with many kinds of fish, and of Trouts especially, which differ in their bigness, and shape, and spots, and colour; . . . and doubtless there is a kind of small trout which will never thrive to be big, that breeds very many more than others do that be of a larger size.'

In Walton's time, scientific theories of taxonomy were much in embryo and remained so until Linnaeus named what in the middle of the eighteenth century was called the Swedish river trout, *Salmo trutta*. He also recognised two other species of trout — *Salmo eriox* (sea trout) and *Salmo fario* (brook trout). His criterion for describing a separate species was simply that all its members exhibited similar physical and behavioural characteristics. It would therefore have been surprising if Linnaeus had not, for example, concluded that the freshwater-dwelling trout was a species totally separate from the large, silvery, migratory sea trout.

Then, Biblical belief in instant creation was almost universal; so too was the idea that a species was immutably fixed and although Linnaeus began to revise some of his ideas in later life his thinking left no room for any possibility of a species changing through the course of time:

'There are as many species in existence as were brought forth by the Supreme Being in the beginning . . . and consequently there cannot be more species now than at the moment of creation.'

During the early nineteenth century, travellers and explorers began to journey all over the globe, generating a massive increase in the body of world-wide scientific knowledge, especially through the collection of plant and animal specimens. These all needed names and with classification by physical characteristics and habits continuing as the accepted procedure, new species proliferated. Often they were described by virtue of the most minimal variations from the accepted norm, their discoverers encouraged not least by the scientific kudos garnered by having their name Latinised in that of the new species.

In 1836 William Yarrell produced a most comprehensive *History of British Fish* in which he accepted Linnaeus' three species but added *Salmo ferox* (the great lake trout) and *Salmo salmulus* (the parr or samlet, for many years considered a separate species but in due course recognised as no more than a young Atlantic salmon). Over the next twenty years individual naturalists elevated any number of different varieties of trout to species status, and by the middle of the century species were being split on the slightest pretext. Typical were the efforts of a Dr Knox who, in 1854, made a whimsical attempt at scientific classification in his *Lone Glens of Scotland*. There he identified seven different species of trout in Britain to all of which he conveniently refrained from ascribing Latin names:

'1. dark spotted lake trout. 2. red spotted estuary trout. 3. red spotted common river trout. 4. pink coloured red spotted river trout. 5. par trout. 6. dark spotted river trout. 7. great lake trout.'

Compilations of scientific information on different species were inevitably haphazard, not least as it was almost impossible for anyone to keep abreast of the deluge of scientific outpourings and competing theories on any given subject. However, in 1866 Dr Albert Gunther, the keeper of the zoological collection of the British Museum, produced a catalogue of its fishes. The author's qualifications made this a much respected compilation of information and species descriptions, and Gunther was undoubtedly more aware than most of his fellow-researchers of the difficulties he faced in attempting to unravel the trout's taxonomy:

'The Salmonidae and the vast literature on this family offer so many and so great difficulties to the ichthyologist, that as much patience and time are required for the investigation of a single species, as in other fishes for the whole of that family. The ordinary method followed by naturalists in distinguishing and determining species is here utterly inadequate; and I do not hesitate to assert that no one, however experienced in the study of other families of fishes, will be able to find his way through this labyrinth of variations without long preliminary study, and without a good collection for constant companion. Sometimes forms are met with so peculiarly and so constantly characterised, that no ichthyologist who has seen them will deny their specific rank; but in numerous other cases, one is much tempted to ask whether we have not to deal with a family which, being one of the most recent creation — no fossil true Salmo being known — is composed of forms not yet specifically differentiated.'

For all his awareness, Gunther was still much influenced by the prevailing trends towards dividing species, and the culmination of his efforts — and his *Catalogue of the Fishes in the British Museum* is a formidable work — was to name sea trout, *Salmo trutta* but also to accept and name four other separate species of migratory trout; these were Orkney sea trout *(S. orcadensis)*, Galway sea trout *(S. gallivensis)*, Welsh sea trout *(S. cambricus)* and Eastern sea trout *(S. brachypoma)*. Of non-migratory trout Gunther called river trout *Salmo fario* and recognised great lake trout *(S. ferox)*, Irish Gillaroo *(S. stomachicus)*, Welsh black-finned trout *(S. nigripinnis)* and Loch Leven trout *(S. levenensis)* as other separate species.

However, while Gunther laboured over the preparation of his Catalogue, strong winds of change began to blow through the scientific community, reaching near gale force with the publication in 1859 of Charles Darwin's *The Origin of Species*. Inevitably some scientists were more receptive to Darwin's radical theories of evolution than others, but eventually it was to become almost universally accepted that consideration of a particular species' ancestry was the most significant means of determining that species' relationships with others. No longer was commonality of physical or behavioural characteristics to be the determining factor in grouping individuals within a species, or species within a genus, but rather commonality of ancestry. And if the identity of the ascendants of any particular species was crucial in determining its taxonomical slot, then equally important were the nature of its potential descendants and the ability to produce them by interbreeding within the boundaries of the species.

Gunther was slower than most to accept these evolutionary theories, and the preparation of his Catalogue was probably too well advanced by the time Darwin's book was published, to admit such a radical change of thought, even if he was privately prepared to do so. A Danish scientist, Hans Widegren, writing with the benefit of Darwin's work, conjectured in 1863 that all supposed European species of trout were in fact varieties of the same one, but the highly qualified English ichthyologist, Francis Day, was the first to assert this with any certainty.

In 1887 Day published *British and Irish Salmonidae,* a magnificent compendium of information and opinion which also contained the results of many years of his own researches. His flexible thinking contrasted strongly with the more dogmatic ideas of Gunther and there was considerable animosity between them which surfaces frequently in Day's book. Their disparate standpoints epitomise perfectly the differences of opinion that initially prevailed within a scientific community confronted by such a radical theory as that proposed by Darwin.

The views Day expounded on speciation in brown trout remained largely unchallenged for nearly 100 years. Two passages from his book clearly show how his ideas differed drastically from those of most of his predecessors, and also how strong was Darwin's influence. Introducing the Salmonidae family, Day gives a hint of his thinking:

'As to the varieties and hybrids of trout. If, as seems probable, we merely possess one very plastic species subject to an almost unlimited amount of variation, that its largest race is found in the ocean, while in order to breed it ascends streams... we at once obtain a clue to the characters of the various so-called species, and relegate these different trout to a single form, in which numerous local races are to be found.'

Then, when moving on specifically to brown trout, he sums up his thoughts quite unequivocally:

'I find myself unable to accept the numerous species that have been described, believing those ichthyologists more correct who have considered them modifications of only one, which as *Salmo trutta* includes both the anadromous and non-migratory fresh-water forms.

For it must be evident when looking through the works of systematic zoologists, that the greatest number of false species among fishes are local varieties . . .; and that local races have been taken for distinct species. If among certain specimens an example is found similar to what exists in another so-called distinct species residing in a different locality, this individual specimen might be an indication that both were descended from a common origin, in short how it may be an instance of atavism, or reversion towards an ancestral form.'

Day went a long way towards convincing his fellow scientists of the good sense of his views, although some still felt that as a 'clumper' he had gone too far. Sir Herbert Maxwell's *British Freshwater Fishes* appeared in 1904 and while its author renounced the claims of species 'splitters', he still described bull-trout or sea trout *(S. eriox)*, salmon trout or white trout *(S. trutta)* and common or brown trout *(S. fario)* commenting that

'While entertaining profound respect for systematic ichthyologists in general and for Dr. Gunther in particular, I am quite unable to share his belief in the constancy of the ten species which he recognises among British trout, and I propose to deal with them as in three species only.'

In 1911 Tate Regan produced his *British Freshwater Fishes* which was to remain the definitive work on the subject for many years to come. There he grouped all British and European trout together, remarking that in the British Isles there was only one species of trout which was identical with the trout of Sweden named by Linnaeus, *Salmo trutta*.

Today the general view is still that all trout occurring naturally in Eurasia and North Africa belong to the one species but the question of speciation in trout is far from resolved. Taxonomists are continually questioning the basis of earlier classifications and using new evaluative methods to re-assess inter-species relationships. Some zoologists still ascribe small relict populations of rare trout on the fringes of the brown trout's range to separate species — e.g. the Atlas trout of North Africa, Lake Garda trout of Italy and marbled trout of Yugoslavia. Moreover, the increasing use of genetic analysis as an additional indicator of biological relationships is now fuelling speculation that previously considered races or sub-species may, after all, merit specific status. However, these views are still those of a minority and for the purposes of this book *Salmo trutta* encompasses all sub-species, races, forms and varieties of trout found naturally east of the Atlantic, migratory or not.

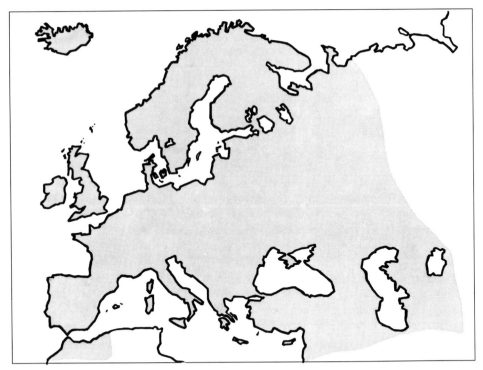

*The brown trout's present natural range.*

Brown trout are mainly a European fish but their natural distribution extends north to Iceland and south through several Mediterranean islands to the north-west coast of Africa. The present eastern limits of their range are more obscure but they were once certainly native to Lebanon and are still found in Turkey and the catchment areas which fill the Black, Caspian and Aral seas, as well as in the streams running off the northern slopes of the Hindu Kush range in Afghanistan and down both sides of the Ural mountains. Yet despite their migratory abilities, unlike their closest relative, the Atlantic salmon, brown trout have yet to colonise the eastern coast of North America — at least voluntarily.

The presence of the species within its natural range is governed by water temperature and the availability of adequate spawning facilities. If both these are suitable, and leaving aside mankind's potential for destroying otherwise habitable environments (Chapter Eleven), there are almost sure to be brown trout, except in some isolated lakes out of reach of the forces of dispersion.

There are many rivers flowing into the Mediterranean sea which harbour trout in the small streams of their upper catchment areas. Lower down, inhospitably warm temperatures now prevent trout reaching the sea where anyway they could not survive. During the chaos of the Pleistocene Ice Ages from which Europe only finally emerged about 10,000 years ago, the whole range of thermal limits suitable for trout and other cold water fish was continually shifting northwards and southwards or up and down mountain ranges. At the extent of maximum glaciation, nearly all the Mediterranean area was perfectly suited for migratory trout but, as the ice retreated and waters warmed, trout were gradually squeezed upstream by the progressive unsuitability of conditions below. Then, no longer able to exercise any migratory inclinations, they were finally confined to the cool streams on high mountains where, as resident brown trout, they remain today. There are populations of three-spined sticklebacks *(Gasterosteus aculeatus)* round the Mediterranean as well as on both sides of the Atlantic and in the Pacific basin, and this intriguing fish's distribution can be explained in the same way.

The composition of the genus *Salmo* has been the subject of just as much scientific controversy as the precise extent of the species' biological parameters. Until recently, the formal view was that three other species shared the genus *Salmo*, but in 1988 the significant, yet questionable decision was made to leave the brown trout with only one congener, *Salmo salar* (L), the Atlantic salmon.

In appearance, habits, distribution and life history, Atlantic salmon are so similar to migratory brown trout that it says much for the observations of Linnaeus and naturalists before him that they were able to distinguish them as two separate species. Since then the species has provided very little scope for argument over its taxonomic classification. There are various land-locked races in Canada, Sweden and Russia which from time to time individual scientists have ranked as separate species, but there is now almost total agreement that all salmon within the Atlantic basin belong to the species *salar.*

Atlantic salmon breed in fresh waters north of latitude 40° on both sides of the Atlantic ocean, as well as in Iceland and Greenland. Like migratory trout, young are hatched in fresh water before migrating to sea two or three years later. There they feed on small fish, sand eels, crustaceans and other open water organisms, growing at a prodigious rate before returning to the headwaters of their home river to breed. Some of these breeding adults reach the sea for a second time — in marked contrast to the Pacific salmon — before coming back to spawn again. As a result of their success in exploiting the deeper reaches of the ocean as a source of food, Atlantic salmon reach far greater average and maximum sizes than the other member of their genus; individuals of twenty kilograms or more are not unusual, especially in Norway.

Prior to 1989, rainbow trout (then *Salmo gairdneri*) and cutthroat trout (then *Salmo clarkii*) had also rested, albeit somewhat uncomfortably, in the genus Salmo, and their removal to the genus of Pacific salmon, *Oncorhynchus*, could not demonstrate more clearly the continually fluid state of taxonomic science and the constant need for re-classification as new information is brought to light. This particular generic relocation was based on the detailed comparison of bones from the jaws and skull of all species of both genera, supported by biochemical evidence from genetic analysis. In many respects it was long overdue, for even in 1914 Regan had argued, on the evidence to be gathered from skull features that

> '. . . the genus *Oncorhynchus* can be no longer maintained unless it be considered that the cranial characters warrant its separation from Salmo; in that case *Oncorhynchus* will include not only the Pacific salmon, but the Pacific trout also.'

Regan's wisdom was long ignored, suppressed largely by the importance attached to both rainbow and cutthroat trout's ability to breed more than once. This supposedly gave them a closer link with their cousins, the brown trout and Atlantic salmon, than with Pacific salmon which (apart from isolated populations of Japanese Masu salmon, *Oncorhynchus masu*) all die after spawning. However, on reassessment, greater significance was finally given to these physiological characteristics than to the more opportunistic differences in breeding strategy. Some taxonomists would prefer to see the Pacific trouts in their own distinct genus but for the time being at least, they belong in *Oncorhynchus*.

Not only have rainbow and cutthroat trout now joined the six species of Pacific salmon, but rainbow trout have also changed their species name. Formerly *Salmo gairdneri*, they are now *Oncorhynchus mykiss* after genetic analysis showed them to be the same species as trout from Kamchatka in north-east Russia which had been given the name *mykiss* (the original Kamchatkan word for them) long before *gairdneri* was ever used for American rainbows.

Both rainbows and cutthroats share a generally similar range and often even the same river in the Pacific basin, up the west coast of North America round the south of Alaska and to a lesser extent into the waters of north-east Asia. Cutthroats (but usually not rainbows) are found in the headwaters of rivers flowing east off the American continental divide. The two species are physically similar, often interbreeding to produce fertile offspring, and only just merit the distinction of specific status. Cutthroat trout have two short red marks down their lower jaws from which they derive their name. Rainbow trout are usually identified by a pinkish band along their bodies which varies in extent and intensity according to sex, age and proximity to spawning. Both Pacific species are most emphatically distinguished from brown trout by their heavily spotted tails.

Like brown trout, rainbows and cutthroats have resident, non-migratory forms which spend all their lives in fresh water, as well as migratory forms, breeding in fresh water then returning to feed in the sea. Sea-going rainbow trout are called steelheads and with such rich food supplies off the Pacific coasts, grow much larger than their river-dwelling brethren. Even the freshwater varieties are voracious feeders which largely accounts for their worldwide popularity as a stock fish.

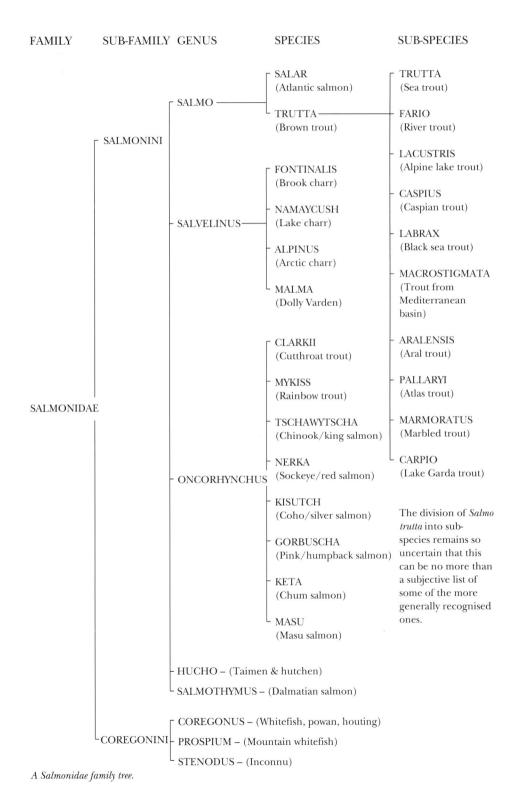

| FAMILY | SUB-FAMILY | GENUS | SPECIES | SUB-SPECIES |
|--------|-----------|-------|---------|-------------|

SALAR
(Atlantic salmon)

TRUTTA
(Sea trout)

SALMO

TRUTTA
(Brown trout)

FARIO
(River trout)

SALMONINI

LACUSTRIS
(Alpine lake trout)

FONTINALIS
(Brook charr)

CASPIUS
(Caspian trout)

NAMAYCUSH
(Lake charr)

SALVELINUS

LABRAX
(Black sea trout)

ALPINUS
(Arctic charr)

MACROSTIGMATA
(Trout from
Mediterranean
basin)

MALMA
(Dolly Varden)

CLARKII
(Cutthroat trout)

ARALENSIS
(Aral trout)

MYKISS
(Rainbow trout)

PALLARYI
(Atlas trout)

SALMONIDAE

TSCHAWYTSCHA
(Chinook/king salmon)

MARMORATUS
(Marbled trout)

NERKA
(Sockeye/red salmon)

CARPIO
(Lake Garda trout)

ONCORHYNCHUS

KISUTCH
(Coho/silver salmon)

The division of *Salmo
trutta* into sub-
species remains so
uncertain that this
can be no more than
a subjective list of
some of the more
generally recognised
ones.

GORBUSCHA
(Pink/humpback salmon)

KETA
(Chum salmon)

MASU
(Masu salmon)

HUCHO – (Taimen & hutchen)

SALMOTHYMUS – (Dalmatian salmon)

COREGONUS – (Whitefish, powan, houting)

COREGONINI     PROSPIUM – (Mountain whitefish)

STENODUS – (Inconnu)

*A Salmonidae family tree.*

The genus *Oncorhynchus* now comprises not only the two new arrivals (some taxonomists considered there were several other distinct species of rainbow-type trout such as golden, Gila and Apache trout) but also Chinook or king salmon *(O. tschawytscha)*, Coho or silver salmon *(O. kisutch)*, sockeye or red salmon *(O. nerka)*, humpback or pink salmon *(O. gorbuscha)*, chum salmon *(O.keta)* and Masu or cherry salmon. The first five are spread widely around both sides of the Pacific basin, but Masu occur only in the Sea of Japan and adjacent waters. Both sockeye and Masu have landlocked races, residual populations stranded in fresh water by geological upheavals, glacial retreats or behavioural changes, which have gradually come to terms with their new environment.

To complete the brown trout's family tree, a branch needs adding to bring in one other familiar genus of the Salmonidae family — the charrs *(Salvelinus)*. Of these there are generally reckoned to be four species — brook charr *(S. fontinalis)*, lake charr *(S. namaycush)*, Arctic charr *(S. alpinus)*, and Dolly Varden charr *(S. malma)*. The classification of these generic components is also fraught with difficulties and the taxonomy is further complicated by the colloquial reference to all except the Arctic charr, as 'trout'. ('Charr' is derived from the Gaelic *tarr* meaning 'belly'.)

All *Salvelinus* species populate varying habitats in cooler fresh waters of the northern hemisphere. Arctic charr are unique in being totally circumpolar in their distribution, occurring in the far north of Europe, Asia and America as well as in Greenland and Iceland. Brook charr are naturally confined to eastern North America, while lake charr spread right across the north of that continent, and Dolly Varden are distributed around both sides of the Pacific basin. All except lake charr have sea-going forms and their anatomy, habits and life cycle are broadly similar to those of true trout.

Arctic charr are native to Britain and Ireland, yet still remain cloaked in an aura of dark mystery. At this southern end of their range (there are also charr in Switzerland's Lake Geneva), they tend to inhabit the black depths of still waters, although this is largely due to the competitive presence of brown trout. There, often as much as 100 meters down, they feed off water fleas, insect larvae and other plankton suspended in open water as well as off small fish, occasionally rising in late summer evenings to take insects from the surface. Being better suited to very cold waters than any other Salmonids, migratory charr would have been the first fish to colonise European fresh waters as the last Ice Age drew to a close, crystallising the geography of the British Isles. When this happened, many populations of charr were isolated in deep remote lakes where they remain today. Some of these populations have evolved quite distinct physical characteristics; Windermere and Loch Rannoch are each home to two separate varieties, breeding at different times of the year and living in quite different habitats. Tate Regan, most forthright in his assertion that all brown trout should be included in one species, identified fifteen separate sub-species of Arctic charr within the one species, some of which were confined to single lakes.

Evolutionary theories usually owe much to speculation and very little to fact, and those on the development of the Salmonidae family are no exception. Nonetheless, the very consideration of a possible evolutionary path may give an insight into the present distribution of the family as well as its division into genus or species units.

Salmonids are described as primitive fish, meaning that they have changed little over a comparatively long time and that present members of the family still resemble their earliest known ancestors very closely. Despite this, an evolutionary history of Salmonidae is clouded by the lack of any really helpful, relatively recent fossil evidence. Fossil records of distant ancestors are found in deposits laid down in Germany during the Miocene period which ended some seven million years ago. Subsequent to the date of these fossils, different genera branched off the line of their common ancestor, one of which would be the founder of *Salmo*, which ultimately split into two species. *Salvelinus* left the ancestral line before *Salmo*, and *Oncorhynchus* afterwards, first losing the common ancestors of rainbow and cutthroat trout before branching out into the six separate species of Pacific salmon we know today. This evolutionary progress can be well illustrated by what is called a 'phylogenetic tree' that also stresses the importance of evolution in the science of taxonomy.

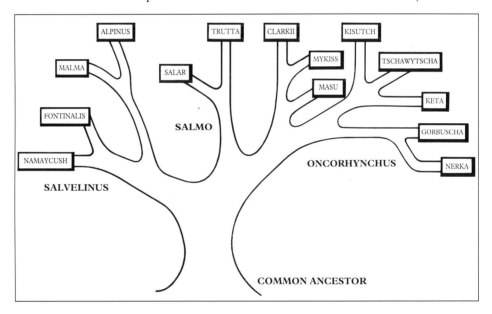

All genera within the Salmonidae family occupy the cooler waters of the northern hemisphere, but linking together their present distribution and evolutionary history requires a vision of a turbulent planet with an ever-changing map which, even quite recently, was very different from the one we see today. It may be particularly significant that until joined by the Panama land bridge, probably only three million years ago, North and South America were separate land masses; and very much more recently the lower sea levels of the Ice Ages exposed a land bridge which joined Alaska and Siberia, allowing humans and large quadrupeds to migrate from Asia to America.

*Oncorhynchus* is the youngest genus of the family and, theoretically at least, as soon as the Bering land bridge was submerged, the colonisation of its present range could have started with a southward spread of fish from a warmer Arctic ocean direct into the Pacific. However, evolution is a frustratingly gradual process and the opening of the Bering strait was far too recent to allow for the subsequent development of so many diverse species of *Oncorhynchus*. It therefore seems much more likely that its forebears moved into the Pacific ocean from the Atlantic before North and South America merged, and when the waters separating them were much cooler than they are now. Then the formation of the Panama land bridge isolated populations of the common ancestor from each other and from then on *Oncorhynchus* began to evolve in the Pacific and *Salmo* in the Atlantic. Pacific and Atlantic populations of Arctic charr have not been separated for long enough to diverge into different species and probably spread south from Arctic seas as soon as the Bering strait opened up, quickly colonising rivers round the upper edge of the Pacific basin.

Geographical separation cannot have been responsible for the gradual split of the Atlantic fish into *salar* and *trutta* since the two species freely occupy the same streams; instead they are more likely to have diverged by exploiting separate ecological niches. Atlantic salmon go far out to sea for their food while brown trout feed in fresh water and, in the case of migratory fish, around the coasts. As salmon ascend their natal river to breed they stop feeding, so neither in sea nor river do adults of the two species compete for the same food resources. Once the young have hatched this ceases to be so but their different feeding habits still do much to keep both species apart.

As with Arctic charr, the end of the last glacial period some 10,000 years ago left various non-migratory populations of *Salmo trutta* geographically isolated from each other. Many of these have slowly evolved into the profusion of varieties which caused the earlier 'splitters' to consider them different enough to merit elevation to specific status. Whether or not any of these varieties have yet gone far enough down the evolutionary trail to deserve such distinction is really no more than a question of semantics; the disparity of colour, habit or form in different varieties of trout, gradually engendered by environmental pressures, still gives a wonderful picture of evolution in action.

No consideration of the brown trout's lineage can ignore the question of whether the species' ancestors were of marine or freshwater origin. The principal argument favouring freshwater beginnings is that all Salmonid species spawn in fresh water, often as far up the river as possible, and many of them, including Atlantic salmon and migratory brown trout, may undertake long and hazardous journeys to do so. Furthermore, each genus within the Salmonidae family contains at least one species, some or all members of which live permanently in fresh water.

The likelihood of a marine origin centres round the wide distribution of the Salmonidae. If the common ancestor was not of marine origin, how could the family have spread round the Pacific basin, both sides of the Atlantic and into sub-Arctic seas, as well as throughout Europe, North Africa and much of Asia? This is a formidable argument but it ignores the possibility that during the repeated periods of de-glaciation, water on the fringes of melting ice was much less saline than the open sea, and freshwater species might well have been able to migrate great distances without encountering true salt water. Nevertheless, the majority view is that Salmonids have evolved from common sea-dwelling ancestors which slowly adapted themselves to life in estuaries. From there they began to move up into the less predator-infested environment of fresh water thus greatly enhancing the survival prospects of their offspring. This evolutionary process was interrupted by massive geological and climatic upheavals, encouraging the development throughout the Holarctic region of a variety of species which, despite their divergence, have all retained broadly similar habits.

The timing of these events has so far proved impossible to assess accurately but was perhaps surprisingly recent and it is likely that the evolution of all Salmonids and their present distribution date back no further than the upheavals of the four great glacial periods of the Pleistocene age during the last two million years. And today in Europe, parts of north Africa and western Asia there now lives a fish which is uniquely varied in colour, form and habit. This fish generally inhabits fresh water but some populations go to sea to augment their food supply, as do all members of its most closely related species, the Atlantic salmon. This fish is the brown trout, *Salmo trutta* L.

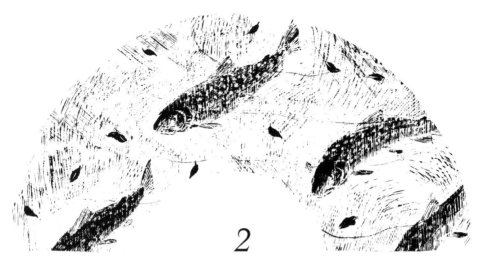

# 2
# *Form and Physiology*

In the course of their evolution, fish have been a dramatically successful group whether success be judged in terms of sheer numbers of living individuals, diversity of species or occupation of different aquatic environments. The word 'fish' describes such a wide variety of animals that it is almost impossible to define concisely. However, 'cold-blooded, aquatic vertebrates' aptly covers the three principal attributes which characterise almost all fish, even if this definition excludes peripheral families whose members may breathe with lungs, lack tails or are able to raise their body temperatures above that of the surrounding water.

Taxonomically, living fish are usually divided into three classes. Much the most important of these is Osteichthyes, (bony rather than cartilaginous fish) which splits into sub-classes dominated by the Actinopterygii (ray-finned fish). Below this sub-class are three super-orders headed by the Teleostei which includes all but some fifty of the twenty thousand species of bony fish, so far described. Within the order Salmoniformes is the sub-order Salmonoidei comprising Salmonidae and six other families. Salmonidae are characterised mainly by their fleshy adipose fin, two bones on each side of the upper jaw, scales on the body but not on the head and by the female shedding individual eggs into her body cavity before spawning. There are usually reckoned to be eight genera in the Salmonidae family, of which one is *Salmo*.

The brown trout's full taxonomical hierarchy may be summarised like this:

| | |
|---|---|
| KINGDOM | ANIMALIA |
| PHYLUM | CHORDATA |
| SUB-PHYLUM | VERTEBRATA |
| CLASS | OSTEICHTHYES |

| | |
|---|---|
| SUB-CLASS | ACTINOPTERYGII |
| SUPER-ORDER | TELEOSTEI |
| ORDER | SALMONIFORMES |
| SUB-ORDER | SALMONOIDEI |
| FAMILY | SALMONIDAE |
| SUB-FAMILY | SALMONINI |
| GENUS | SALMO |
| SPECIES | TRUTTA |

With every step down this hierarchy the differences between the separate units at each particular level are gradually reduced. Salmonidae is distinguished from other families within the same sub-order by the distinct skeletal peculiarity of three flattened, upturned vertebrae at the end of the backbone. Yet down at species level, migratory brown trout are only physically differentiated from their congener, the Atlantic salmon, by unremarkable differences in scale numbers, tail and anal fin shape and dentition. And so by the time the science of taxonomical classification has filtered down through its pyramid of distinctive groupings (taxa), to the species unit at the base, all relevant characteristics have emerged which differentiate brown trout from every other fish. An outline of a fish's anatomy and senses cannot but resemble an excerpt from a zoological textbook. However, it is indispensable to any understanding of the ways of the trout and what follows is a general description of the form and physiology of *Salmo trutta* which together make it the distinct species that it is.

**Skeleton**

The skeleton is the frame to which the muscles of the trout's body are attached. It can be roughly divided into three sections — skull, backbone and the peripheral bones supporting the fins.

The skull houses and protects the trout's brain and sensory organs. It is made up of several bony plates overlying layers of cartilage, which are formed before the skeletal exterior is fully developed. The plates may grow disproportionately leading to slight changes in skull shape as trout age; these are particularly noticeable in the development of the aggressive looking, hooked lower jaw (kype) in older male fish, which are also recognisable by their generally more elongated heads.

At the skull's base is the fixed upper jaw. Round its edge there are almost parallel rows of teeth embedded in the two palatine bones. Down the centre of the roof of the mouth — and easily felt by running a thumb along it — is a third toothed bone (vomer, or sometimes ploughshare bone) whose structure is central to the ascription of individual species to the genera of *Salmo*, *Oncorhynchus* and *Salvelinus*. Early taxonomists relied upon the vomer's dentition to identify separate species of trout. The shaft of a brown trout's vomer is usually densely toothed but teeth are always falling out and it is therefore an unreliable guide.

A trout has a formidable array of teeth — a clear indicator of its carnivorous habits. As well as its upper set, it has two rows on its lower jaw and usually ten or twelve teeth on its tongue. All point backwards enabling prey to be secured better, but this inward slanting arrangement, in conjunction with the restricted up and down movements of the jaw, inhibits chewing and food is therefore usually swallowed whole. Something as large as a crayfish may need to be shaken or turned round first but the ability to swallow smaller creatures quickly, allows trout to take advantage of sudden influxes of particular prey.

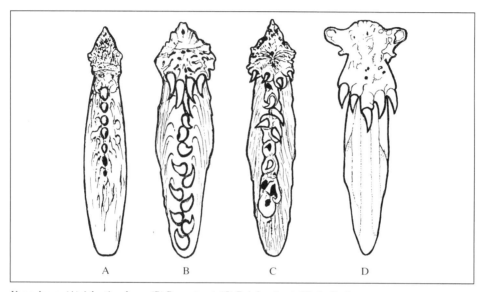

*Vomer bones. (A) Atlantic salmon. (B) Brown trout. (C) Rainbow trout. (D) Arctic charr.*

Behind the skull, running down the full length of the rest of its body are the vertebrae which make up the backbone. Their number may differ between individuals of the same species, making them an unreliable pointer to species identification. Anything from fifty-seven to sixty is considered normal for brown trout while charr from British waters normally have between fifty-nine and sixty-three. Greater numbers of vertebrae add to a fish's flexibility as well as to its general mobility in the water; the rigid members of the perch family (Percidae) only have around thirty but serpentine eels *(Anguilla anguilla)* wriggle through the water with the help of over 100.

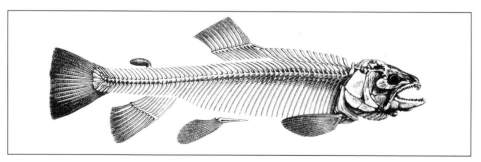

*Skeleton of a trout.*

The first vertebra is fused to the skull while subsequent ones are attached to their neighbours by connective ligaments. The structure of each vertebra changes gradually down the spine in accordance with its function. Those at the front have two rib-like projections which curve downwards, bending round to form a cavity to protect the internal organs. However, towards the tail, behind the fish's vent, where maximum lateral flexibility is required for efficient swimming, the vertebrae only carry a single downward pointing projection.

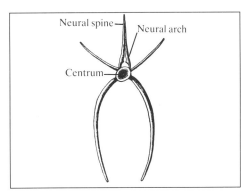

*Abdominal vertebra of trout.*

The core of a vertebra is called its centrum and together these form a long, solid cylinder running the length of the backbone and from which ribs and other projections branch. Just above each centrum is a circular cavity (neural arch) creating a tunnel to protect the spinal cord. Vertebrae towards the tail also have an arch below the centrum forming a shorter tunnel which carries blood vessels. All vertebrae have a single neural spine projecting upwards along the length of the backbone and those at the front have additional projections branching out into the muscles at the top of the back. The projections of the last three vertebrae are splayed out to form the flat plate of bone to which is attached the tail (caudal fin), and which characterises the Salmonidae family.

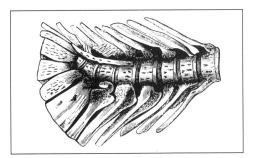

*End of a trout's backbone.*

The remaining bones in the trout's body support its other fins. Along the back, above the neural spines and set into the muscle, is a line of bones (interneurals) whose function is to uphold the dorsal fin. Underneath, behind the vent, is a similar set supporting the anal fin while in front of the vent are two small floating bones to which the pelvic fins are attached. Then, secured by ligaments to the lower part of the skull are nine pairs of bones forming the pectoral girdle (corresponding with human shoulders) which provides an attachment for the pectoral fins.

## Fins

The brown trout, in common with all other Salmonids, has eight fins, including its tail. They are composed of tough membrane, all interlaced with stiff bony rays except for the stubby little adipose fin which, as the name indicates, is made of more fatty tissue. Its general fin arrangement makes the trout a versatile feeder, able to manoeuvre quickly in any direction to take advantage of available prey.

The dorsal fin, strengthened by between twelve and fifteen rays (ten to twelve in salmon), helps the fish maintain its upright position. The dorsal fin arrangement along the backs of different species of fish is remarkably diverse. Perch *(Perca fluviatilis)* have a second smaller dorsal fin behind the first while the rear dorsal fin of the zander or pike-perch *(Stizostedion lucioperca)* is larger than the front one. The pike *(Esox lucius)* has a single dorsal fin just in front of its tail which is an aid to faster swimming as well as stability.

One of the distinctive characteristics of the Salmonidae is the small adipose fin which may be a vestige of a more pronounced second dorsal fin that existed in the earlier stages of the family's evolution. The fin serves no recognised purpose and its clipping as part of a research and recovery programme appears to have no detrimental effects on successful growth.

The large tail, firmly attached to the flattened end of the backbone, provides the main impetus to a trout's forward movement. With the aid of its lateral movements trout can swim at significant speeds and make spectacular leaps up weirs and waterfalls. The end of a trout's tail is slightly forked although usually less so than that of an Atlantic salmon. This can help identify the species, as can the salmon's thinner wrist (caudal peduncle) which makes it easier to grasp in front of the tail. Stocked trout may often be identified as such by the rough, rounded edges to their tails caused either by continued contact with the sides of tanks or cages in which they were reared, or by fin rot and fin-nipping in their early life.

Almost directly below the little adipose fin is the much larger anal fin which helps a fish maintain its position in the current as well as being far enough back to contribute to forward propulsion. It also plays an important part in the spawning process, enabling the female to feel the texture of the stream bed and to test the depth of the nest which she excavates with vigorous flexions of her tail.

The remaining four fins are paired, two pelvic or ventral fins in the middle of the trout's body and two pectoral ones behind its gills. These fins equate to a mammal's four legs or the legs and wings of a bird and are mainly responsible for the trout's manoeuvrability and balance, although neither is seriously affected if one of these four fins is cut off to mark a fish.

## Muscle, Movement and Buoyancy

The greater part of the trout's body weight comprises muscle tissue. The actual percentage varies considerably, depending how close the fish is to spawning, but this — the edible part of the fish — may account for up to seventy per cent of its total weight, especially at the height of summer before testes or ovaries are well developed.

Body muscle is divided into a series of zig-zag shaped, interlocking segments, all attached to separate vertebrae. These are just sufficiently jointed to bend with the flexions of the attached muscles. Messages to each segment of muscles are received in sequence from the spinal cord running down the neural arches of the vertebrae. Thus segments are actuated in sequence to produce the undulations of the trout's body which combine with the lateral movements of the tail to propel it forwards.

Most of the trout's muscle is light coloured, 'white' muscle like the white meat of chicken. Relatively poor in blood supply, it is usually utilised for sudden urgent spurts of energy either to escape danger or capture prey. Sometimes, especially in sea-feeding trout, this muscle may actually be coloured pink or orange, depending upon the fish's diet. Many food items, particularly crustaceans, contain carotene in their shells which colours the muscle of predatory fish, and trout or salmon farmed for the table may actually be given food containing natural or synthetic carotenoids. There is no real evidence that carotene itself affects the taste of the muscle it colours, probably just enhancing its visual appeal.

There is also a thin layer of 'red' muscle under the trout's skin — its equivalent of the red meat of the legs and wings of a chicken. This muscle owes its darker colouring to greater blood supply and is used in continued, routine activity such as holding position against a gentle current. In pelagic species of fish like tuna (*Thunnus* spp.), which are continually cruising through the water, most muscle is red.

Each fin also has its own separate muscles and there are individual sets of muscles for eye and jaw movements. In addition, involuntarily operated muscular systems are responsible for the functioning of the heart, digestive system and other internal organs.

A trout swims by making repeated muscular undulations of its body; these are accentuated towards the end, effecting the broad lateral sweeps of its tail which are the main source of forward propulsion. If its tail is amputated, a trout can still swim but uses far more energy in extra oscillations of its body to compensate for the missing propeller. Dorsal and anal fins enlarge the undulating surface areas and thereby help increase swimming speed while the paired fins play a key role in upwards or downwards movements, reversing and braking. Pectoral fins can also be used like oars for slow swimming and precise manoeuvres.

Maximum swimming speeds depend on a fish's size, shape and the frequency with which it can sweep its tail. Bigger fish can swim faster and, by using the same number of tail beats, one trout can swim approximately twice the speed of another half its length. As a general guide, fast-swimming species of fish such as trout can swim about ten times their length in one second. Precise maximum speeds are difficult to ascertain among bigger fish which cannot be easily timed under artificial conditions. However, large trout may be able to achieve maximum speeds up to twenty kilometers per hour over short distances and a determined cruising speed might be around one third of that. Sea trout migrating upstream through a series of runs and pools have been timed at two kilometers per hour.

Body shape also affects ease of movement in the water. Trout are elegantly streamlined fish with a fusiform shape which implies a round or oval cross-section and a body which is generally thinner behind than in front.

One other aspect of trout physiology which influences manoeuvrability is buoyancy. Water is over seven hundred times denser than air, depending much on temperature and salinity. This makes floating in water a comparatively simple matter but, taken as a mass, a trout's body is still heavier than water which means that, unless regulated by some other influence, it would sink. Indeed, some cartilaginous fish such as skates or sharks have no mechanism to adjust their buoyancy and therefore either live on the sea bed or must constantly keep moving to avoid sinking. To counteract their tendency to sink, trout and most other bony fish have a swim-bladder whose centre is also the centre of the fish's gravity. When inflated, it accounts for between six and eight per cent of body volume giving the trout completely neutral buoyancy and enabling it to remain at any depth without regulatory fin movements. Because salt water is denser than fresh, trout in the sea need only inflate their swim bladders to around five per cent of body volume to achieve neutral buoyancy.

To move up or down in the water, a trout can alter its specific gravity by respectively absorbing or expelling gas from the swim-bladder and then re-regulating its buoyancy once it has reached the new level. As a general rule the pressure inside the swim-bladder needs to be reduced by fifty per cent for each ten meters of increased depth. The swim-bladder is linked to the oesophagus and air is forced out orally if a fish is sinking deeper. Fish that want to move upwards can gulp in air once they have reached the surface, but this is a potentially dangerous exercise which exposes them to a whole new range of predators. More effective is regulation of the swim-bladder through the introduction of gases from the network of capillaries lining its walls.

**Skin, Scales and Colour**
The trout has two layers of skin — a thin, outer epidermis and a thicker, inner dermis. Within the epidermis are glands which constantly secrete slimy mucus providing a protective shield against bacterial infection or fungal growth, and also serving to reduce friction between the fish and its element as it swims.

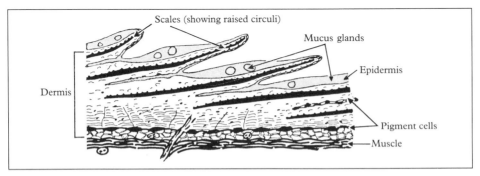

*Cross section of a trout's skin.*

Embedded in the dermis are the long overlapping discs which are the trout's scales. Very little of each is visible as the amount of overlap is so great, and as the scales do not protrude through the epidermis, trout feel much less rough to the touch than, for instance, grayling *(Thymallus thymallus)*. A young fry has no scales until it is about four centimeters long when traces begin to appear along the lateral line, spreading slowly above and below until eventually scales cover the whole body. As trout increase in size they do not produce additional scales unless replacing lost or damaged ones. Therefore, if they are to continue to act as a protective covering, a trout's scales must grow proportionately with its body making them an invaluable indicator of growth cycles and age (Chapter Four).

The trout's colouration is controlled by three different types of special cell (melanophores, lipophores and guanophores), collectively called 'chromatophores'. These contain the pigments which generate the spectrum of colours in the skin of trout as well as the astonishing variety in the colouration of different populations. The chromatophores also control the colour and extent of spotting, creating a unique pattern on each individual.

Chromatophores are fundamentally under neural control and can either increase or decrease the supply of their particular pigment to alter colouration. The amount of light entering a trout's eye serves to suppress or stimulate the supply of the dark pigment, melanin, in the melanophores, so enabling a trout's surroundings to affect its colouration. Trout from brown, peaty lochs or from rivers overhung with thick vegetation are likely to be much darker than those from the clear, light-filled waters of chalk streams. Similarly, nearly blind trout are almost always blacker in colour than their fellows and the gradual darkening of fish as they age is often the result of deteriorating eyesight.

The reds and yellows in a trout's skin are due to the presence of the pigment carotene in the lipophores. This is the same pigment that colours a fish's muscle and its supply in the skin is also governed to some extent by diet. The silvery sheen, so characteristic of sea trout and sometimes brown trout from large open lakes, is created by guanin which is a light-reflecting crystal secreted by the guanophores. Its secretion increases proportionately with the decreasing production of other pigments and in this way sea trout establish their protective silvery-blue camouflage as they reach the sea where dark brown pigmentation would be a great disadvantage. Increased thyroid activity is linked to the migratory urge and also to the production of melanin, and on return to fresh water sea trout become noticeably darker as the silvering induced by the guanin fades and melanin supply increases.

All trout are paler on their undersides than on their backs. This is known as 'countershading' and when the fish is naturally lit from above, gives it an even tone that blends with the water and makes it less visible to both predator and prey. The darkest part of a trout is the ridge along its back which needs to blend with the lake or river bed while different coloured spots help diffuse its distinctive outline. Fish that live on the bottom or among thick vegetation like common carp *(Cyprinus carpio)* or Tench *(Tinca tinca)* are usually brown or green all over so they merge with their background.

A fish's basic colour pattern is established by heredity and the distribution of different chromatophores throughout its skin is fixed at hatching. Much of the distinctive variegation of separate trout populations is genetically controlled and has, theoretically at least, evolved as the most effective camouflage for the particular habitat they occupy. However, environmental factors also play their part. The amount of carotene in a trout's diet may affect the development of red spots or the intensity of the golden colouration along its flanks; and trout moved from one water to another can to some extent adapt their colouration, chameleon-like, to fit better into their new environment.

Nature might almost have allowed herself the luxury of indulging an artistic streak when colouring fish. The variations in pigmentation that pushed early taxonomists to the conclusion that there were many distinct species of trout, are so extra-ordinarily wide that the precise advantage of each in its particular environment is sometimes difficult to appreciate.

The gillaroo (from the Irish *Giolla ruadh* meaning 'red fellow') of western Ireland are golden-brown with a jumble of dark brown and bright red spots. This colouration may well be accentuated by a carotene-rich diet of molluscs and crustaceans. Gunther christened them *Salmo stomachicus* on account of their thick stomach walls which are seemingly adapted to crush the shells of their prey in the same way as the gizzard of a bird. At the other end of the spectrum are Loch Leven trout (formerly *S. levenensis*) and sonaghen or black-finned trout (originally *S. nigripinnis*). Loch Leven fish are silvery with plenty of black but almost no red spots. Sonaghen are steely blue with black fins and also very few red spots. Their home is Lough Melvin in western Ireland which they share with gillaroo although living in deeper, more open water, leaving gillaroo to feed among the stones round the shallow edges of the lough. Marbled trout *(S.t. marmoratus)* of Yugoslavia have a mosaic of black lines on their greeny bodies and are so unusually coloured that if colour alone was a reliable guide, they would seem more genetically distant than any other isolated population of brown trout. Yet many of these distinctive liveries are not firmly established and are soon lost if fish are moved from their natural environment to new waters. Distinctive pigmentation is often also threatened by the artificial introduction of alien strains of brown trout with which indigenous fish freely interbreed.

**Digestion and Excretion**

Once in the trout's mouth, large prey is gripped between the teeth before being swallowed. Food is not chewed but there are taste buds on the trout's tongue to help identify prey which it may not otherwise have clearly recognised. Any water taken in with food is expelled through the gill openings just as in breathing. No digestive juices are secreted into the mouth but mucus lubricates swallowing which a fish does simply by raising the bottom of its mouth.

From the gullet (oesophagus), food passes into the stomach. This is V-shaped with muscular walls which literally break down food by their repeated contractions. The muscular nature of the stomach wall also permits considerable expansion, allowing trout to take advantage of a brief but prolific hatch of fly, a shoal of smaller prey fish or other glut of food. The stomach also secretes hydrochloric acid which aids the chemical breakdown of food before it is squeezed through the pyloric sphincter into the intestine.

Attached to the upper end of the intestine are a number of worm-like appendages (pyloric caecae). These are blind tubes which lead off the intestine and probably serve to increase its surface area thus also increasing the exposure of food to the digestive properties of the intestinal wall. They are very noticeable when gutting a trout and their number varies immensely, different dissections having revealed as few as twenty-seven and as many as ninety. Early taxonomists relied on variations in numbers of pyloric caecae, vertebrae and fin rays as the basis for the description and identification of different species of trout. It is possible that separate populations inherit varying numbers of all these features, giving rise to distinct diagnostic characteristics, but data is still insufficient to establish this with certainty.

The caecae and intestine themselves produce digestive enzymes and the liver secretes the greenish bile which is stored in the gall bladder from where it is discharged into the intestine to reduce the acidity of the stomach contents and help digest fats. The pancreas also introduces digestive juices into the intestine through numerous pancreatic ducts. This chemical mixture works slowly on the contents of the intestine which are gradually pushed backwards by peristaltic contractions. Proteins, fats and carbohydrates are broken down into amino and fatty acids and sugars, which are all absorbed into the blood and lymph systems through the intestinal wall. Eventually these absorbed nutrients reach the liver where sugar is removed and converted into glycogen to be stored as an energy reserve for the future. Amino acids, which are the basic components of body-forming protein, are used in growth and cell replacement, and fatty acids are stored as fat reserves for later conversion into sugars. Any indigestible remains are slowly compacted in the rectum and expelled intermittently through the vent in front of the tail.

At optimum temperatures, food takes between ten and twelve hours to digest fully but might take as long as five days in very cold weather. This has great significance to fishermen since the rapid processing of food in warmer weather means trout can then eat much more food and their keener appetites are likely to make them easier to catch.

Waste from the chemical reactions in the trout's body is also eliminated through the kidney. This is the long dark red streak immediately below the backbone and which usually remains behind after gutting. It has two parts, the head kidney which is concerned with the production of blood cells and the posterior kidney which filters out waste products from the bloodstream, as well as surplus water. In fresh water a trout takes in large quantities of excess water through the thin, permeable tissues lining its gills and mouth. This is absorbed osmotically as a result of the trout's body fluids being more chemically concentrated than the surrounding fresh water. Excess water thus absorbed is then filtered through the kidneys and expelled in the form of copious quantities of very dilute urine, passing through twin ureters to a bladder which discharges through the urino-genital opening behind the vent.

Migratory trout undergo dramatic physiological changes on reaching the sea where the water is far richer in natural chemicals than are their body tissues. There, the osmotic process is reversed and the tendency is immediately for water to be lost rather than gained, through the extensive surfaces of the gills and mouth. A fish may compensate for this loss by swallowing sea water which is absorbed into its system through the stomach wall. The kidneys must then reverse their fresh water function, excreting excess salts in small quantities of concentrated urine as well as through specialised gill cells, and conserving water to make up for that lost through the surface of the gills.

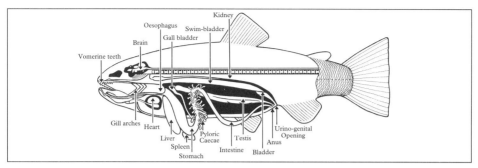

*The main internal organs of a trout.*

**Blood and Breathing**

Like all other animals except certain micro-organisms, trout must have oxygen to remain alive. This creates chemical reactions with substances derived from their nourishment, thereby fuelling all metabolic processes. Trout need more oxygen than nearly all other fish and because water's potential oxygen content increases as its temperature drops, they are most often found in cold, well aerated conditions.

Oxygen accounts for between eight and fourteen parts per million of water and is absorbed during respiration by rows of gills lying underneath the gill covers (opercula) on either side of the trout's head. Each row of gills consists of a double line of feathery filaments attached to the four gill arches. Under microscopic examination each filament is seen to comprise huge numbers of tiny projections (lamellae); these greatly increase the surface area of the gills exposed to the water and therefore their capacity to absorb oxygen. In front of the gill arches are projections like the teeth of a comb (gill rakers) which act to keep larger morsels of food off the delicate surface of the gills. The gill rakers of trout, which eat comparatively large prey, are short and thick, unlike the longer, more flexible projections of fish such as Arctic charr that feed on smaller creatures.

Water reaches the gill chambers from the mouth before being strained through the filaments and then passed out through the gill openings behind the opercula. Gills are bright red because blood is so clearly visible through the thin membrane covering their filaments. This fragile membrane is only one cell thick, allowing oxygen to pass freely into the bloodstream but making the gills particularly susceptible to damage, especially as a fish is unhooked before being returned to the water. The breathing system is so effective that at least seventy-five per cent of the dissolved oxygen in the water may be absorbed in this way, in marked contrast with the twenty-five per cent extracted in human respiration. At the same time, carbon dioxide from the blood stream passes out through the gills; so does nitrogenous waste, usually in the form of ammonia, which results from the breakdown of proteins by the trout's digestive system.

The mouth and opercula operate together like a pump. Water is sucked in through the mouth as its bottom lies flat, while the opercula are closed; these then open, the mouth closes and its bottom is raised to expel the water past the gills and out through their openings. In fast flowing water, where trout lie facing upstream, much of this operation can be left to the current but in stiller waters active pumping is essential to ensure an adequate oxygen supply. The pumping rate accelerates whenever more oxygen is required for sudden surges of activity. The efficiency of this oxygen extraction system is enhanced by the arrangement whereby blood flows through the lamellae in the opposite direction to the flow of incoming water. This ensures that blood about to leave the gills is last in contact with fresh, fully oxygenated water, while blood entering them first meets the less oxygenated water being expelled through the opercula. In experimental conditions where water flow is reversed, the amount of oxygen fish are able to extract from the water falls dramatically.

After passing through the gill membranes into the blood system, oxygen combines with the red blood pigment (haemoglobin) to form oxyhaemoglobin and is thus carried together with other nutrients and hormones to the different body tissues. Blood is distributed by the regular pumping actions of the heart, which is at the front of the body cavity behind the gills and just above and forward of the pectoral fins. It comprises two muscular chambers (auricle and ventricle), and a third (sinus venosus) which acts as a reservoir for deoxygenated blood returning from the body tissue before entering the heart.

Once in the heart, blood is pumped by the auricle to the ventricle and then, still depleted of oxygen, out through the ventral aorta. From there it diffuses into the vast network of lamellae in the gill filaments to receive its oxygen supply from the water. Then, fully oxygenated, some blood is taken up by arteries leading to the brain but most runs back through the main dorsal aorta which branches into a number of smaller arteries. These all take blood, through the spreading network of capillaries, to the muscles and internal organs. There the oxygen is used up in the course of the various bodily functions before the blood brings back carbon dioxide and other waste materials through returning capillaries and veins. Blood which has absorbed nutrients from the intestinal wall returns via the liver to the heart; that from the muscle fibres is filtered first by the kidneys before being recycled with the rest of the fish's blood through the heart and out again to the gills.

The quality of the blood supply is regulated by the head kidney as well as by the spleen which is loosely attached to the stomach. Both function to ensure the replacement of worn out red and white blood cells.

**Reproductive Organs**

The organs responsible for the perpetuation of the species, *Salmo trutta*, are the two male testes and the female's similarly paired ovaries. In both sexes, these lie between the intestinal tract and swim bladder. As they start to mature, the testes are creamy white in colour and contain the white seminal fluid or milt which sustains the spermatozoa. When released, these little tadpole-shaped cells propel themselves with the aid of their tails (flagellae), which they shed after entering the egg of the female at the culmination of spawning.

The ovaries of immature females comprise two inconspicuous strings of cells, but as these develop in the spring, small orange spherical eggs start to show. These eggs are nourished within the ovaries by follicle cells supplied with food from the blood. When almost fully developed, the eggs begin to press on internal organs and at this point the thin membrane which surrounds the ovary ruptures. The loose eggs may then remain in the body cavity for some days before being finally ejected through the urino-genital opening during spawning.

The eggs of a ripe female trout may account for as much as twenty-five per cent of body weight — far more than the mature testes of a male. Quantity and size of eggs varies mainly with the female's weight (Chapter Three). Environmental factors as well as genetic make-up may also influence egg numbers and appear particularly to affect small fish in crowded upland waters where mature females may not lay more than 150. These eggs are, perhaps perversely, often larger than those laid by much bigger fish but in such a highly competitive environment large eggs have a much better chance of hatching successfully. At the other end of the scale, a chalk stream hen fish in her third breeding season may lay over 3,000 eggs. A male needs to produce many times more sperm than a female produces eggs if most of his mate's eggs are to stand a reasonable chance of being fertilised.

**Chemical Control**

The trout's behaviour is largely regulated by chemical hormones released into the blood by endocrine glands. These hormones are responsible for the gradual processes in the fish's metabolism and development, as opposed to its more immediate actions and reactions which are controlled by the responses of its nervous system.

In overall control is the pituitary gland, just below the brain, which produces hormones to stimulate the activity of other glands such as the thyroid, adrenal and pancreatic. Hormones secreted by these junior glands have a diverse range of effects on colouration, growth, sexual maturity, and reproductive and migratory urges and on the production of adrenalin and insulin. In some respects the various glands function quite independently but in the general scheme of a fish's development their activities are closely interrelated although still little understood.

**Brain and Nervous System**

Viewed from above, the brain's most obvious features are its two olfactory lobes, behind which are the larger, paired optic lobes and then the single cerebellum. Nerve fibres from olfactory membranes terminate in the olfactory lobes which are almost exclusively concerned with the trout's sense of smell. Optic lobes control not only vision but also the reception of information from other sensory nerve endings in the taste buds and in the complex audio/lateral line system. Lying behind these optic lobes, the cerebellum co-ordinates muscular activity. Behind and below the cerebellum, tapering into the spinal cord, is the medulla which regulates many of the automatic nervous responses controlling digestion, heart beat and respiration.

The trunk of the nervous system is the spinal cord, which emerges from the back of the brain, passing down the backbone through the tunnel formed by the neural arches of the vertebrae. From this central spinal cord paired nerves branch off between each of the neural arches, bifurcating again and again, like twigs on a tree, to create a comprehensive web of nerves throughout the trout's body. Sensory nerves gather information from the sensitive nerve ends in body tissue and near the skin and relay it to the brain. This determines the appropriate responsive action and duly informs the body through motor nerves that convey messages from the brain back to the muscles.

Considerable conjecture as well as a great deal of wishful thinking, surrounds the question of whether or not its nervous system is sufficiently developed for a trout to feel much pain. The main problem in trying to make such an assessment is the difficulty of considering the question from other than a human standpoint. A man with a hook embedded in the side of his mouth and being driven deeper into the flesh by the exertion of great force in a particular direction would obviously experience considerable pain. Simple analysis of his situation would stimulate him to take positive action to minimise the suffering; it would also enable him to appreciate that salvation almost certainly did not lie in pulling hard against the hook. The reaction of a hooked fish almost always to swim directly against the source of pressure is sometimes used as an argument favouring the assumption that the fish cannot therefore be responding to pain. However, a trout's brain is unarguably far less developed than a human's and its basic instinct to flee from the direction of perceived danger is likely to supersede any conceivable rationalisation of the cause and effect of its predicament.

Examples of fish that have been caught, released and quickly re-caught are also cited in support of the argument that therefore they cannot have felt pain during capture. Yet experiments with carp have shown that after being caught, tagged and released, their recapture rate was so much lower as to prove almost conclusively that they positively endeavoured to ensure the experience was not repeated. Trout caught twice in quick succession are more likely to provide evidence of their own deficient memories than of total disregard for the trauma of capture.

It has also been demonstrated that trout are sensitive to electric currents as well as to artificial temperature changes, actively seeking out water within their preferred thermal range. They have complex and highly developed nervous systems with elaborate webs of sensory nerves which must chiefly serve to warn of impending or actual bodily damage or internal disorder. To this end, while not appreciating its cause and being unable to react other than by instinct, trout must feel some degree of pain. If they did not, much of their nervous systems would be superfluous to the conduct of their lives.

**Sight**
Sight is crucial to the fundamental survival activities of feeding, sensing and avoiding danger, moving and breeding. Indeed, much of the trout's way of life is conditioned by its visual abilities which themselves derive from the anatomical structure and positioning of its eyes and from the behaviour of light in water.

Superficially, a trout's eye resembles its human counterpart. Both have an outer transparent cornea, the trout's protruding slightly from the side of its head. Beneath the cornea is the coloured iris which surrounds the pupil. A trout's pupil is simply a hole in the iris that allows light through the clear lens in the eye, then to be focused on the retina. In the retina are millions of photoreceptive cells. These are either rods or cones and contain pigments that react chemically to light, thereby transmitting nervous impulses to the brain where the information received is transformed into an image.

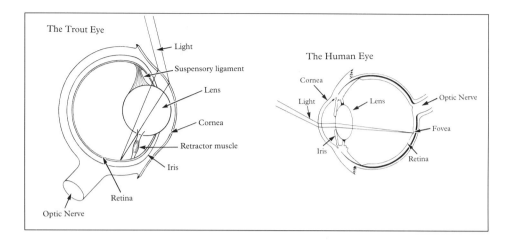

Rod cells are in constant use, especially during periods of poor light; they cannot discern colour but are particularly important in the perception of minute detail. Rods may be up to one thousand times as sensitive as cones which can detect colours and function when light is particularly bright. In the retinas of fish living in murky, light-starved waters on the sea bed there are often only rods and no cones. They are therefore colour-blind although their eyes are often acutely sensitive to the deep blue wavelengths of light which penetrate the depths. Trout's eyes are adequately supplied with both rods and cones giving them potentially good colour vision in a bright enough environment. Water first absorbs red light waves, then orange, yellow and green. Less than ten per cent of red light penetrates as far down as four meters, so wet flies dressed with red materials soon lose their colours in quite shallow water; orange and yellow last to greater depths but not as far as green which holds out quite as far as any artificial fly is likely to sink.

Light is quickly absorbed by water and the eyes of fish are better adapted for vision in poorer light than those of land-dwelling vertebrates. In twilight and semi-darkness a trout's sight is far superior to a human's. However, in optimum lighting conditions human sight is many times more powerful than that of trout which must come very close to their prey to confirm its identity.

Unlike the human eye, a trout's has no eyelids and there are three other principal areas of distinction — the shape of the lens, its focussing mechanism and the distribution of rods and cones in the retina. All are consequential differences of the trout's shape or of its aquatic environment.

Light passing into a human eye travels from air into the much denser matter of the cornea; there it bends by refraction in the same manner as light entering water. The human cornea is responsible for much of the initial focusing which is then fine-tuned by the lens. Light entering a trout's eye does so directly from an equally dense medium — water — and therefore there is no refraction at the cornea and all focusing is undertaken by the lens. This is extremely powerful and actually protrudes through the pupil enabling the trout to look almost straight up and down as well as backwards and forwards. It also makes the lens more susceptible to accidental damage.

The focusing mechanism of the human eye centres round the lens' ability to change shape, using muscles fixed to its top and bottom. A trout does not possess this ability, instead focusing by moving the entire lens forwards or backwards, as in a telescope, to create the required clarity of image on the retina. The amount of light entering a human eye can be controlled by adjusting the iris, which expands or contracts the size of the pupil; however the protrusion of the trout's lens through the iris precludes this and there are particular retinal cells to counteract the otherwise potentially damaging effect of a sudden invasion of brighter light.

Rods and cones in a trout's eye are uniformly distributed over the retina — a direct consequence both of the fish's inability to move its head easily from side to side and of the positioning of its eyes which give almost all-round vision. In a human eye, cones are densely concentrated round a central point in the retina (fovea) which results in acutely sensitive daylight vision within a small arc of about five degrees. By moving the eyes but not the head, visual acuity becomes noticeably less but this is easily overcome by simply turning the head so that most of the light continues to focus on the fovea. The cones in a trout's eye are far more evenly distributed, giving it much greater all-round vision without any head movement but no area of acutely perceptive daylight sight.

A trout owes its power of all-round vision not only to the distribution of the cones in its retina but also to the actual positioning of its eyes. Just like any bird that has eyes on the side of its head, this gives trout an area of binocular vision in an arc of some thirty degrees in front of it and a blind spot of a roughly similar arc directly behind; immediately in front of its head and for an inch or so above, a trout has no vision and it has a corresponding but larger blind spot directly below it. Between these blind spots in both the vertical and horizontal planes are wide arcs of monocular vision. These are enough for general visual scanning and the detection of movement, but not sufficient to perceive distance, detail and perspective. For this, a trout must bring its binocular vision into play by pointing its head, usually through movement of its whole body, at the particular object on which it wishes to focus. Trout must continually avoid becoming a meal for some larger predator as they seek out their own food, and their eyes are designed to provide maximum all round awareness. Pike, which have little to fear from aquatic predators other than their own kind, have their eyes well forward, giving a large area of easy binocular vision but also a bigger blind spot behind their head.

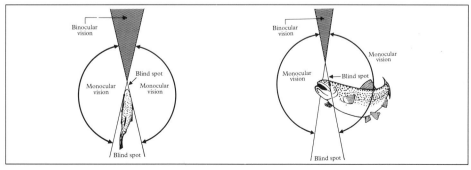

*A trout's vision.*

At rest, both trout and human eyes are focused on infinity, but the former's depth of field is considerably greater with the result that all objects more than about seventy centimeters away are simultaneously in focus. This greatly enhances a trout's ability to perceive movement, food or other details outside its immediate vicinity. When focused on something only a short distance away, depth of field is minimal and only sudden movements or changes in light intensity are detectable outside this immediate area of close-up focus, whether in the water or the air beyond.

A fish's perception of objects in the air is dominated by the refractive behaviour of light as it passes from air to water, clearly demonstrated by the apparent bending of a stick that is stuck into the water at an angle. This has given rise to the concept of the trout's 'window' which describes what and how it can see above the surface of the water.

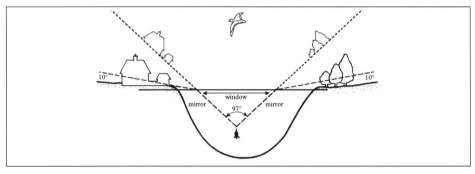

*The trout's window and mirror.*

The degree of refraction of light rays entering water depends upon the angle at which they strike its surface. Below ten degrees from the horizontal almost no light penetrates the surface. Thereafter, as the angle increases so does the amount of light entering the water. At the same time, distortion decreases until light directly above a fish enters the water with no distortion at all — so the stick standing upright in the water appears quite as straight as it is. The effect of this refraction is that light from an arc of about 160 degrees above the surface (ten degrees off the horizontal on either side) is compressed into a window of ninety-seven degrees within the water. Objects on the perimeter of that arc, such as the tip of a rod, look compressed and blurred in the window, while those in the centre are detected with greatest clarity and minimum distortion. However, the colour of a fly silhouetted against the sky directly above a trout's head is obviously less discernible than if it was floating down nearer the edge of the window.

The apex of the triangle creating the trout's window is fixed at ninety-seven degrees irrespective of the fish's depth in the water. So the deeper a fish's position, the greater the area of its window, although visual ability is reduced with depth simply by the absorption of so much light by water. At a depth of one meter a trout's window is just over two meters across and at double the depth, the diameter of the window is also doubled. Sensing danger, a trout will sink lower, not only to put more distance between itself and the source of its unease but also to give it a wider field of vision.

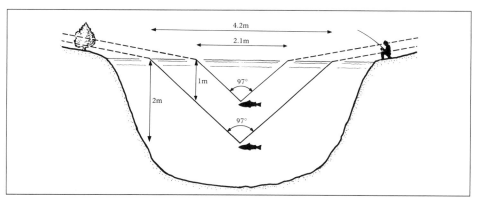

*The width of the trout's window*

Confined as it is to viewing only through a circular window, it follows that a trout is unable to see through the surface of the water anywhere beyond the window's edge. This area is called the 'mirror' and reflects the bottom of the lake or river bed on the underside of the surface film. Any object on the surface of the water, outside the area of the window, is quite undetectable but a trout almost certainly uses the optical effect of the mirror of its world as an aid to catching underwater prey reflected in it.

Both mirror and window only operate effectively when the surface of the water is relatively calm. If ruffled by current or wind, visibility in both is seriously reduced making feeding a much more haphazard undertaking — and fishing far less of a challenge.

**Taste and Smell**

Despite the lack of any anatomical connection between their nasal sacs and mouth, the trout's senses of taste and smell are much more closely connected than those of land vertebrates. This is because both can be stimulated by substances dissolved in the surrounding water. A trout has distinct taste buds in its mouth which are probably sensitive to the basic stimuli of sweet, sour, bitter and salt. It is also likely that it has some form of taste buds around the outside of its body enabling it to 'taste' the presence of food before seeing or swallowing it.

Alfred Ronalds described intriguing experiments on trout's senses in his *Fly-Fisher's Entomology* published in 1836. Trout are now actually given credit for a more sensitive palate than Ronalds suspected but there is no denying the thoroughness of a researcher who

'once threw upon the water, from my hut (by blowing them through a tin tube) successively ten dead house flies, towards a Trout known to me... all of which he took. Thirty more, with Cayenne pepper and mustard plastered on the least conspicuous parts of them, were then administered in the same manner. These he also seized . . . From these and similar experiments, such as Trout taking flies dipped in honey, oil, vinegar etc I concluded that if the animal has taste his palate is not particularly sensitive.'

The trout's sense of smell is extremely well developed, as the size of its olfactory lobes would suggest. Nostrils on the front of the head lead into nasal cavities. There water is propelled round by the action of slender cilia, stimulating the epithelium, which transmit stimuli back to the brain to effect any necessary response. Water is then expelled back out through the nostrils and the process continually repeated.

Trout can certainly detect worms or maggots on the end of a fishing line well below the depth that light ceases to penetrate. Some fishermen also believe trout can sense human smell left on a fly after it has been tied onto the cast, and experiments with Pacific salmon have shown them to react strongly to bear scent, as well as to seal, sea-lion and human odours. However, the most striking illustration of the olfactory powers of Salmonids is their remarkable ability to return from the sea to spawn in their natal stream. This is now attributed to the detection, by sense of smell, of the peculiar chemical composition of the waters of their stream of origin and appears all the more impressive because of the frequent contamination of these waters by industrial and human outpourings. The migratory travels of Atlantic salmon are the most spectacular but the shorter journeys of sea trout, which feed closer inshore than their congener, still demonstrate the sensitivity of the trout's sense of smell. Tagging experiments with sea trout parr or smolts have occasionally produced fresh water recaptures outside the river system of birth, but there is no doubting the ability of sea trout to return with extraordinary accuracy to their native stream, even to a particular stretch within it (Chapter Eight).

### Balance, Hearing and the Lateral Line

A trout's ear has no external opening, consisting only of an inner ear recessed into a cavity in the skull. It serves a dual purpose, both maintaining the fish's balance and providing it with the ability to hear.

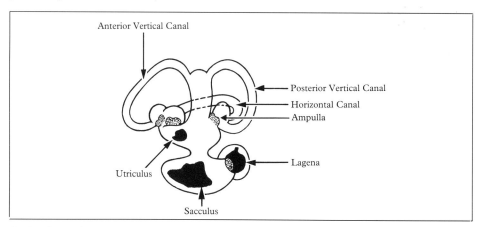

*Interior of a trout's ear.*

Sight is an important contributor to the maintenance of a fish's equilibrium but balance is principally achieved by the function of three fluid-filled semi-circular canals — two vertical and one horizontal. At the end of each is a small swelling (ampulla) lined with sensitive cells that respond to the fluid's stimulus. These cells send messages

(*Above*) Gillaroo (*Salmo stomachicus*) and (*below*) Great Lake Trout (*Salmo ferox*) as illustrated in the Rev W. Houghton's *British Freshwater Fishes* (1879) in which they are both described as separate species. (*I.F.E*)

A trout egg hatching (*above*) and eyed and uneyed trout eggs (*below*). (*I.F.E.*)

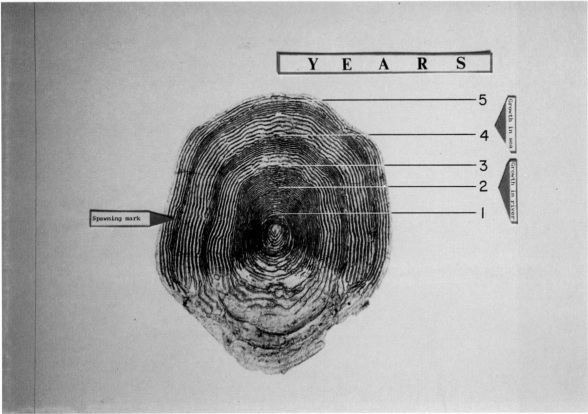

An alevin still with its yolk sac unabsorbed (*above*) (*I.F.E.*) and (*below*), the scale of a five year old sea trout showing a distinctive spawning mark in the fifth year after two years in the sea. (*Ardea*)

A trout stream in the Middle Atlas Mountains in Morocco (*above*) where there are still indigenous brown trout. (*Christine Osborne*). (*Below*) Lough Melvin in western Ireland, home of the distinct Gillaroo, Sonaghen and Ferox forms of brown trout. (*Author*)

The rich waters of the River Kennet in Berkshire (*above*) and the barren upper reaches of the River Tees in County Durham (*below*). (*Author*)

Competitors — grayling (*above*) and perch (*below*). (*N. Giles*)

Algal bloom on Windermere (*above*) and cutting weed on the River Frome in Dorset (*below*). (*I.F.E.*)

Blind Tarn in Cumbria (*above*), a 'new', rugged, oligotrophic lake and (*below*) Blelham Tarn, also in Cumbria, an eroded, eutrophic lake. (*I.F.E.*)

to the brain which may in turn signal a muscular response to effect a change in the fish's motion or position. Below the semi-circular canals are three membranous sacs (utriculus, sacculus and lagena) in each of which is a calcareous stone (otolith). Movement in any plane makes the otoliths, especially that in the utriculus, press on the sensitive cells which line the sacs, thereby transmitting a message to the brain in a similar manner to the action of fluid in the semi-circular canals.

Some fish, but not Salmonids, have a complex system of bones and membranes (Weberian apparatus) linking their ear and swim bladder. This mechanism enables their swim bladders to act as additional sound detectors and such fish hear very much better than those without it. The little sacculus and lagena sacs may also play a restricted role in the reception of sound waves, but all fish's hearing is greatly enhanced by the receptive abilities of the lateral line, which is part of the audio/lateral system. In trout, this line is a distinctive indentation running up both flanks from tail to head where it divides into three branches which then link with the brain.

The lateral line is a hollow mucus-filled channel within the skin from which branch short offshoots that emerge between the scales. The mucus in these offshoots is receptive to slight changes in water pressure which stimulate special cells (neuromasts). Nerves link these neuromasts to the larger lateral line nerve which collects information from all neuromasts down the line and transmits it to the brain. The lateral line system is particularly responsive to low-frequency sound waves and is most useful in detecting the sort of vibrations or pressure changes made by a fish or other animal swimming through the water.

The first reported experiments on the hearing powers of fish were conducted at a Benedictine monastery where carp, which possess the Weberian apparatus, were reputed to respond to the sound of a bell. Further research showed that their response was actually to the appearance of a monk which invariably coincided with the ringing of the bell. Alfred Ronalds also experimented.

'In order that we might be enabled to ascertain the truth of a common assertion, that fish can hear voices in conversation on the banks of a stream, my friend, the Reverend Brown of Grawich, and myself selected for close observation a Trout poised about six inches deep in the water, while a third gentleman, who was situated behind the fishing house, diametrically opposite to the side where the fish was, fired off one barrel of his gun. The possibility of the flash being seen by the fish was thus wholly prevented, and the report produced not the slightest apparent effect upon him. The second barrel was then fired. Still he remained immovable, evincing not the slightest symptom of having heard the report. This experiment was often repeated, and precisely similar results were invariably obtained. Neither could we ever awaken symptoms of alarm in fishes near the hut by shouting to them in the loudest tones, although our distance from them sometimes did not exceed six feet. The experiments were not repeated so often that they could become habituated to the sound.'

As Ronalds surmised, nearly all airborne sound is deflected off the water's surface and trout can hear none but the loudest noises originating outside their own much denser environment. But sound travels five times faster through water than air and vibrations are much easier to sense under the surface. Outboard engines, the tramp of heavy footfalls on banks, rowing or baling out a boat, dislodging stones by careless wading in a fast current — all these may generate vibrations which pass straight into the water where they can be detected by fish. If fish associate the noise with danger, then fright and flight are likely to follow.

Trout may use their limited ability to perceive water-borne vibrations in order to detect food, predators or other trout. Not only do swimming insects give off vibrations but some, such as dragonfly and caddis larvae, water bugs and water boatmen, actually make sounds. Often, trout merely duplicate the perceptions of their eyes in sensing objects through changing pressures, sound waves or lower frequency vibrations. However, in the comparatively lightless medium of water, sound and more especially vibration, is detectable by the audio/lateral system far outside the fish's visual range (which may be one reason why spinning baits are so successful). This makes a trout's ability to respond to these changing pressures or vibrations a vital part of its survival mechanisms, and nearly blind fish may even be able to remain alive exclusively by utilising the combined senses of their ears and lateral lines.

So, while the trout is a primitive fish in evolutionary terms, it is remarkably well adapted for life in a variety of freshwater environments, as well as for existence in the vastly different world of salt water. Its body carries a web of interdependent systems which function in unison to give that body life. A bony skeleton is surrounded by broad layers of muscle, the whole manoeuvred with the greatest precision through the water by eight different fins. Organs used in breathing, digestion and excretion all process matter from the trout's environment to promote growth, tissue replacement and other metabolic functions. Throughout the body tissue a network of blood vessels carries oxygen and other essential inputs to the cells and returns with waste matter for eventual expulsion. Responding to external stimuli are sense organs and a nervous system conveying messages to the brain which analyses their contents and then initiates any necessary muscular response.

These bones, muscles and internal organs make up a body so shaped as to maximise mobility and minimise resistence to the strong currents which dominate so much of the trout's habitat; and round this body is a protective skin, almost unparalleled in diversity of colour and pattern.

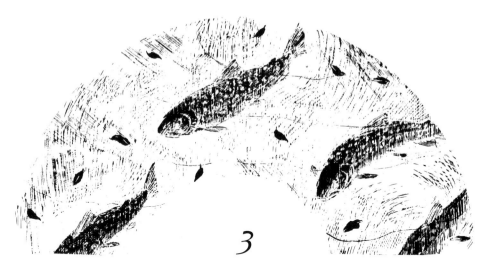

# 3
# Breeding and Heredity

Breeding is fundamental to the continuation of all animal life, ensuring not only the perpetuation of the species but also a diversity of progeny which is itself the basis for gradual evolutionary change. Fish have developed an extraordinary variety of different reproductive methods. The eggs of some species, including many sharks, skates and rays, are fertilised inside the female by copulation before they are laid (oviparous); in others, such as guppies *(Poecilia reticulata)* eggs are retained and hatched internally before birth (ovoviviparous), in almost mammalian fashion. Some individual fish are hermaphroditic and even capable of self-fertilisation, but far the most common method of reproduction is for the female to lay her eggs which are then externally fertilised by the male, and this is the way of the trout.

In their natural range trout breed in late autumn and early winter, but long before they reach the spawning grounds both sexes begin to undergo quite dramatic physiological changes. These begin several months before spawning with the gradual enlargement of the reproductive organs.

Late in winter, the female's undeveloped ovary consists of two long strips of transparent tissue to which are attached the disintegrating remains of any eggs unshed during the previous autumn's spawning. By the end of March, the full quota of eggs has been determined and each is surrounded by a sac of cells (follicle) which nourish the developing nucleus of the egg. During summer the follicles absorb nutriment from the blood stream, much of it resulting from the conversion of fat from the walls of the intestine and caecae. Such nutriment is then passed to the egg cell as yolk.

At the same time, the male testes are also developing. In early spring these are thin, pinky strips of tissue but fatten out during the summer, gaining the more familiar creamy colouring which they retain until spawning. Testes are made up of long, coiled seminiferous tubules containing the sperm and their nutritive Sertoli cells that perform the same supportive function as the ovarian follicles. Sperm are much smaller than eggs and even though the male produces many more sperm than the female does eggs, testes never expand to fill the body cavity to the same extent as do the female's ovaries. However, in both sexes the development of sex cells takes a heavy toll of the body's resources, and growth slows right down as spawning time approaches.

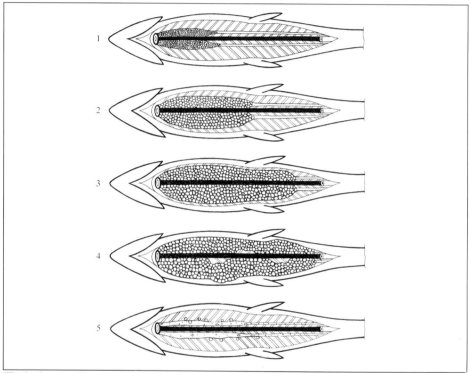

*The development of a trout's ovary. 1-3 show the ova gradually ripening. In 4 the membrane surrounding the ova has ruptured and the eggs are now loose in the body cavity. In 5 the fish has spawned and one or two unshed eggs remain behind.*

In addition to their prime function as producers of eggs or sperm, the reproductive organs also control much of the hormonal activity which precipitates other metabolic changes associated with breeding: the fish's skin darkens and becomes slimier, the male's skull may elongate and older male trout often develop pronounced kypes at the end of their lower jaws. Both sexes also show marked changes in behaviour as their inclination to feed is gradually repressed by stronger migratory and courtship urges.

Spawning times are partly affected by inheritance, causing some populations of trout to breed as early as October and others as late as February. The external influences of dropping temperatures, reduced daylight or increased water flow also play an important part in stimulating the breeding urge. This is nowhere better demonstrated than by the behaviour of trout exported as fertilised ova from their native northern climes and introduced into rivers in the southern hemisphere.

The first successful shipment of fertilised trout ova was to Australia, arriving in April 1864 (Chapter Ten). Shortly afterwards, the eggs hatched and the mature fish eventually introduced into the Plenty river in Tasmania soon established themselves as spawners during the antipodean winter. This was quite contrary to any influence of inherent rhythm, which would naturally have tended to promote spawning in the months of the northern winter, and environmental factors clearly overrode any inherited inclination to breed between November and February. Since then, experiences with exported ova have repeatedly demonstrated that any inherited tendency to spawn at a particular time of year is soon suppressed by environmental influences.

The shorter days of approaching autumn may be the main trigger to the onset of the trout's spawning urge, and experiments have shown that unnatural light conditions can accelerate or retard breeding maturity. Falling water temperatures are also likely to spur the upstream migration which often precedes spawning; so too may the increased flow of water brought on by the start of autumn rains. In equatorial Kenya, where day length hardly varies and monthly average temperatures are much more consistent, there are two spawning periods coinciding with the rainy seasons of April/May and October/November.

Many of the possible stimuli to spawning are so closely interconnected that isolating the influence of any particular one may be almost impossible. A drop in atmospheric pressure inevitably accompanies the onset of rain and the relative effects of each of these closely related meteorological changes cannot be dissociated. It is equally difficult to predict whether it is the actual fall of either water temperature or atmospheric pressure which brings about changes in the trout's behaviour, rather than the attainment of a specific level of one of these.

Prompted by one or more of these environmental stimuli, as spawning time approaches, trout in still waters usually start to move up the small streams feeding their native ponds and lakes. The timing of these upstream migrations varies from one water to another and they can begin several months, or merely a few days, before spawning is due to take place. Trout in rivers may also migrate up smaller tributaries to more suitable spawning grounds than they can find in the main stream.

Effective spawning depends on a number of specific requirements chiefly relating to the substratum of the breeding area and the flow of water over it. Water temperature is crucial to the development of ova, but is not so critically important for actual spawning. In any event, because trout breed in autumn in the northern hemisphere and tend to migrate upstream to do so, the need during ova development for water cooler than that required for normal life is likely to be naturally satisfied. The requirement for plenty of oxygen is also fulfilled by the lower water temperatures as well as by trout's preference for a reasonable current over their spawning beds.

Sluggish water tends to leave silt on the stream bottom. This is very unwelcome in that it may cover gravel beds suitable for spawning and also choke ova by depriving them of oxygen during development. A swifter current carries silt away with it as well as creating a more uniform water temperature; it may also help trout in their excavation of suitable nests. A flow rate of around two kilometers per hour (just over half a meter per second) will contribute to optimum spawning conditions. However, in a lake with no feeder streams large enough to swim up, trout may occasionally try to breed in the gravelly, windswept shallows where wave motion can to some extent compensate for lack of current. Then breeding is usually less successful but may eventually result in a stock of fewer, but larger fish rather than overpopulation by many smaller ones.

Floods may ruin any chance of successful spawning, dirt in the water choking eggs or the stronger current disturbing them on the stream bed. Too little water in autumn can be equally disastrous, disrupting breeding either because trout have difficulty in moving up their spawning stream or because the chosen area is too shallow. Lower water levels also induce warmer temperatures, less oxygen and higher concentrations of acid or other pollutants.

The suitable composition of the chosen spawning area's substratum is the most indispensable factor for successful breeding. A female hollows out her nest ('redd' is usually applied to a group of several nests or the area of gravel where they are excavated) with her tail, the pressure changes created by its repeated flapping lifting the gravel which is then carried downstream by the current. The process is known as 'cutting'. For trout to excavate suitable nests, the stream bed must comprise stones small enough to be displaced by the fanning actions of their tails and then later flicked back over the fertilised eggs. After spawning, water should continue to percolate between the stones covering the nest, so as to provide ova with a constant supply of oxygen during pre-hatching development. Therefore stones must not be so small that they choke the ova by preventing percolation and yet should be heavy enough to withstand the increased pressures of winter floods. By virtue of water's high density, stones on a stream bed are much easier to dislodge than those on dry land. Large trout can displace pebbles up to six centimeters in diameter, but the ideal redd is composed of gravel pieces between one and three centimeters across.

A female trout may reach her selected spawning ground several days before she is due to lay her eggs and, on arrival, begins to explore the stream bed with gentle flicks of her tail and anal fin. There are often suitable spawning areas at the ends of small pools where flow is gradually increasing before water runs out into the riffle at the top of the next pool. Bigger fish may choose deeper, faster flowing areas where gravel is coarser but can still be shifted by the exertions of their larger bodies. This exploratory work may take several days or only a few hours, but having selected an appropriate site the female then begins cutting, eventually excavating a deep enough nest in which to release her eggs.

Even though males migrate upstream first, they play no part in the early cutting of the nest. This is the female's work which she tackles by turning on her side while facing upstream, and bending and straightening her whole body in a series of violent movements which produce an exaggerated fanning motion of her tail. At times it appears as if her tail actually touches the gravelly substratum, but most of the stones are actually dislodged by the pressure waves created by its vertical flexions. Careful observation of the cutting movements shows that, while the tail's downward strokes scatter some of the smaller pebbles through the increase in water pressure, it is the suction effect brought about by its upward strokes that displaces most of the stones.

Cuts each consist of several strenuous tail flexions which shift stones from the nest and push them downstream. At the same time, each cut edges the female trout a short distance upstream from where she either drifts back over the nest or turns round and swims downstream to approach it from below. Using her eyes to appraise her work and her anal fin to test her progress, the female continues cutting until fully satisfied with the nest's construction.

As excavation continues, cuts tend to become more violent and it is now that the male, somewhat belatedly, begins to take an interest in the opposite sex. The female is so preoccupied with her nest making that she has little energy or opportunity to exercise much choice in selecting a partner. Therefore successful pairing is usually accomplished by a male ready to spawn attaching himself to a female in similar condition and keeping at bay any other males showing an interest in his chosen mate. Successful males can react violently to threats from other males — lunging or snapping at interlopers and sometimes actually biting them. To this end, fitter, stronger and more aggressive males are more likely to succeed as breeders. Those that successfully attach themselves to females are often referred to as 'dominant' males in contrast to the non-breeding, usually smaller, satellite males lurking on the edges of a redd awaiting their chances to intrude.

The time taken to make her nest depends particularly on how long the female spends on preliminary exploration and casual excavations. However, once she has selected a site, cutting continues for up to two hours before egg laying starts. As cutting increases in intensity, so do the dominant male's attentions which are particularly apparent from his violent quivering as he lies near the contortive female. Together, this cutting and quivering constitute a form of mutual courtship which continues until the nest is large enough for its purpose.

Completed nests are always longer than the trout that made them, sometimes considerably so, and usually slightly deeper. In shape nests are either circular or oval with the heap of displaced stones forming a small mound at the downstream end. They are often conspicuous on the stream bed by the paler colour of the excavated gravel. The depression of the nest and the raised heap of stones behind it set up a system of currents which protects the eggs, once laid, from being swept downstream before the female has covered them over.

Finally satisfied that her work is complete, the female then settles down into the nest, arching her body so her head is raised and her vent nestles close onto the gravel bed. If the substratum allows she will also slip her anal fin between the stones. Then, properly settled, she opens her mouth and the male, who has remained alongside his mate during this final cutting, also settles into the nest, and opens his. The female opening her mouth is probably the final stimulus to the male. It also signals the impending extrusion of the female's eggs because as her mouth opens to its fullest extent a muscular spasm causes her eggs to squirt out onto the gravel below. Simultaneously the male ejaculates milt which then mingles with the eggs.

Eggs must be fertilised by the male within little more than a minute from extrusion, otherwise they become inactive. So do sperm, which can only survive contact with fresh water for a similar period, quickly dying unless they can fuse with an egg. Immediately after they are laid, eggs are soft and slightly sticky but swell up as they absorb water, becoming harder and much less adhesive. On their surface is a tiny aperture (micropyle) which quickly closes as the egg expands through water absorption, making almost instant fertilisation so crucial. Sperm swim by wiggling their tails and are probably attracted to eggs by chemical stimuli. Once a single sperm has entered through the micropyle, this closes up automatically so ensuring that not more than one sperm fertilises each egg.

The male and female's almost simultaneous orgasm, which is the main prerequisite for successful fertilisation, is not by any means the inevitable culmination of courtship and cutting. A male often leaks much of his milt during the preliminary stages or ejaculates before the female does, thereby effectively wasting both his sperm and her eggs. There may also be a number of false starts when successful spawning by both fish appears about to take place but for some reason does not immediately do so. Yet despite this seemingly haphazard spawning behaviour, in suitable conditions and aided by the massive surplus of sperm to eggs, well over ninety per cent of ova are successfully fertilised before their micropyles close up. In imperfect conditions the percentage is obviously smaller but even a partially successful mating is likely to ensure the fertilisation of many eggs.

Once extruded, whether fertilised or not, the moisture absorbed by eggs almost immediately makes them heavier than the surrounding water, causing them to sink to the bottom of the nest and, if the stones are large enough, down into the cracks between them. The female then immediately moves upstream of the nest and with further vigorous cuts of her tail, covers up the eggs with gravel. The eggs are now hard and not damaged as the small stones are spread over them, providing protection both from predation and from any danger of being washed away by the current. Bigger trout are able to displace larger stones and can therefore bury their eggs deeper in the nest, so increasing their chances of hatching successfully.

Perhaps to counter the possibility that for any reason a single spawning might prove unsuccessful, females usually make more than one nest, laying successive clutches in each. Any depression created in the process of covering eggs in the first nest may provide the basis for a second one and so spawning is repeated until the female has shed most of the eggs from her body. A male can also expel milt in a succession of matings but usually abandons the female as she starts to cover up her eggs. During subsequent nest excavations she may be accompanied by a different mate which is at least an effective way of increasing the different genetic combinations of her offspring.

After spawning, a female may remain near her nest for anything from a few hours to several days, driving away intruders which are usually other females wanting to spawn nearby. Where suitable redds are scarce, the competition for breeding space is often intense and successive females frequently stir up the nests of previous spawners. Sometimes eels, young trout, grayling or other species of fish nose around the redds foraging for stray eggs. Beyond this rather casual post-spawning protection from the female, eggs, and subsequently the newly hatched fish, receive no parental care whatsoever. However, to some extent, the enormous over-production of eggs from which so few young survive to maturity compensates for this.

The fundamental requirement to maintain a constant population of any animal species (assuming an equal proportion of both sexes) is for each female during her lifetime to produce two offspring which themselves survive to breed. The eggs of cod (*Gadus morhua*) are simply extruded into the open sea and to ensure at least one or two (depending on how often in her life a female breeds) are fertilised and survive to maturity the female usually lays more than a million at a time. By contrast, a coelacanth's twenty eggs are internally fertilised and hatch inside their mother, while female bitterling *(Rhodeus sericeus)* from eastern Europe, deposit theirs only between the gaping shells of freshwater mussels by means of the long egg-tubes they develop before spawning. The disadvantage of such specialised behaviour is that successful spawning depends on finding a mussel, but the hatching rate is so high as a result of the protection thus afforded to the eggs that the female bitterling need only lay about fifty to maintain a level population. Because both salmon and trout build nests and cover their eggs after laying, their eggs stand a better chance of hatching than cod's, but not than bitterling's, and both *Salmo* species are reckoned to lay between 1000 and 1500 eggs per kilogram of body weight. If a female spawns twice in her life, just one egg from each spawning which matures into a fertile adult suffices to keep the population constant.

The number of eggs a female trout lays depends not only on body weight but also on her length, age and the particular aquatic environment. Figures vary from less than 200 eggs to over 3,000 but larger fish generally lay larger eggs and in greater numbers. Sometimes small early-maturing trout in overpopulated upland waters appear to lay fewer eggs than even their reduced size would suggest; however, these are usually larger and therefore stand a better chance of surviving in waters where food is scarce and fish may live shorter lives. For the corollary of the need to produce enough eggs to maintain a stable population is of course that it is a waste of energy to produce too many.

It is self-evident that under normal conditions members of a species elect to mate with each other, and trout are no exception. Indeed, one of the definitions of a species is 'a group of actually or potentially interbreeding populations, isolated by reproductive, but not necessarily geographical, barriers from other such groups'. However, under certain natural conditions an animal of one species may still attempt to breed with one from another closely related species.

Below species level, interbreeding between different forms, races or even sub-species is perfectly possible since by definition those groups are not yet reproductively isolated. Brown trout and sea trout may be regarded as separate forms of the same species but are far from being reproductively isolated from each other. Wherever sea trout are found, so are non-migratory brown trout, and both forms may even emerge from the same clutch of eggs (Chapter Eight). A cross between the two forms produces fertile offspring and if one usually favours a mate from the same form it is more because of generally differing breeding habits than any genetic incompatibility. Both forms in the same stream may reach breeding maturity at different times of the year and this also militates against interbreeding.

The brown trout's closest relative is the Atlantic salmon and, given the considerable overlap in their native distributions, natural hybridisation between them is theoretically possible. Salmon usually breed later in the year than trout; they also need deeper water to do so which often means they spawn lower down the stream making use of redds where stones are larger. But despite Nature's efforts to separate the species at spawning time, natural hybridisation occurs fairly often. Different tests on a large number of British salmon showed that up to four per cent were salmon/trout hybrids. The reasons why the species interbreed are still unclear.

Perhaps where individuals of one or other species are scarce, it is at least preferable to expel eggs or semen by mating with a fish of a different species rather than simply waiting for them to be reabsorbed.

The ability of two species to interbreed successfully is theoretically a sign of their genetic proximity and the more closely related they are the more likely are the resulting hybrids to be fertile. Atlantic salmon/brown trout crosses are usually infertile whereas closely related rainbow and cutthroat trout interbreed in the wild, often producing fertile offspring, although mortality among fry is abnormally high. Strangely though, in the slower reaches of many British rivers roach *(Rutilus rutilus)*, rudd *(Scardinius erythrophthalmus)* and common bream *(Abramis brama)* all freely interbreed despite belonging to different genera; the resulting offspring are often fertile and may cross with either parent species.

With the aim of improving fish either for the table or for stocking purposes, or even in the course of pure scientific study, researchers have subjected various species of Salmonidae to any number of artificial hybridisation experiments. Almost all crosses have resulted in some successful hatchings, but an especially significant phenomenon is the marked difference in using a male of one species and a female of another against the results of reversing the sexes.

One of the most successful artificially bred hybrids, often called 'tiger trout', comes from the inter-generic cross between brown trout and brook charr. In the breeding of tiger trout, mixing brown trout eggs and brook charr milt produces far more tiger trout with totally different colour patterns than does the reverse process, whose offspring are sometimes called 'leopard trout'. Similarly, with the most successful inter-species Salmonid cross of all, which are hybrids between congeneric brook and lake charr (colloquially called 'splake'), female lake and male brook charr produce many times more offspring than if the sexes are reversed. When correctly bred, splake are so genetically stable that not only can they successfully breed with one another but also with either parent species. Both brook and lake charr have the same number of chromosomes (eighty-four) in each cell, which may give them a distinct advantage over hybrids between species whose chromosome numbers are unevenly matched.

All species of animal have a distinctive number of chromosomes in most of their cells; man has forty-six, Atlantic salmon sixty and brown trout eighty. As with all animals that reproduce sexually, during the development of a brown trout's testes or ovaries a process known as meiotic division takes place whereby sperm and eggs split into two cells whose nuclei each retain forty chromosomes — exactly half the number (haploid number) of every other cell.

Within the chromosomes are genes, which are chemical compounds controlling the inherited characteristics of individuals of any species. Genes are composed of varying lengths of a complex molecule (DNA — deoxyribonucleic acid). During breeding between members of the same species, equal numbers of chromosomes are contributed by sperm and egg to make up the full complement (diploid number) in the developing progeny. In this way the male and female contribute their respective genes that both compete and combine to influence the make-up of their offspring.

Early geneticists assumed the existence of one gene for each particular inherited characteristic, such as colour, size, fertility or longevity. Certainly some traits may be largely influenced by one specific gene, but the vast majority of inherited characteristics are now known to result from the combined influence of many different genes, of which there are thousands in every cell of each animal. These combinations promote the possibility of wide variations within any one particular characteristic; thus a trout's colouration may vary not only within the range of brown and gold but also in the number, distribution and colour of spots, as well as in the different markings on its fins.

The genetic make-up of a particular population of any animal species is collectively referred to as its 'gene pool', and it is this pool of potential influence that shapes the form and behaviour of each individual within that population. The specific environment of any one geographically separated population of trout will tend to favour particular inherited qualities suitable for that environment; at the same time it will select against unfavourable ones such as low resistance to prevalent diseases, pale colouration in dark waters or a tendency to late maturity in an overpopulated stream. An individual's genetic constitution is passed on to its offspring and gradually, generation by generation, natural selection discards unfavourable qualities, promoting more favourable ones so that any natural population slowly begins to fit itself for its particular environment. At the same time, other geographically separated populations of trout are also adapting themselves for survival in their own peculiar environments which may result in very different sets of inherited characteristics gradually gaining dominance. So, with almost imperceptible slowness the genetic composition of different populations begins to take on a distinct identity as different forms, varieties or races of trout emerge. In time these may differ sufficiently to merit the very arbitrary distinction of a sub-species and eventually the slightly less subjective status of a separate species.

Sometimes chance intervenes to disturb the gradual selection process by upsetting the structure of a particular DNA molecule. Such an event is called a mutation and may trigger a quantum leap forward in the evolutionary advance of a particular species. It is strange that it takes a genetic accident to provide the raw material for evolutionary progress, yet while mutations are rare, their influence seems undeniable.

In most cases, the ascription of an individual specimen to a particular species means checking its physical characteristics with the established description of that species. However, anatomical features may be very uncertain indicators and a more effective method of identifying species or ascertaining relationships between individuals is by chemically testing their genetic constitutions.

The genetic profile of an individual of a species is established by testing body tissue for different proteins, using a system known as electrophoresis. By establishing this protein composition it is possible, within limitations, to ascertain the genetic control over the formation of these proteins and therefore the make-up of the genes of any given individual which exercise this control. Far more accurate would be a direct analysis of DNA itself rather than of its products (akin to the genetic fingerprinting techniques used to identify criminals), but the techniques for doing this have not yet been perfected. Both facilities have had a major impact on the science of taxonomy, having already contributed to the removal of rainbow and cutthroat trout from genus *Salmo* to that of *Oncorhynchus*, and also having shown both species to be most closely related to the Japanese Masu salmon. These tests have also opened up many of the old arguments for promoting certain forms or races of brown trout to the rank of species.

The best example of genetic differences between brown trout populations comes from the justifiably much-quoted research at Lough Melvin in western Ireland. Here there are three distinct forms of trout — gillaroo, sonaghen and ferox. The richly coloured gillaroo with their thickly muscled stomachs live mainly off a diet of molluscs, crustaceans and fly larvae which they nose off the stones round the shallow edges of the lough. The little sonaghen are steely blue in colour with black fins and are seldom more than thirty centimeters long or half a kilogram in weight; they feed mainly off animal plankton, filtering water fleas and midge larvae out of the open waters of the lough by swimming along with their mouths open like miniature whales. Adult ferox trout are almost exclusively piscivorous, preying on Arctic charr, perch and young trout although in some Scottish lochs salmon smolts also feature seasonally in their diets. These three separate forms of trout hardly ever interbreed in Lough Melvin and their differing habits, together with their distinctively different genetic profiles, give rise to a strong argument in favour of their being treated as separate species. This would be a return to a classification very similar to Gunther's in 1866 in which he named respectively, *Salmo stomachicus*, *S. nigripinnis* and *S. ferox*.

From the formation of genetic profiles by means of electrophoretic testing or DNA analysis it may also be possible to determine relationships between geographically separated populations of trout. Lough Melvin ferox and those of the deep highland lochs of Scotland show distinct genetic similarities and could be descended from common ancestral stock, but the genetic make-up of sonaghen is very different to that of the superficially similar black-finned trout from certain lakes in north Wales.

The present natural distribution of trout in all their different forms can be largely attributed to the glacial history of Britain and Ireland. The last Ice Age began about 60,000 years ago and probably reached its most southerly extent 40,000 years later, by which time ice covered nearly all of Britain and probably most of Ireland; any land not then coated in ice would have been covered with a layer of permafrost. Under such conditions few fish are likely to have survived, and therefore the arrival of nearly all freshwater species most probably started as the glaciation began to retreat. Gradually the fresh waters of Britain and Ireland were colonised by species from northern Europe and by Salmonids migrating northwards in the sea. These latter would gradually have found the Mediterranean and southern Atlantic seas too warm and slowly moved northwards, colonising suitable fresh waters as they did so. During the 10,000 years it took the ice to thaw, several distinct invasions of migratory fish are likely to have spread through Europe, and the different forms of trout in Lough Melvin and elsewhere may be descended from these separate waves of immigrants.

However, the process of diversification is a laboured one and the 10,000 years since the end of the last deglaciation has hardly been long enough for these three, and all other forms of trout throughout Britain and Ireland, to have diverged from a common migratory stock. The major climatic upheavals during the last two million years almost certainly created many opportunities for the geographical isolation of different populations of any one species, and DNA analysis can also help calculate how long ago a particular form or species split from its ancestral lineage. The initial conclusions from such tests are that ferox trout have been reproductively isolated from all other forms of trout far longer than the 65,000 years during which gillaroo have been isolated from sonaghen. If these results are correct, the three forms of trout began to evolve along separate paths before the start of the last Ice Age. Then, 40,000 years later, the ice melt's chaotic effect on the topography would have distributed populations of each of these forms throughout various parts of Britain and Ireland, with all three finding their way to Lough Melvin. Perhaps too, if some of these different trout really did diverge from their ancestral stock as long ago as it seems they may have done, early taxonomists were doubly justified in considering them separate species.

Genetic analysis of sea trout populations in Britain and Ireland has also shown that the classifications of Gunther and others may not have been so wide of the mark after all. To admit five separate species of sea trout, as Gunther did, was probably an exaggeration of species splitting. It is nevertheless now generally agreed that today's sea trout populations are descended from at least two clearly identifiable, separate invasions of distinct forms of trout. The first influx was of fish that, until the ice began its retreat from the limits of maximum glaciation perhaps 20,000 years ago, found the climatic conditions in southern Europe ideal. These are now referred to as the 'ancestral' race and are the predecessors of many of the migratory populations of sea trout, characterised by their long life and slow growth, on the west coast of Britain and Ireland. This ancestral race is genetically similar to the long-lived ferox trout and may also have founded many of the landlocked populations of brown trout which became isolated by the geological consequences of so much melting ice. Then, as Europe warmed further and the ice all but disappeared from Britain 10,000 years after it began to melt, a second influx of trout appeared in British fresh waters. These came from elsewhere in northern Europe, perhaps from the North Sea, and are called the 'modern' race. They tend to grow much faster than the ancestral race but not to live as long.

While the genetic influence of inheritance on the anatomy and behaviour of any individual trout is paramount, the environment's influence cannot be ignored and it is often difficult to dissociate the two. The native trout in Scotland's Loch Leven have almost no red spots, but if removed to a new habitat or reared under artificial conditions such spots may soon appear. Therefore the absence of red spots on Loch Leven trout is a genetically unstable characteristic and due more to the effects of the environment — in this case probably diet — than to the effects of heredity. Tiny trout from moorland waters, where a 250 gram fish would be considered unusually large, easily grow to one or two kilograms if introduced to the rich diet of chalk streams; their size is therefore governed by food supply rather than by genetic influence, and the same trout would also soon lose their dark peat-induced colours and take on the more golden hues of chalk stream fish. Similarly, trout hatched from ova exported to Australia quickly discarded any inherited inclination to breed during the northern winter months and instead bowed to the environmental influences of the colder weather and shorter days of antipodean winters.

A trout inherits the physiological ability to adapt to life in salt water. Such ability would be wasted if it did not also inherit an inclination to utilise it by migrating to sea to feed. However, unknown environmental factors either suppress or encourage the exercise of this inclination. Fish bred under artificial conditions from non-migratory parent stock and introduced to foreign waters often quickly migrate to sea, while some offspring of migratory parents never leave fresh water. And between the two ends of the migratory spectrum is the widest possible range of intermediate behaviour both within a given population and between separate ones. There are communities where only females migrate to sea and others where some but not all males remain behind in fresh water. Some trout make relatively extensive migrations within their home stream but never leave fresh water, while others reach the brackish waters of the estuary but travel no further.

Electrophoretic tests on different individual trout that exercise all these migratory options have shown them to have very similar genetic make-ups, and yet some undiscovered trigger provokes this whole range of behaviour within different individuals of the one species. So, while the comparative influences of nature (inheritance) and nurture (environment) remain obscure, the trout's behaviour is ultimately the product of the two. A specific genetic make-up is necessary before the environmental trigger can precipitate a particular behaviour pattern, but the precise workings of the trigger mechanism itself remain little understood.

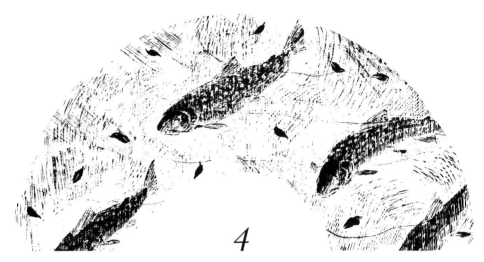

# 4

# *Life and Growth*

A trout's life begins with the fusion of sperm and egg that is the culmination of successful spawning. Once a sperm has passed through the micropyle, this closes up and the egg starts to absorb water, gradually increasing in volume by about one third, before reaching its full size twenty minutes later.

As eggs swell, they quickly become heavier than water and sink to the bottom of the nest. During their first hours, newly fertilised eggs can tolerate sudden shock or movement with little risk of damage and are not harmed by the female's further cutting actions as she covers them over with gravel. Any eggs not properly covered or inadvertently excavated by a second female attempting to lay on an earlier nest will not usually hatch and are likely to be swept away and eaten by other species of fish or even other trout.

Once safely inside an egg, the sperm immediately comes into contact with the tiny germinal disc on the outside of the yolk sac. This contains the key to those characteristics a fish inherits from its female parent and fuses with the sperm which contributes the male's. As cells multiply, this genetic identity is disseminated through every one in the embryo's body to create the unique entity of an individual of its species.

As its embryo starts to develop an egg becomes extremely delicate and susceptible to damage, remaining in this fragile condition until the retina of the eye begins to show as a dark blob on either side of the developing head. At this stage, less than half-way through the incubation period, eggs are said to be 'eyed' and from then on can withstand shocks and sudden movements.

A plentiful supply of oxygen is essential for the embryo's successful development and for this reason water must be able to percolate freely among the nest's gravel lining; a layer of silt can lethally harm eggs by depriving them of oxygen. The other factor critical to embryo growth is water temperature, which must remain within certain distinct limits. Between these limits, higher or lower temperatures significantly accelerate or retard embryo development and therefore vary the length of time before hatching.

The discovery of the importance of water temperature during the incubation period was stimulated by the repeated failure of early efforts to transport trout to Australia (Chapter Ten), through ova hatching prematurely on board ship. Only after considerable research into incubation periods at differing temperatures and the development of satisfactory refrigeration techniques using large blocks of ice, was hatching sufficiently delayed until the ova reached their destination.

The maximum water temperature for successful incubation and hatching of brown trout eggs is about 16°C. Above that figure mortality increases dramatically despite the fact that, once hatched, trout can live in water several degrees warmer. The lower lethal limit for egg survival is close to freezing point but at 1°C many eggs fail to hatch and incubation is almost indefinitely prolonged.

At the upper lethal limit of 16°C brown trout eggs hatch just over twenty days after laying but mortality is high. As water temperature decreases so the number of days to hatching increases and if eggs hatch at all at 2°C they take over 150 days to do so. For maximum hatching, optimum temperatures range between 5°C and 12°C, and if possible ova in fish hatcheries are kept at around 10°C when hatching occurs within about forty days.

These are approximate incubation periods for brown trout eggs under different temperatures:-

| ° Centigrade | Days of incubation |
|:---:|:---:|
| 2 | 150+ |
| 3 | 128 |
| 4 | 108 |
| 5 | 90 |
| 6 | 75 |
| 7 | 63 |
| 10 | 40 |
| 12 | 27 |
| 16 | 20 |

Ova can expect constant water temperatures only in an artificial environment or if their nest is very close to a spring. Under natural conditions, temperatures fluctuate not only within the day but also throughout longer spans of time, as the seasons ebb and flow. Therefore, when fish are breeding in the wild these figures must be read as average temperatures during the whole incubation period.

The likely span of the incubation period will largely govern the time of year trout spawn. Fish in consistently warm, spring-fed chalk streams normally breed in

December or January, even as late as February. That being the case, the arrival of young trout, ready and able to feed for themselves (which is several weeks after hatching), coincides with the increased food supplies appearing in March and April. Trout in cold upland waters may need to spawn in late October or early November if their offspring are to be mature enough to start feeding in the spring. It also follows that unseasonal weather may delay or advance hatching.

Within a given population of trout, the first to hatch have a distinct advantage over their siblings in that they are also first to establish their feeding territories and should therefore have access to the best of them. Because trout use less energy in cooler temperatures, early hatchers may also gain by utilising more of their yolk sac in growth than those emerging when the water is warmer. Still, it is a critical balance, for fish that hatch too early may find themselves having to feed before food supplies are abundant enough to sustain them.

Prior to hatching, because its surrounding membrane is impermeable, the developing embryo must subsist exclusively on the various nutrients in the egg yolk. Hatching is triggered by internal enzyme activity. First the egg's outer membrane ruptures and gradually the young fish (alevin) wriggles out of its shell with its yolk sac attached below its throat, giving it a rather tadpole-like appearance. Its beating heart is clearly visible as is a network of blood vessels and prominent black eyes on either side of its head.

At this stage, the young alevin remains inactive and, burdened by its yolk sac and highly vulnerable to predators, tends to stay nestled down among the stones. However, its eyes are sufficiently developed to distinguish changes in light intensity. This helps the alevin to orientate itself towards the comparative security of the stream bed where it remains, self-contained in nourishment, for between three and twelve weeks depending on water temperature. At an average of 10°C, a young trout emerges from its gravel about five weeks after hatching but takes nearly twice as long to do so at 5°C. As its body matures the alevin's yolk sac is gradually depleted so that when the stock of nutrition is almost exhausted, its anatomy is sufficiently developed for it to feed for itself: by then it is just over two centimeters long.

An alevin that has made the transition from dependence on its yolk sac to reliance on external food supplies is called a 'fry' and goes through the process of 'swim-up', which means leaving the protection of the stream bed and swimming up into the open water to establish a feeding territory. In all probability, swim-up is finally stimulated by changes in the alevin's response to light. Instead of frightening it into shelter among the darkness of the gravel, the brighter light at the surface now becomes attractive, gradually luring the young fish upwards to begin the most intensely vulnerable stage of its life.

To begin with, fry hesitate to leave the security of their nest, making occasional tentative forays a few centimeters out into the current in pursuit of some passing morsel. Gradually they become more adventurous and eventually forsake their protective gravel for the open water. There they are guided by nothing but their inherited instincts and must contend with a full range of predators, intense competition from their fellows and the fundamental difficulties of life in a comparatively swift current. Some fry never start feeding for themselves and quickly die. Others may not be able to establish their own territories and starve to death more slowly as they struggle to survive on the edge of spaces already occupied by their peers, or in water unsuited for catching passing prey. Fry which succeed in establishing territories must defend them strenuously against encroachment. If they are able to do so they will flourish, but at the expense of the lives of many of their siblings: for the essence of the trout's breeding strategy is to compensate for lack of parental care by producing numbers of young far in excess of those which could possibly survive to maturity.

When fry swim up from the stream bed to begin feeding on their own, their initial choice of territory is governed by its fitness as a feeding station. Sites behind a small stone or in the water cushion in front of a rock are excellent, combining a plentiful food supply and sufficient protection from the current to allow fish to remain stationary with minimal expenditure of energy. Sometimes trout find a good feeding station on the quieter edges of a fast current which brings plenty of food down past them.

A territory is usually heart shaped with the fish lying at the downstream point facing upstream, continually aligning its position against some focal feature on the stream bed. Territory and fish size being directly related, a first feeding station may cover an area of about ten centimeters across or even less if food is particularly abundant. In crowded conditions, fry that first acquire prime territories soon start to gain in size and strength over their siblings, provided the food supply is sufficient for them to do so. As they grow, so do their food requirements, and to satisfy these fry need to expand their territories. This can only be achieved by ousting their neighbours, who are likely to die as a result. Thus, in classic Darwinian fashion, fewer and fewer individuals survive through each successive stage in development. And by the time they reach maturity, the minimum number of strongest individuals remains to breed again and sustain the population at its established level.

The early development of young trout, as their yolk sacs are absorbed and feeding territories established, is similar in all different types of stream. Thereafter however, there is an enormous difference between the behaviour and growth of trout as determined by the environmental extremes of small, peaty upland streams or slow, calcareous lowland rivers. For this reason, any single description of the life and growth of trout unavoidably includes a great many generalisations, not least because between these two extremes is a whole continuum of intermediate environments — of both still and running waters — that promote a correspondingly wide variation in the habits and development of the fish within them.

Naturally the greatest number of eggs hatch when breeding conditions are close to ideal. Then competition for available feeding territories is fiercest. This means many young fish (usually called 'parr' once the distinctive finger marks on their flanks start to show) are driven downstream to areas where conditions may be suitable for the establishment of new feeding territories but not for breeding. Thus territorial instincts gradually promote the distribution of similarly aged trout throughout the river, thereby maximising the benefits from the food supplies within it.

Having established their first territories, young trout remain at their feeding stations, darting out to seize any likely looking prey and then returning to the exact position they left. If current-borne food is not carried through their territories they will simply starve, for at that age they are unable to move away and seek out prey.

Trout expend considerable energy in counteracting the force of the current so as to remain within their feeding stations and starvation will gradually weaken them to the point of being swept downstream — usually to their death, unless they are fortunate enough to reach a large still pool or lake before they die.

As the ever decreasing number of survivors grow in size so do their territories, and with an enlarged feeding area comes the development of foraging behaviour whereby parr actively search for food instead of merely awaiting its arrival. At the same time, they can take in a wider range of prey, larger than the tiny larvae and pupae to which their size restricted them in the early weeks. As trout develop the ability to forage, they may be able to abandon the stronger currents of their first territories and seek quieter waters. There food can still be snapped out of the current but fish may also search for shrimps or insect larvae lurking on the stream bed or among rooted vegetation. When trout spread throughout the stream, their territorial requirements change little but there may be additional considerations such as the need for a refuge, perhaps outside their territories, to which they can flee if danger threatens.

Young parr leaving their nursery areas to colonise new parts of the river will inevitably move into the existing territories of older trout. Established residents seem prepared to tolerate these intrusions of younger fish, perhaps because these new arrivals consistently feed on smaller food items which larger fish tend to ignore. All animals must unconsciously balance the energy expended in securing food against the nutritional benefit derived from eating it; and if the former outweighs the latter, there is clearly a net energy loss in that particular feeding foray.

In still waters, the absence of current generally makes foraging the only means of feeding. There, trout are much harder to study than in small streams but are less influenced by their territorial instincts. Feeding may still be restricted to loosely defined areas, but one such area is likely to support a great many fish. Trout hatched in the smaller feeder streams flowing into ponds and lakes may spend one or two years in these relatively predator-free sanctuaries before moving down to the deeper still waters. Once there, they disperse evenly throughout the area and may become vulnerable to attacks by larger trout or pike, but prey is usually more plentiful and such bounty more than compensates for both the extra energy spent in catching it and the added dangers of predation. When mature, trout move inshore to the better feeding grounds in shallow water before returning to breed where they were born.

A combination of factors, whose relative effects are still uncertain, determine numbers of trout of different age groups in any given area. Young fish make their first impact on the existing trout population when they hatch, but until swim-up this is negligible. Once away from their nest, the number of fry that then establish territories depends significantly on the topography of the stream bed and the availability of feeding stations. The rougher more varied substratum of an upland stream creates far more of these than the flat gravelly bottom of a lazy lowland chalk river, although the latter's weed beds may provide valuable feeding stations for young trout in early summer.

Fry mortality is massive during and immediately after swim-up when over three quarters of a hatching may perish. The percentage survival through the summer depends largely upon how many trout initially established territories in any given stretch of stream. At that stage, survival is said to be "density-dependent" in that, by the end of summer there is a maximum number of fish of any one age group that a particular area of water can support (carrying capacity). If ten times more fish than that carrying capacity initially established territories, then their mortality rate through the summer would be ninety per cent but if only twice as many did, it would drop to fifty per cent; in other words mortality — or survival — is then dependent on population density.

Throughout the summer, survival is also affected by water level and temperature. Extremes of either can be fatal to many first year fish. Spring floods carry away whole broods of newly hatched fry. Then, as the water warms, a trout's metabolic rate accelerates and its food requirements increase. Consequently, if food supplies are already marginal, fish may die as temperatures rise. Moreover, lower levels of warmer water mean less current to bring down food, fewer feeding areas as the stream bed contracts and less dissolved oxygen in the water. Low water levels also render young fish more vulnerable to predators as well as possibly raising acidity or concentrations of pollutants to danger levels.

By the end of summer, the population of first year fish is likely to have stabilised at the stream's maximum carrying capacity. From then on, mortality no longer depends on population density, but is controlled by factors unrelated to existing numbers. Throughout its first winter the population of an age group may halve and then level off during the second summer before a further sharp drop in the second winter. At the end of their third summer, mature trout may breed for the first time but more often do not do so until a year later; thereafter they usually try to breed every year until death.

So, taking a hypothetical stream under average conditions — an unsatisfactory yet unavoidable proposition — where one hen fish lays 1000 eggs of which 900 are successfully fertilised, the survival rates of fish hatching from her eggs may be something like these. From the fertilised eggs, 800 alevins hatch of which 200 establish feeding territories with varying degrees of success. Throughout the summer, 160 of these die as a result of the remaining forty (which is the maximum carrying capacity of this hypothetical stretch of water) expanding their territories and growing to face the winter. In the general dispersal during winter months half of the forty die, leaving twenty alive the following spring. None of these breed and six more die during their second summer. Four more die during the second winter and out of the ten left at the beginning of the third summer one female attempts to breed in the autumn but is unsuccessful. By the following year, only six of the original 800 trout are still alive. Of these, three are females, two of which breed successfully. Only one female and one male trout survive into their fifth year.

From this huge surplus of young fish, it is clear that the brown trout's ability to repopulate a stream is almost infinitely elastic. Under normal circumstances, because so few fish survive, numbers of eggs have hardly any direct effect on the total population at the end of the year. Yet trout numbers can rapidly recover from a population crash, simply through the survival of more young fish from the following year's hatching. This perhaps implies that too much importance is attached to preserving breeding stocks of mature trout; if such stocks are reduced by, say, one third, there are still more than enough offspring from the remaining breeders to occupy the feeding stations unfilled by any progeny of that third.

So great are the variations in the factors influencing fish growth between one water and another that the hypothesis of trout in an average stream under average conditions must be continued. Temperature and chemical composition of the water, food supply and possibly even some genetic variability between populations may all combine to promote differing rates of development. Nevertheless, there remains a general pattern of growth applicable to trout in all waters.

Unlike birds and mammals, trout do not reach a maximum size but instead are able to continue growing throughout their lives. A graph of their growth indicating annual proportionate increase in length (and therefore unrelated to actual length) shows clearly that maximum proportionate growth occurs during the first two or three years of a trout's life. Thereafter the curve starts to flatten out as growth slows down. Young fish are voracious feeders and assuming an average length of 2.25 centimeters when they first swim up to start feeding, they are between two and five times that length by the end of their first year. Length may double during the second year and thereafter both proportionate and actual rates of growth slow noticeably, with an average proportionate increase of between one third and one half in the third year. From then on growth rates usually decline so that fish surviving to their fifth or sixth years show only minimal length increases unless there is a sudden change in their feeding strategy.

An example of the enormous variation in growth rates between different populations of fish illustrates both the necessity for, and dangers of, limited generalisations. A sample of trout from the river Kennet in Berkshire averaged 11.5 centimeters in length at the end of their first year, nearly twenty-four centimeters at the end of their second and thirty-four centimeters by the end of the third. Fish surviving through to the end of their fourth year were thirty-nine centimeters long, but curiously grew more in their fifth year than in their fourth. Further north, several studies in the small streams feeding the upper reaches of the river Tees on the Pennines in Cumbria, painted a very different picture. By the end of their first year these trout were five centimeters long and exactly doubled to ten centimeters during their second. In their third year they grew to just under fourteen centimeters and by the end of their fourth, averaged seventeen centimeters. During the next four years Tees trout increased in length by an average of 2.5 centimeters a year to give an eight year old fish an average length of twenty-six centimeters — only just longer than a two year old Kennet trout!

Length is not the only component of a trout's size because increase in length is almost invariably accompanied by increase in weight. In perfect circumstances, a trout's overall shape remains unchanged as it grows (except for a slightly disproportionate lengthening of its skull). Thus the approximate weight of a well-conditioned trout in relation to its length can be calculated by a simple formula based on the notion that weight is proportionate to the cube of length. This is:-

$$\frac{\text{gram weight x } 100}{\text{centimeter length}^3} = 1.0$$

which can be rewritten as:

$$\text{gram weight} \times 100 = \text{centimeter length}^3.$$

This formula has given rise to an indicator of a wild trout's physical well-being (condition or 'K' factor) which, although not appliable to fry, provides a useful guide for older parr and mature fish. If weight and length can be measured and both figures inserted into the formula, then a resulting figure greater than 1.0 indicates a fish in better than average condition while a figure of less than 1.0 suggests otherwise. For example, a 500 gram trout in good condition should be just under thirty-seven centimeters long. If it is only thirty-five centimeters its condition is exceptional, even unnaturally so. Much longer than thirty-seven centimeters, then perhaps food supplies are inadequate or some internal disorder or parasite is adversely affecting its well-being. The condition factor is related not only to the amount of flesh on a trout's body; it is also affected by the weight of any eggs or milt inside the fish which will tend to exaggerate condition just before spawning and underrate it immediately afterwards.

Breeding exacts a heavy toll on a trout's resources and results in a very marked growth check. During the first two or three years of its life, growth is unhampered by sexual development. When the reproductive organs start to form, growth is inevitably slowed, which is the main reason why its curve gradually flattens out as fish become sexually mature.

Because a trout's weight is roughly proportionate to the cube of its length, each subsequent increase in length therefore brings about a lesser proportionate weight gain but a greater actual one. When young fry grow two centimeters they increase in weight several fold, but only by a few grams. Yet a similar increase in the length of a much older fish engenders a far greater actual weight gain but a much lesser one in relation to total body weight.

The average numbers and weight of trout in any given age group can be correlated to show the total number and weight of trout in any given stretch of water. This can help calculate the amount of trout that the water is able to support. In the hypothetical example above, the 800 alevin which hatched may together have weighed 200 grams. The forty parr left at the end of the first summer may each be several times heavier than they were when hatched but the total trout weight of that hatching (at least in the Tees) is far less than it was at birth. By then the mortality rate has dropped dramatically and by the start of the third summer the collective weight of the ten survivors in the Kennet far exceeds the weight of the total hatching at birth, although in the Tees it is still only half that figure. The total weight of the year group continues to rise and peaks around the end of the third year, at which time food requirements are also maximised.

Much of the information presented in these pages is summarised on the table opposite. This gives figures for the two extremes of growth in the rivers Tees and Kennet, but should be read as relating to an initial spawning by four trout in the river Tees as a single fish would hardly ever grow large enough to lay 1000 eggs.

Food requirements vary directly in relation to weight, so at similar temperatures those of a 500 gram trout are ten times those of a fifty gram fish. As ever with figures relating to trout growth and populations this is a generalisation and is not accurately applicable to very young fish. Food intake is utilised in two ways. Some of the energy derived from a trout's diet is required merely to replace existing body tissues and to sustain the physiological activities which combine to keep it alive. This has been

| TIME OF YEAR | NUMBER OF SURVIVORS | INDIVIDUAL LENGTH (centimeters) | | INDIVIDUAL WEIGHT (grams) | | TOTAL TROUT WEIGHT (grams) | |
|---|---|---|---|---|---|---|---|
| | | TEES | KENNET | TEES | KENNET | TEES | KENNET |
| Egg laying (Nov - Tees Jan – Kennet) | 1,000 | | | | | | |
| Fertilisation (Nov – Tees Jan – Kennet) | 900 | | | | | | |
| Hatching (March) | 800 | | | 0.25 | 0.25 | 200 | 200 |
| Establishing Territories (April – Kennet) May – Tees) | 200 | 2.25 | 2.25 | 0.30 | 0.30 | 60 | 60 |
| End First Summer (September) | 40 | 4 | 8 | 0.75 | 5 | 30 | 200 |
| End First Year (March) | 20 | 5 | 11.5 | 1.25 | 15 | 25 | 300 |
| End Second Year (March) | 10 | 10 | 24 | 10 | 166 | 100 | 1660 |
| End Third Year (March) | 6 | 14 | 34 | 27 | 393 | 162 | 2358 |
| End Fourth Year (March) | 2 | 17 | 39 | 49 | 593 | 98 | 1186 |

*Figures for the two extremes of growth in the rivers Tees and Kennet.*

referred to as the 'maintenance requirement' and represents the bare minimum needed to maintain a fish in its existing condition. Larger fish have greater minimum food requirements but, expressed as a proportion of body weight, they remain constant. Food in excess of the basic maintenance requirement is utilised in growth and the rate of growth therefore depends on the amount of this surplus. In rare times of copious food supplies, trout sometimes fail to convert all this bounty effectively and then growth is no faster than if the surplus had been less.

The nutritional value of food intake varies according to the components of the trout's diet. Ideally, such a diet is made up of a maximum of fifty per cent protein and much smaller quantities of fats and carbohydrates which the trout's digestive system is less able to break down. In fish farms trout are fed as close to an ideal diet as possible to raise them to maximum size with minimum expense as rapidly as possible. The quantity of food required to produce a given increase in trout weight can be expressed as a conversion ratio (sometimes called a 'coefficient of nourishment') which may be as low as 3:1. This means that under perfect natural conditions thirty grams of food could produce a ten gram increase in a trout's body weight, the additional twenty grams either being utilised for body maintenance or excreted. Where diet is less ideal and more energy is expended in catching food as well as in simply staying alive the conversion ratio is likely to be much higher; then 7:1 would be more usual, rising as high as 10:1 in winter.

The disparity in growth rates of different trout populations that has given rise to the concept of an 'average trout' in this chapter is due to a number of different environmental factors. The most important of these are temperature, water chemistry, water flow and food supply, but they are so interdependent that it is misleading to rely too much on the apparent effects of any one of them.

Trout, being cold blooded, have a body temperature which is always the same as that of the surrounding water. Within their ideal thermal range, this gives them a great advantage over warm blooded animals in that precious energy is not expended on maintaining constant body temperature. Even so, as a fish's body temperature rises with that of its environment, so does its metabolic rate and the energy required to fuel bodily functions. Therefore, subject to certain limitations, more food is required in warmer water than in cold to satisfy the basic maintenance requirement, before any surplus can be directed towards growth.

Below 4°C, activity and growth are negligible. Above this level trout become increasingly lively as temperatures approach the optimum range of between 12° and 15°C. (Some researchers suggest that 10°-12° and 15°-18°C are the two preferred ranges and that the intermediate temperatures are in fact less ideal.) Above 15°C, activity decreases quickly so that when water is warmer than 19°C trout become lethargic and disinclined to feed.

The combined effect of these thermally controlled rates of metabolism and activity seems to be that increased feeding activity more than compensates for the fish's need for more food in warmer waters. Furthermore, maximum growth occurs between 12° and 15°C rather than at the lower temperatures which might be expected to promote it.

The amount of dissolved oxygen that water can hold in solution is also controlled by its temperature, making this latter doubly important to trout. Water containing the maximum amount of dissolved oxygen is said to be saturated, and saturation point falls as temperature rises. Water is often not fully saturated. At 1°C fully saturated water contains fourteen parts per million of oxygen, at 10°C only eleven ppm and when temperature rises to 20°C the maximum amount of dissolved oxygen is down to nine ppm. Trout are able to extract over seventy-five per cent of the available oxygen from water passing through their gills. Therefore, while trout need more oxygen for the very process of living when temperatures are higher, there is already less in the water. As temperature increases, fish breathe faster using more energy to extract the reduced amount of oxygen. This only serves to stress the importance of cool, but not too cold, well-oxygenated water for the successful growth of trout.

So important are the effects of temperature on trout growth and metabolism that their different directions of influence should be repeated. Trout need oxygen to survive. Oxygen dissolves better in colder water. Trout must work harder to extract the lesser amounts of oxygen present in warmer water and to do this they need even more oxygen and more food. At low temperatures, except at spawning time, trout tend to be lethargic. As the temperature rises, they become more active and require more food to fuel this activity. At optimum temperatures food intake provides surplus for growth. Above and below this optimum, trout feed less and grow more slowly.

The factors of water chemistry and flow are to a great extent connected with that most crucial of all regulators of a trout's development — food supply. Without food, trout die, although they may take a long time to do so, and without more than the basic maintenance requirement they cannot grow. Variations in water flow directly affect the amount of food carried down a stream. At the same time, if water levels drop, more of the stream bed is exposed to the atmosphere, killing aquatic invertebrates which would otherwise have provided fish with food. When this happens, trout are also constricted into a smaller area of water forcing them to compete more aggressively for the basic energy-producing requirements of food and oxygen. Because trout are forced to use more energy in feeding, the surplus available for growth is depleted. So from a reduction in water flow stems a wide variety of interlinked considerations which can all combine to stunt fish.

Rivers susceptible to droughts are often equally prone to severe flooding, when food is wasted by being washed downstream, and young fish may die as they too are swept away or find themselves stranded when the floods recede. Rain falling on permeable rock can filter through the rock strata before being trapped by subterranean aquifers, eventually to be forced up and out through springs. In these spring-fed rivers, flow levels are less erratic and conditions for sustained trout development are far more favourable.

Permeable rocks are often calcareous and so an even flow of water and a chalk substratum are usually combined. Relatively constant water flow also does much to encourage plant life which would not thrive in alternating droughts and floods. In addition, spring-fed rivers maintain a more constant and generally higher water temperature than surface-fed ones and this also helps fish grow.

Trout are almost exclusively carnivorous, but rich aquatic plant growth is important in that it provides both food and shelter for the invertebrates which form the bulk of their prey. Therefore, within reasonable limits, more abundant plant life in the water sustains greater supplies of food for trout which are likely to grow larger as a result. Various factors influence successful aquatic plant growth. In particular, underwater vegetation needs sufficient daylight for successful photosynthesis, and nutritional mineral salts in the water to act as natural fertilisers. Daylight freely penetrates most streams and rivers but may be insufficient in the deeper parts of still waters for plants to grow well.

Calcium compounds in the water, as well as nitrates and phosphates, encourage more luxurious plant growth (Chapter Seven). These also stimulate the growth of microscopic plant plankton which are food for tiny zooplankton, preyed upon either directly by trout or by other small animals themselves eaten by trout. So, as well as stimulating plant growth and indirectly animal life, nutrient salts also form the base of a food chain of which trout are near the top. Although it has never been proved, trout may also benefit directly from the presence of calcium and other nutrients which may stimulate healthy physical development and particularly the formation of bones and scales. Dangerously low levels of calcium could stunt young trout just as they do mammals, and sterile, almost nutrient-free water contributes little to the growth of either plants or animals.

The topography of the stream bed is clearly crucial to successful spawning but also indirectly contributes to much of the variation in size and growth between different populations of trout. Smooth gravelly streams of minimal gradient, even flow and little variety in underwater topography tend to encourage more even growth of generally larger trout. Such waters offer fewer opportunities to secure particularly advantageous feeding stations. However, a rocky, tumbling stream with alternating rapids, shallow runs, deep pools and waterfalls provides much greater opportunities for more divergent rates of growth among the trout that live there.

All these influences on trout growth are so interconnected that it would be both difficult and misleading to try to dissociate one from another. Put simply, there are a wide range of natural circumstances which may directly and indirectly affect a trout's increase in size. Together, these may combine to produce a three-year-old fish, ten centimeters long, weighing ten grams or one well over twice that length weighing 160 grams.

Populations and growth rates of trout are each easily described separately, but the relationship between the two is complex and difficult to interpret. It may seem axiomatic that trout grow bigger where there are fewer of them but why should there be fewer if food supplies are so abundant? And why do there always seem to be far more trout in small, impoverished upland waters where fish want for both space and food? For many fishermen these are crucial questions which remain unanswered and the problems they pose are all too frequently solved simply by stocking the water with imported trout of catchable size. This is usually to the marked detriment of the indigenous stock and as the river's food supply is quite unable to sustain large numbers of introduced fish, most of them will die if they are not caught within the first season.

Overcrowding begins on the redds. If breeding areas are conducive to the successful hatching of a high percentage of alevins from many different nests, an overcrowding problem immediately arises. The problem persists if the topography of the stream bed encourages the establishment of many small feeding territories. Food supplies may just exceed the basic maintenance requirements of numerous small fish, but will be insufficient to foster any more than minimal growth. In such circumstances, very few trout will grow big enough to drive away competitors from neighbouring territories, resulting in the gradual creation of a population of many stunted, uniformly-sized fish. Even as they edge downstream from the breeding areas, the surviving parr continue to be squeezed for food and space by the older survivors of previous spawnings. However, those fish that eventually leave the small feeder streams for still waters and rivers less suitable for breeding, are rewarded with far larger territories than they could ever have found near their redds of birth.

Where overcrowding is severe, much more energy is expended on maintaining territories and securing what little food is available, than in a less stressful and less competitive environment where such energy can be more productively diverted to growth. Therefore, once the cycle of overcrowding has started, it becomes — naturally at least — almost impossible to break. By the time the next spawning season comes round, the ideal redds which encouraged successful breeding in the first place are once again visited by large numbers of diminutive adult fish, with the unconscious objective of further supplementing the trout population of an already overcrowded stream. Eventually, small trout in these crowded environments may evolve some inherited predisposition to breed smaller fish although so far research has not supported this proposition. Any experiments involving the translocation of stunted, mature fish into unstocked waters have shown them to have retained the potential for excellent growth if food supplies in their new environment are sufficient to promote it.

As most trout continue growing throughout their lives, the size a fish ultimately reaches before it dies depends also on age. On average, the few trout that reach maturity die aged five or six having first spawned when they were three or four. There is no distinct correlation between type of water and longevity; if anything, trout that grow quickly in mineral-rich waters do not appear to live as long as slower-growing fish even though they often seem to mature earlier in crowded conditions than where space is at less of a premium. In lower temperatures, fish metabolise more slowly and it may be that by doing so they live longer than those which grow faster in warmer waters but quickly burn themselves out in the process.

Maximum age naturally tends to be greatest among trout populations with a propensity to longer life. It may be as high as fifteen although normally fish of ten would be considered old. Size at death depends on the workings of the influences on growth. In later years trout may start to decline in condition and therefore also in weight, as food consumption scarcely matches the minimum maintenance requirement, but once attained, a given skeletal length is never lost. Growth rates decline as old age approaches and in acidic streams where food supplies are sparse but breeding facilities excellent, a trout aged six may not weigh more than 150 grams. This might rise to 500 grams if breeding facilities are limited or even more if, due to the absence of any suitable feeder streams, trout must try to spawn in the far from ideal environment of gravelly lake shallows. On the edges of mineral-rich still waters or in slow-flowing chalk streams, where food supplies abound but spawning facilities are less perfect, conditions may be ideal for maximum growth.

There, competition from other fish species, as well as increased predation, may combine to reduce numbers of juveniles, and after six years a trout may weigh as much as three kilograms.

The British rod-caught record brown trout enjoying current recognition is 8.8 kilograms, that of nearly eighteen kilograms from Loch Awe in 1866 having been discounted. In Ireland the record fish is one of nearly twelve kilograms. The world rod-caught record, from Patagonia, is over sixteen kilograms and a seventeen year old trout of twenty-five kilograms was found after draining a lake in Yugoslavia. Sea trout, which exploit much richer feeding grounds in estuaries and off the coast, usually grow far larger. In some populations, mature sea trout average little over half a kilogram, but in others, fish of between two and three kilograms are quite common. The biggest British sea trout was caught in the nets off the mouth of the river Tweed and weighed thirteen kilograms (Chapter Eight) but sea trout migrating up Scandinavian rivers from the Baltic sea frequently weigh more than that.

Many of the generalisations regarding age and size are contradicted by the strange phenomenon of ferox trout. These frequently weigh more than five kilograms and were originally regarded as a separate species, given the specific name *Salmo ferox* by Gunther and others. Some scientists still consider certain ferox populations to be genetically distinct from other trout with which they cohabit, and more closely related to ferox from different waters. This view is based on the premise that ferox colonised their various native waters before the arrival of other forms of trout from which they have remained reproductively isolated ever since. Other researchers regard ferox as no more than large, predatory brown trout with almost exclusively piscivorous tastes. After starting their lives, feeding in the normal way off invertebrate prey, these trout then simply survive long enough to reach a size that enables them to make the change to a diet of other fish.

Up until the age of six or seven, ferox appear to grow at quite normal annual rates, proportionate increases in weight declining slowly in their fourth, fifth and sixth years just like other trout. Then some of those that survive to six or seven suddenly appear to make a critical dietary transition to fish, probably for two reasons. Firstly, they are by then large enough — usually around thirty centimeters — to catch prey fish. Secondly, if they do not do so, their size is already such that alternative food sources in the water are insufficient to support their basic maintenance requirements and they will therefore die. It is also suggested that ferox may be very late maturing fish that have been able to direct their energies to growth rather than to spawning, for much longer than other trout which first bred aged three or four. Spawning is a massive drain on energy reserves and any fish able to channel that energy to growth instead will rapidly outgrow fish that cannot. Whatever the reason, once having started to catch other fish, their growth rates suddenly show such massive increases that ferox may actually double in weight in the first year on their new diet and show substantial but lesser increases each year of their lives thereafter.

Once ferox begin feeding on fish they continue to do so almost exclusively. Usually they prey on Arctic charr whose habit of foraging in shoals in deeper regions of still waters makes them easier to catch, although perch may also feature in ferox diets as may salmon smolts. The remains of young trout are surprisingly seldom found in their stomachs, perhaps adding credence to the argument that ferox are indeed genetically distinct, having already begun to prosper on a diet of different species of fish before they were joined by other forms of trout. Irrespective of its precise components, a diet of fish provides great nutritional advantages. Prey fish have already broken down their invertebrate food into the necessary components for successful growth of fish flesh and can themselves then be converted into ferox flesh with much less wastage. The conversion ratio of a fifteen centimeter charr to ferox weight gain is far lower (more efficient) than if the same trout had to catch the 4,500 midge larvae which are estimated to weigh the same; and this ratio also ignores the colossal amount of energy expended in tracking down so many larvae compared to the energy needed to catch one fish.

Ferox invariably grow bigger and older than other trout in the same lake. They also live longer than trout from other waters where food supplies, while less nutritious than a diet of fish, are apparently abundant enough not to prompt a change of diet. From this it can be argued that food supply is the principal factor controlling longevity, and certainly trout reared under artificial conditions and fed regularly have been kept alive for over twenty years. Dead ferox (or any other trout that have died from natural causes) are seldom discovered, and for that reason alone maximum size and age under natural conditions are hard to predict. One ferox trout from Scotland was estimated to be twenty-three years old and an age of fifteen is certainly not unusual. The two oldest recorded brown trout were captured together in a gill net in Norway — a female of thirty-eight and a male of thirty-four whose respective condition factors of 0.83 and 0.88 indicated lean, poorly nourished fish whose deaths were probably imminent anyway.

Data on weight and length of live or dead trout is easily acquired when the fish are to hand. Under hatchery conditions, age and growth can also be monitored and recorded but the calculation of age and prior annual growth rates of wild fish involves the extrapolation of information contained in their scales. Each one of these tiny discs contains sufficient evidence to tell a detailed story of a trout's life.

On young trout, scales first show as slight projections underneath the dermis but once a parr is about four centimeters long, actual scales start to appear on either side of its lateral line, slowly spreading upwards and downwards until they eventually cover its whole body. When a fish has grown a complete set of overlapping scales, it retains them for the rest of its life, only replacing any that are damaged, by growing new ones in the pocket of the dermis. Therefore, in order that this protective layer continues to act as such, each scale must grow more or less in proportion with the fish; and because of the scales' uneven increase in size much can be learned about the life history of the particular trout from which they derive.

Scales of bony fish are generally of two kinds, the smoother cycloid scales of those such as members of the salmon and carp families and the rough, spiny, ctenoid scales of perch or grayling. Some fish, like dabs (*Limanda* spp.), have a combination of the two. A trout's layer of cycloid scales is covered in a relatively thick outer epidermis which further enhances the fish's smooth feel. Each cycloid scale is made up of a fibrous inner layer and a hard calcareous outer covering of bony material similar to the dentine of a mammalian tooth.

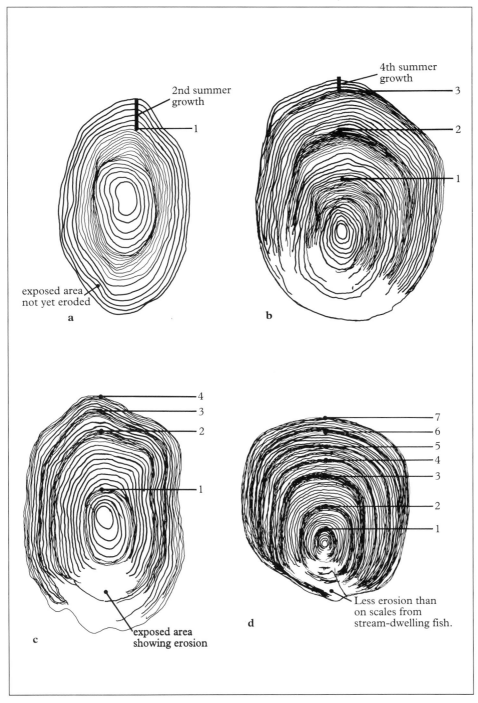

*Scales from trout. (a) Young trout. (b) Fast growing chalk-stream trout. (c) Slow growing trout from an upland stream. (d) Trout spawned in an upland stream and eventually caught in a lake which it probably entered at the beginning of its third summer.*

As a fish grows and its scales proportionately enlarge, bony material is gradually added to the edge of the scales' outer covering in a series of concentric rings. These rings show up under a microscope as a succession of bands, interspersed with distinctive ridges known as 'circuli', one practical function of which is to help secure the scale in the skin. The distances between them vary greatly and circuli are probably created when calcium supplied to the scale's outer layer exceeds the scale's capacity to absorb calcium in growth, the surplus then being deposited by way of bony ridges on its surface. This explanation is supported by the fact that in periods of plentiful food and sustained growth, circuli are usually relatively far apart, but may be almost contiguous when growth is slower.

Scales from an older trout which has spent all its six years in fresh water might appear under low magnification, where all circuli were not individually visible, as a series of six dark rings on a slightly lighter background. These dark check rings (annuli) represent periods of slow winter growth when calcareous circuli were laid down close together. Annuli present a very similar pattern — and for similar reasons — to the annual rings of xylem in the trunk of a tree. Between these annual rings in the tree trunk and on the trout's scale are paler bands representing faster growth. Their relative width can indicate a fish's annual growth, and the comparative placing of dark winter annuli can also help in assessing its size at the end of any given year. A scale increases proportionately with the fish's length therefore, by expressing the distance from the scale's centre to a particular winter ring as a fraction of its total radius, it is easily possible to apply the same fraction to the length of the trout.

Greater magnification of scales may reveal further checks in a fish's growth besides those associated with the effects of climate or reduced food supply. On the scales of older fish there are often one or more very distinct marks, each of which indicates a spawning. These may be particularly noticeable on scales from trout introduced to countries nearer the equator; there average temperatures and food supplies are more constant than in more temperate areas and there are no real check rings to indicate slower growth. However, the absence of spawning marks is not necessarily evidence that a fish has never bred, because fish from some waters have very distinctive marks while on the scales of those from others, they are barely visible.

Spawning marks are created as scales erode through changes in the body's internal metabolism. There are two main reasons for their appearance. One is simply the negative effect on a fish of the depressed appetite that precedes spawning. The other is a process of calcium absorption by the trout's body which may need extra calcium for the development of ova or milt when it is already stressed by lack of food. Spawning marks are particularly conspicuous on salmon which normally only spawn once and on which the whole breeding process takes a massive physiological toll. A salmon does not usually feed for several months before spawning and calcium absorption during the whole of its stay in fresh water leaves a very distinct scar on each scale.

Sea trout are likely to show more distinct spawning marks than brown trout, and their scales can also indicate quite dramatically the relative periods of growth in fresh and salt water. The freshwater circuli of their early years appear closely interspaced, but as soon as a fish reaches the sea, the rich feeding there shows up as broad flat bands between the ridges of the circuli, often giving no indication of slower growth in the winter. On return to fresh water the bands narrow again and spawning marks may show as well. Scales can also help to identify whether a fish is a salmon or sea trout (Chapter Eight), or to differentiate between trout and salmon parr.

Scales for analysis are usually taken from just in front of a trout's tail or from its 'shoulder' near the dorsal fin, which is actually one of the last parts of its body to grow them. Scales that have replaced damaged ones are of little use as they do not indicate pre-damage growth. Those with too distinct a spawning mark are also unreliable aids in calculating the size of a fish at any given time of its life, because many of the circuli may have been absorbed during breeding before the scale began to grow again. Otoliths from within a trout's semicircular canals form alternating dense and opaque zones at different times of the year and can also be used to determine age. However, despite its limitations, scale reading is able to provide a microcosmic history of the chapters of a wild trout's life, in far more detail than can any other indicator.

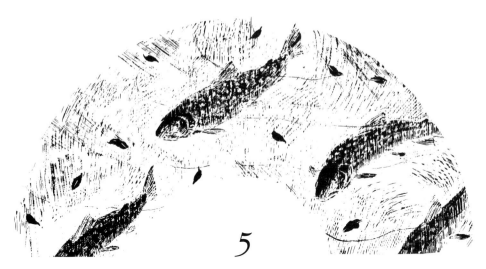

# 5

# Competition, Predation, Disease
# and Death

From the moment they swim up from the gravel as tiny fry to begin feeding for themselves, trout must compete for the available resources of food and space in order to survive. Intra-specific competition is fiercest in the first weeks of trout's lives. Then, mortality is massive (Chapter Four) and only about five per cent of alevins survive to the end of their first summer. Thereafter, competition from other trout eases off and death strikes from other directions, although with such devastating effect that little more than one from every hundred that hatch breed successfully.

The intensity of competition between individuals of the same species, and the strain they impose on the resources of the environment, varies with population density. Indeed, competition in the ecological sense only exists when there is an actual shortage of a resource, such as food or space, and not merely when individuals of the same or different species happen to eat similar food or occupy the same habitat. Once any stretch of water's carrying capacity is exceeded, death of surplus trout is inevitable, and will continue until the balance between available resources and their consumers is gradually restored. After eggs have hatched in small upland streams ideal for spawning, carrying capacity is quickly exceeded but in wider lowland rivers where space is at less of a premium and breeding facilities are scarce, trout mortality as a result of overpopulation is far less likely.

Not only must individuals of one species compete with each other, but they may also encounter competition from different species. Naturally, the more similar the requirements of any two species, the more likely is the prospect of their competing, usually for food, but also for space either for feeding or breeding.

Generally, no two species exploit precisely the same environmental niche within any one area; if they did, both would not survive. Geographical separation often provides the impetus for speciation, although many fish in the sea or the Rift Valley lakes of East Africa have diverged into the modern catalogue of different species without such stimulus. However, geographical separation from its peers gives any population of a species a much greater opportunity to evolve its own distinct physiological and behavioural characteristics. Then, much later, topographical or climatic changes or other natural pressures may bring species together which are by then sufficiently disparate to coexist without competing lethally for the same resources.

The more specialised the habits of any one species, the less likely is it to encounter serious competition, although over-reliance on any particular food source makes a predator highly vulnerable to the vagaries of its prey. Thin-lipped grey mullet *(Liza ramada)* are highly specialised in their feeding habits rather than their selection of food, sucking in mouthfuls of estuarine mud from which they filter out algae and small invertebrates. To extract the maximum goodness from this mainly algal diet a thirty centimeter mullet is endowed with an intestine over two meters long. Some African cichlids live exclusively off a diet of other fish's scales but absence of inter-specific competition is an evolutionary luxury not afforded to animals with more catholic feeding habits such as brown trout. These are remarkable for their wide-ranging diet and the ease with which they adapt to living conditions in still or running fresh waters, as well as to the totally different environment of the sea. But the biological price for such opportunistic behaviour, to which they owe so much of their success as a species, is inevitably that throughout their lives trout must compete for nourishment with other species of fish — and even occasionally with insectivorous birds.

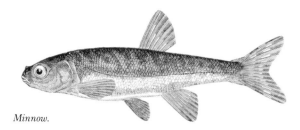

*Minnow.*

A fish's size obviously influences the potential diversity of its diet, in that bigger fish are able to catch a wider variety of prey. When trout fry begin feeding, their size restricts them to tiny midge larvae and other immature insects brought down by the current. At that stage they compete directly with minnows *(Phoxinus phoxinus)* which can live almost exclusively off algae if they have to but by choice are mainly carnivorous, preying on an almost identical range of food as young trout. However, minnows are not territorial, instead living in shoals on the edge of the current or near weeds in the shallows. Spawning in early summer, they also observe a totally different breeding season from trout. Competition between the two species is therefore naturally limited by their differing habits but may still be significant in small rocky streams where food supplies are already marginal.

Bullheads (or miller's thumbs — *Cottus gobio*) have no swim-bladders and live on the stream bed, coming out at dusk to search for freshwater shrimps and insect larvae, rather than relying on organic drift to sustain them. They need a stony substratum covered with clean, shallow water and in the warmer reaches of their range sometimes spawn several times a year. Bullheads are known to take occasional trout fry and, like minnows, are suspected of eating trout ova, although they could not possibly shift the gravel which covers well-buried eggs. Nourishment is often sparse in their preferred habitat, and then bullheads may compete actively with trout that have left their first feeding stations and begun to forage for their food.

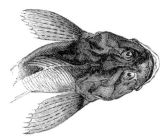

*Bullhead.*

In the warmer, lower reaches of streams and rivers, bullheads are replaced by gudgeon *(Gobio gobio)*. The adults are exclusively bottom-feeders, as are stone loaches *(Noemacheilus barbatulus)* and both species may compete with trout for larvae and shrimps. Three-spined sticklebacks are one of the smallest British freshwater fish and build nests of vegetation, silt or sand. This habit restricts their distribution but through much of their range they coexist with trout, competing with fry and parr for small morsels of prey.

These small species of fish are all potential competitors of similarly sized trout, especially in running waters. However, the trout's territorial habits and its preference in early life for faster water keep direct competition to a minimum. And, while these other fish may plunder the same larders as young trout, in the greater context of a complex food web, these competitors may eventually form an important part of older trout's diets. Some three-spined sticklebacks migrate to sea becoming prey for trout that also do; and non-migratory trout that grow large enough, freely devour sticklebacks, minnows, bullheads and loaches with which, as young parr, they once competed.

Mature Atlantic salmon, feeding far out to sea, compete for neither food nor space with non-migratory brown trout, but young salmon may certainly do so. Where the two species occur together, trout usually spawn first and are therefore also first to hatch. This gives them a formidable advantage over salmon which is often never lost in fresh water, trout remaining larger and stronger than their more streamlined congeners of the same age group. Despite this, salmon parr may still provide trout with the most intense direct competition they ever experience.

As parr, salmon and trout are extremely difficult to tell apart but even at that tender stage exhibit certain distinguishing characteristics which often become more pronounced as fish mature. Already apparent is the salmon's deeply forked tail with its more pointed tips and thinner 'wrist' in front. Along the body of both species are distinctive parr marks, like fingerprints. Their numbers were once considered a diagnostic feature in separating the two species but while salmon sometimes have one or two more than most trout, they are not an accurate pointer and individuals of both species have been found with as few as eight or as many as thirteen. A young trout's mouth is larger than a salmon's and the upper jawbone (maxilla) of a trout extends level with the back of its eye while that of a salmon only reaches as far as its pupil: this is one of the most distinctive differences as may be the more intense spotting on a trout's gill covers and dorsal fin. Colouration also differs, trout often having more red or orange spots on their bodies and adipose fins. Salmon parr have more pronounced pectoral fins, shaped like butterfly wings, which sometimes support them on the river bed — perhaps as an aid to underwater feeding. It takes close examination to count the rows of scales between the back of a fish's adipose fin and its lateral line, but this can be the surest way to distinguish the species: between ten and thirteen is usual for salmon and from thirteen to sixteen for trout.

*Salmon parr.*

Not only do these parr look confusingly alike but their similarity extends to diet and feeding behaviour. Young trout take winged and terrestrial insects from the surface while salmon parr eat more bottom food, but the overlap between their ranges of prey is still sufficient to make some direct competition inevitable.

Young salmon tend to congregate in loose shoals after hatching. This may be because the earlier hatching trout have secured all available territories, although salmon often spawn further downstream. Alternatively, as eventual downstream migration is inevitable in the lives of young salmon, the security of feeding territories is probably less important to them. Salmon parr prefer faster riffles than trout which may also be a consequence of their general downstream drift. The collective strength of a shoal perhaps enables it to invade the established territories of larger trout on the spawning grounds, or further downstream, with relative impunity. Thus, by remaining in a loose association with other members of its species, the young salmon's chances of survival are enhanced.

As they gradually drift away, salmon parr leave the resident trout behind to redistribute themselves around their natal stream. Then trout begin to suffer limited competition from fish of species larger than the minnows, bullheads and loaches that snatched away the food of newly-hatched fry, and with this they must contend throughout their adult lives. However, such inter-specific competition is far less oppressive than the combination of competitive pressures endured by juvenile fish already engaged in a struggle for survival with their siblings. Older trout are more adaptable feeders and must coexist with other species if the natural balance in their particular aquatic community is to be maintained. So, while more than one species may certainly consume the same prey, a different set of preferences usually ensures that such competition is kept to a minimum.

Many of the colder still waters of northern Britain and Europe, as well as rivers in Iceland and sub-Arctic Scandinavia, contain populations of Arctic charr. In rivers, charr are usually anadromous, migrating to salt water where they feed even closer inshore than sea trout. Stillwater charr spend most of their lives in the cold, lightless depths, feeding mainly off tiny zoo-plankton, although they move upwards if their prey does and in the absence of trout easily spread throughout the whole of a lake. They move in shoals and their different diet and habits make serious competition with trout unlikely, but to some extent such differences are forced on charr by the competitive presence of trout. Both species often eat tiny crustaceans, but the only trout down at these deep levels are likely to be piscivorous ferox which depend almost exclusively upon charr for their survival. Trout and charr may also breed at the same time but charr can successfully do so in the shallows round lake edges, and while there may be limited competition for space on the redds of inflowing streams, it is unlikely to restrict the successful spawning of either fish.

Perch are occasionally found alongside charr — e.g. in Windermere and Lough Melvin — but ideally prefer slightly warmer, less acidic water. Often however, they have to tolerate very marginal conditions simply because they owe their presence to mankind's efforts. Almost exclusively carnivorous, perch have wide-ranging appetites that extend to a perverse preference for their own fry. They live in shoals of particular age groups which contract as numbers of component fish drop off, and compete with trout for certain prey. Nevertheless, older trout feed voraciously off young perch which more than compensates for any limited competition from fully-grown fish. The presence of perch may also benefit trout by providing pike with alternative prey. Like all so-called coarse fish, the perch's early summer breeding season ensures that there is never any competition with trout for spawning space, as does its need for vegetation among which to lay its eggs.

The interaction between mature trout and other fish within the same environment is more apparent lower down rivers where the water is still cool enough for trout and marginally warm enough for certain other species. Fast-flowing, well-oxygenated upland waters comprise what is sometimes called the 'trout region' (Chapter Seven) and further down where these small streams merge and the river flattens out into longer, deeper pools, the grayling region begins.

Grayling have no close relatives in Europe although there are reckoned to be five other species of the genus *Thymallus* in Mongolia, Siberia and North America. Trout are still the dominant species in much of the grayling region but both compete for invertebrate food. In prime southern English chalk streams, grayling are netted out in large numbers in the belief that too many of them adversely affects both numbers and growth of trout. Netting usually takes place in autumn but regardless of man's efforts to control them, grayling numbers soon seem to recover to established levels, probably because of the huge surplus of young fish which quickly take over the spaces vacated by their departed parents.

Despite the extent of their mutual distribution, it is still not clear to what extent grayling and trout are determined competitors for food, and the grayling's reputation as a predator of trout eggs has been neither effectively established nor refuted. Analyses of the stomach contents of both species and a wealth of river-bank observations show that (as would be expected of two species with such catholic carnivorous tastes) the range of prey in both their diets is broadly similar. However, dietary preferences vary greatly and this, as well as the gregarious habits of grayling compared to the essentially solitary nature of the trout, makes for relatively peaceful co-existence.

At the lower end of the grayling region, where trout may still survive, the dominant species belong to the carp family, Cyprinidae. This is the largest family of fish in the world with over 2000 species of which sixteen occur in the British Isles. Cyprinids range in size from the common carp which may weigh more than twenty kilograms and the rather smaller barbel *(Barbus barbus)*, down to tiny gudgeon and minnows of a few grams. At these higher temperatures it is generally dace *(Leuciscus leuciscus)*, chub *(Leuciscus cephalus)* and roach *(Rutilus rutilus)* that vie with adult trout for food supplies.

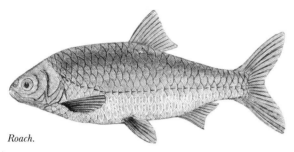

*Roach.*

Most European members of the carp family are at least partly herbivorous. Dace are like small chub and live in shoals in streamy shallows. In a manner uncharacteristic of their family, they rise to flies on the surface although most of their food is taken underwater and includes a variety of aquatic invertebrates as well as some vegetation. Chub move into faster-flowing reaches in the summer months when they too take adult insects on the wing and, like dace, can be caught on a dry fly. They also eat insect larvae and plant matter and having grown large enough to prey upon small fish, perhaps take occasional trout fry. Roach freely tolerate a wide range of aquatic habitats, from fast-flowing streams down to brackish estuaries. Their diet is particularly varied, depending upon where they live, but in the upstream limits of their range roach may compete superficially with trout.

In some rivers where trout live and breed successfully, there may be as many as eight other resident species of fish in any one stretch. Not only might these all, at some time in their lives, compete with trout for particular food items, but they must also compete with each other. For all their importance to fishermen, trout are only one small piece in the great interlocking jigsaw of their underwater world. Smaller species compete with young trout fry for available food but those trout that survive to maturity may one day include their former competitors in their own diets. Older trout may also prey upon the young of some of those species with which, as adults, they compete for the massive production of underwater invertebrates. And so productive is this aquatic environment, both in terms of variety and numbers, that while limited competition between two species is inevitable, direct competition is avoided by the differing dietary priorities of each. Were this not so, the long term consequences for one or other, in their particular sphere of coexistence, would be fatal.

Limited competition, both within and between species, is part of the wider laws of nature which combine to ensure the survival of the strongest members of a species, as well as equilibrium between different species within the same community. Trout prey on smaller animals lower down their food chain. As most of these animals figure in the diets of other fish, competition ensues. However, if there is enough of a particular food resource, competition is only theoretical and has no practical influence on the growth or numbers of that resource's consumers. And trout, for all their carnivorous habits, are themselves only a middle link in this aquatic food chain. At its base are mineral salts sustaining plant matter which is directly or indirectly converted into flesh by herbivorous animals; some of these are eaten by trout. Higher up the chain are a range of fish, birds and mammals which all regard trout as an item of greater or lesser importance among their own ranges of prey. Therefore between predators, there may be competition for the dietary contributions of trout.

Predation is part of the trout's lot, even before birth. During spawning, eggs may be washed downstream by the current or incompletely covered with gravel. Those swept away from the nest are seized by almost any fish, including other trout which often also eat up loose eggs on the redds. The presence of breeding trout discourages other species of fish from approaching nests but the redds are soon deserted once spawning is over. From then on the weight of gravel over buried eggs is their only protection from the predatory attentions of other fish or water shrews (Neomys fodiens). These small black creatures with long tails and white underparts nose much of their food off the river bed and occasionally cause considerable damage on the redds, either by eating eggs or newly hatched alevins. Dippers (Cinclus cinclus) which can swim and walk underwater, are also suspected of eating trout eggs but so small a bird could never uncover a well made nest and only accounts for a few stray or half-buried eggs.

At the swim-up stage, young fry are extremely vulnerable, having just emerged from the safety of their gravel for the first time to take up feeding stations and fend for themselves. Then, mammals, birds, fish and even young insects may all take their toll. As well as water shrews, little grebes (or dabchicks Podiceps ruficollis) search redds for eggs and fry. Even large dragonfly larvae may occasionally grab parr, and eels are accused, probably falsely, of doing great damage to stocks of young trout.

Eels are carnivorous scavengers with such wide-ranging diets that theoretically they compete with mature trout as well as preying upon their eggs or fry. Historically, they were branded as one of the trout's most destructive predators but more recent observations suggest this reputation is largely undeserved. During winter, When trout spawn, if not actually hibernating, eels' metabolic rates are so reduced that their food requirements are minimal. They are therefore unlikely to forage for eggs on the redds with anything more than desultory interest. By the time fry have swum up, eels are feeding avidly but seem to prefer sticklebacks, minnows and loaches to young trout. They may eat some freshwater crustaceans and insect larvae, but not to an extent likely to affect food supplies available for trout. Indeed, indirectly eels may even benefit trout, preying on competitors in those rivers where other species of fish proliferate. During spring and early summer when coarse fish are spawning, eels eat large numbers of eggs and continue feeding on the young fish — even pike fry — after hatching. They also eat underwater carrion, effectively cleansing the river of dead fish and other animals.

*Eel.*

Small trout are naturally more vulnerable to a wider range of predators than mature fish, which are much harder to catch. Grayling, chub and perch all eat occasional trout fry, and kingfishers *(Alcedo atthis)* can take parr at least six centimeters long — nearly half their own length. These birds are very territorial, each pair usually requiring a minimum of two or three kilometers of river. Over ninety per cent of their diet consists of fish but kingfishers are great consumers of coarse fish fry which are usually hatching at the same time as their own young and therefore, like eels, where competition from other species of fish is severe, they may actually benefit trout.

Predation on the massive surplus of young trout, when populations are still density-dependent, has no noticeable effect on the numbers of fish surviving to maturity. Indeed, one of the very effects of the surplus production of ova, fry and parr is that it allows the population to withstand such intense predation. Slowly however, trout outgrow the ability of many of their predators to catch them, although even on reaching the relative safety of maturity they continue to represent food for other larger, more efficient predators. These may do most damage to the stability of trout stocks by consuming mature breeding individuals, although the huge surplus of eggs laid by each female still provides great scope for population recoveries. Man, as the prime predator, has a chapter to himself but otters *(Lutra lutra)*, grey herons *(Ardea cinerea)*, and most especially pike, all feed largely on fully grown fish. Where there is a choice, they are just as likely to select other fish as they are to take trout, but if trout are the dominant species, any one of these predators may kill significant numbers of them.

Otters living along the banks of rocky, upland waters in which the only sizeable fish are trout or salmon, can decimate adults and may actually kill more prey than they can eat which is about their total body weight in a week. Eels are probably otters' favourite fish although they may be most easily caught and therefore appear so. In warmer waters they also take pike and other coarse fish. However, in most of Britain otters are now so scarce that mink *(Mustela vison)* pose a more likely danger to trout.

There is a mink native to Europe *(Mustela lutreola)* but it is now confined to France and Germany and the species that endangers wild fish in Britain was imported from America in the 1920s to satisfy the demand for its fur. First reported in the wild in Lancashire after the Second World War, it has since escaped or been released from captivity so often that it is now firmly established in the wild throughout much of Britain and Scandinavia, as well as in Iceland where it has caused huge damage on the breeding grounds of waders and waterfowl. The American mink is a hardy, adaptable creature and its wide-ranging diet of fish, birds and other animals makes it a threatening competitor of many more specialised indigenous carnivores. Trout often feature in its diet and in parts of England hounds once used for hunting otters now concentrate their efforts on mink.

Grey herons are probably the trout's worst avian enemy. Confined by their fishing techniques to catching fish in shallow water, they can be especially damaging on redds or in small streams with few deep pools offering trout sanctuary from airborne dangers. Because of their communal nesting and roosting habits, any streams near a colony are likely to be visited by several herons which can create havoc among fish stocks. Herons can catch fish of up to one kilogram, but prefer smaller prey which they try to pierce behind the head, severing its backbone. They are reported to fish at night but there is no evidence that they prefer trout to any other species.

For a wide variety of other birds, trout are a food source of varying importance. As many as fifty different species are recorded as taking freshwater fish but few of these are likely to make any noticeable dent in a trout population. The damage birds cause depends largely on how many are feeding in a particular stretch of water and the importance of fish in general, and trout in particular, in their diets. A family of goosanders *(Mergus merganser)* or red-breasted mergansers *(M.serrator)* on a short length of river, or a pair of black-throated divers *(Gavia arctica)* nesting on a small Scottish loch, could wreak havoc on trout stocks confined to those restricted areas, exacerbated by the ease with which they all pursue fish underwater. However, trout numbers in a large lake will be almost unaffected by a single pair of ospreys *(Pandion haliaetus)* nesting nearby. Cormorants *(Phalacrocorax carbo)* are increasingly common on inland lakes, especially in winter; on average they eat over half a kilogram of fish daily — twice as much as an osprey — and a nesting colony can mean disaster for trout in nearby still waters. Other divers, grebes, gulls and terns may all take more than the occasional freshwater fish, but if they catch trout these are usually only smaller ones which are part of a huge natural surplus ordained by Nature to die in order that the few survive.

*Pike.*

Inhabiting the same element as their prey, other species of fish have a distinct advantage over birds and mammals, as predators of trout. Pike are the only widespread threat to mature trout in British fresh waters, now that there are probably no burbot *(Lota lota)* left, but their presence can be very damaging. They dislike fast-flowing water, probably also avoiding this because of the related dearth of underwater vegetation among which they lay their eggs and also lurk in wait for prey. From their youngest days pike are carnivorous, feeding first on small invertebrates until they are large enough to catch the alevins and fry of other species. Male pike very seldom weigh more than four kilograms but both these and the larger females, can easily eat a fish one third their own size. They also appear to show a distinct preference for a more efficient diet of fewer, larger fish rather than of many smaller ones. Their partiality for mature fish makes pike potentially far more damaging to trout stocks than smaller, less piscivorous species of coarse fish which concentrate their predatory efforts on fry and parr.

Because of their preference for slower water, pike are seldom found in fast-flowing rivers where trout and salmon would be their only suitable prey. In their more sluggish chosen habitat there are nearly always several different species of prey fish with which pike can vary their diet; in rivers, grayling, dace, roach and chub may all serve to do so and shoaling perch and Arctic charr are usually easier to catch in lakes than the solitary trout. However, if they can catch them, pike show a distinct preference for trout which are less scaly and bony than coarse fish and lack any pronounced spines on their dorsal fins. In an effort to counter over-population with small trout, pike were introduced into many lochs and lakes where they can be especially dangerous to trout waiting to run up spawning streams in October and November.

The annual natural food requirement to maintain a pike at a given size has been variously estimated at between 0.8 and 1.4 times its weight but there is greater consensus over the idea that an increase in one unit of pike weight requires five units of food. So if a pike is to increase its weight from four to five kilograms in one year, it must consume, say, four kilograms for its minimum maintenance requirement and an additional five kilograms for growth. The pike's preferred prey size is between ten and twenty-five per cent of its own weight. Taking the lower end of this range would mean a four kilogram pike consuming ten 400 gram fish to maintain existing condition and a further twelve for conversion into growth — twenty-two fish in a year. Pike also take small mammals and young birds, but many of the trout they eat have already survived the usually lethal gamut of competition or predation, to reach maturity. When they finally fall prey to pike such trout may be old enough to spawn and for this reason the predatory impact of pike on trout stocks may be particularly harmful.

The only other freshwater fish that regularly prey on trout are other trout. Sustained cannibalism can never be part of any successful survival strategy as it would soon lead to the disappearance of the species concerned. Even so, many fish are strangely partial to their own kind and trout fall foul of their fellows, as do pike, at nearly all stages in their development. Eggs that were not effectively buried in their nest, being swept downstream by the current, are grist to the digestive mill of any trout that finds them. By hatching time, larger trout have left the redds and examples of cannibalism are rare in breeding streams. However, if fish have successfully bred in still waters, shoals of young fry may be chased by older marauders that find them unexpectedly easy prey.

Once at the parr stage, trout are usually safe from the predatory attentions of other trout, apart from ferox. These almost legendary creatures have an unjustified reputation as cannibals, in part due to the general misuse of the word 'cannibal' to denote any trout that eats fish. Ferox have a marked preference for Arctic charr, and also catch perch and salmon parr (Chapter Four). True cannibalism is therefore probably much less common than might be supposed but in the absence of other prey fish, ferox will certainly not shrink from attacking their own kind.

Trout that migrate to sea benefit from a vastly increased range of food sources but to do so run the risk of attack by a whole different range of predators. There is a sufficiently wide variety of fish around European shores to sustain large numbers of predators without these having any'marked effect on the population of any one prey species. Anyway, because most sea fish are to some extent migratory, predators that are not must accept a varied diet or starve. So, while trout at sea suffer from predatory attacks by an assortment of other fish, birds and mammals, the effect of any one of these on trout numbers is seldom catastrophic.

Trout have always been frustratingly elusive once they reach the sea and reliable information on their behaviour, or on the habits of their predators, is almost impossibly difficult to gather. Much detailed study of birds, which are relatively easy to watch as they fish or return to their nest, has still revealed little information on the precise identity of their prey. Despite this, some evidence of underwater predation can be gathered from analysis of scars and other injuries to sea trout, caught either in nets along the shore or, back in their native rivers, by sport fishermen.

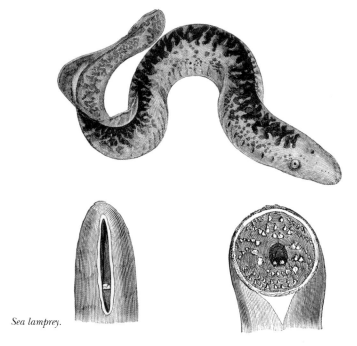

*Sea lamprey.*

Sea lampreys *(Petromyzon marinus)* spawn in fresh water but are vicious predators at sea, fixing their suckers onto the flanks of sea trout and rasping away pieces of flesh with their circular rows of teeth. Attacks on a fish's underside are likely to be fatal, but are not inevitably so if the lamprey attaches itself to a more muscular part of the body. A circular wound shows clearly after a lamprey has detached itself, usually healing in time to leave a distinct scar. Salmon and basking sharks *(Cetorhinus maximus)* are also favoured prey of lampreys off British coasts, but their potential for damaging fish stocks was most frighteningly illustrated with the construction of the Welland canal to circumvent Niagara falls, thus for the first time allowing lampreys up into the Great Lakes system. Once there, these parasitic creatures began to deplete the populations of lake charr which has sustained the local Indians for centuries. In all the Great Lakes except Superior a combination of lampreys and pollution gradually forced these deep-dwelling Salmonids to the edge of extinction and the fishing industry collapsed. Now, scientists have perfected a selective poison that has brought lamprey numbers under control but so far, massive efforts to re-establish breeding stocks of lake charr have been depressingly unsuccessful.

Many other sea fish prey on smolts and perhaps larger sea trout, but there is very little reliable evidence of the extent to which they do so. Furthermore, such underwater predation seldom leaves fish scarred but alive to provide later proof of their escape. Common porpoises *(Phocoena phocoena)* sometimes attack sea trout as may killer whales *(Orcinus orca)* and various dolphins (Delphinidae) although analysis of the contents of porpoise stomachs shows they prefer true sea fish.

Seals have often been blamed for local declines in sea trout numbers around the west coasts of Britain and Ireland. Both grey seals *(Halichoerus grypus)* and the less widespread, common seals *(Phoca vitulina)* are protected and show a distinct preference for salmon and sea trout if they can find them. Grey seals consume up to eight kilograms of fish flesh every day and may leave much of a large fish uneaten. Migratory fish, massing in the estuaries of their native rivers, are alarmingly vulnerable to seal and, to a much lesser extent, otter attacks. A good flow of fresh water allows sea trout to move straight up, but long periods without rain regularly confine them to the estuaries. They are less dependent than salmon on a spate of fresh water to stimulate the start of their breeding migrations and are also prepared to continue swimming upstream when the river is much lower. However, if it is down to drought levels, even sea trout may be reluctant to begin their journey, and fish often find themselves unable to exercise their migratory urges for long periods every summer.

Seals seldom fail in their attacks on sea trout and even if they are only partly successful, their prey are unlikely to survive. Even so, trout and salmon caught by coastal net fishermen occasionally show evidence of seal damage. Sometimes seals attack fish already trapped in nets but because they are largely protected, information on their diets is only available from uneaten prey. The occasional culling of seals has provided vague and predictable evidence as to how seriously they threaten sea trout stocks, showing only that seals are a real danger in estuaries but further out at sea their diet is far more varied.

There is little detailed evidence of the extent of bird predation at sea, although returning sea trout are often caught bearing scars on their backs. These marks are likely to evidence narrow escapes from attacks by cormorants, shags *(Phalacrocorax aristotelis)* or even gannets *(Sula bassana)* which fish spectacularly by folding up their wings before diving head first into the sea. Around their huge nesting colonies no fish under forty centimeters is safe from attack but gannets seek their food in deep clear water and do not threaten sea trout in the murky safety of an estuary. There, herring gulls *(Larus argentatus)* and cormorants are likely to be the most significant airborne dangers, at least to small sea trout smolts on their way out to face life in the open sea.

The only outcome of a successful attack by a predator is the sudden demise of its prey. By contrast, the attentions of parasites, both internal and external, are far less dramatic and not necessarily lethal. Nevertheless, they may seriously affect a trout's wellbeing, leading to loss of condition, starvation and sometimes death.

Every animal large enough to do so harbours parasites of one kind or another. Of these, sea lampreys are the most obviously destructive with which trout must contend, but they easily move from one fish to another and are far less dependent on any individual host than smaller, less mobile parasites. Many of these have the most intricate and specialised life histories, depending on more than one kind of host during different stages in their development. Biologically, parasites include nearly all disease-inducing organisms, as well as the larger flukes, worms and lice which fit the more colloquial use of the word. These larger parasites are multicelled organisms, often visible with the unaided eye; some attack trout externally while others live inside the dark security of the fish's body.

The most common parasites are those which subsist in the trout's digestive tract. They are usually wormlike creatures living off the contents of the stomach and intestine, and varying in length from a few millimeters to several centimeters. They often have the effect of reducing a trout's food supply by diverting part of it to their own use. This in turn can lead to serious deterioration in the fish's condition, although sometimes trout carry large numbers of small worms without any noticeable affect.

Worms are either flat or round and nearly all rely on more than one host during their life cycle (digenetic). It is the adults that are usually found in trout, implying the fish are secondary hosts that have eaten prey such as snails, shrimps or sticklebacks which were then acting as primary hosts during the worms' larval stages. The presence of particular parasites in a trout's digestive system can therefore act as an indicator of its diet.

Trout pick up different species of roundworms (Nematoda) in salt or fresh water. These sometimes affect their condition but more damaging can be flatworms, the most harmful of which are tapeworms (Cestoda) whose long segmented bodies break off at the end as the worms grow. They can seriously weaken their host, especially around spawning time when trout have almost stopped feeding and, with their resistance lowered, are already more susceptible to disease. However, killing off its host is not usually in the best interests of any parasite. Rather, it must achieve a delicate balance which allows it to flourish, yet ensures its presence is not so debilitating that the host dies before the parasite's life cycle is complete. Internal parasites are most often found in trout from rich still waters where shrimps, snails and prey fish are abundant, and less well-nourished trout from oligotrophic lakes may actually live longer because there are fewer carriers of parasites in their habitat.

External parasites are more self-evident but often lead less complex lives. Because they survive on a fish's exterior, they can find a host by simple contact, without having to develop inside a food source in order to gain access to a digestive system. Many of these parasites therefore need only one host during their life cycle (monogenetic).

Flukes and many other small worms are monogenetic, attaching themselves to skin or gills where, if the infestation is serious, they can cause severe damage. The most infamous external parasites are sea lice *(Lepeophtheirus salmonis)*. As these little crustaceans live and breed in the sea, only migratory trout (and salmon) suffer from their attentions as they stick to the skin of their host during the fourth of ten distinct life stages. They may suck blood from their host but feed mainly on particles of its skin. Sea lice cannot tolerate fresh water, usually surviving for only two or three days before they fall off and die, and their presence on a trout is an unmistakable indicator of its only recently having left the sea. All the same, if the fresh water is exceptionally cold they may cling to their host for up to six days before finally releasing their hold. Trout stocked into rich lakes where there are large numbers of coarse fish may suffer from infestations of carp lice *(Argulus* spp.*)*. There, other species of fish carry the parasite but are less affected by its attentions which can wipe out entire trout populations if unchecked.

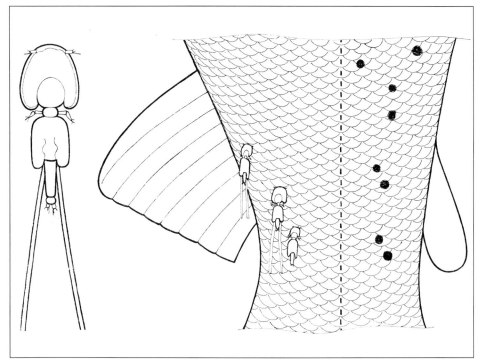

*Sea lice on a sea trout.*

There is also a fluke *(Diplostomum spathaceum)* which attacks a trout's eye during what is actually only one stage in a complex life cycle. The mature organism lives in the gut of a gull, osprey or other water bird which excretes the fluke's eggs. As long as these fall on water, they will hatch and the larvae then enter the body of an aquatic snail, remaining there for three further distinct life stages. On emerging, they swim freely in the water, but to survive they must make contact with a fish's skin and then move gradually up to infect its eye. When this happens, the eye lens starts to whiten over, usually blinding the fish which darkens in colour and eventually dies. In this case the host's death is actually necessary to ensure the continuation of the parasite's life, because a bird must then eat the remains of an infected fish for the cycle to begin all over again.

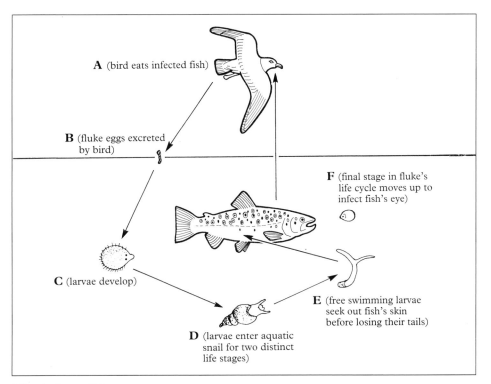

*Life cycle of an eye fluke.*

Parasitic infestations may cause disease in trout, as may viral and bacterial infections. These are responsible for most of the contagious diseases that are particularly prevalent under hatchery conditions, where trout may be infected by each other and their own waste, but which seldom threaten natural stocks of fish. In the wild, trout space themselves out to maximise the benefit from their food supplies and are therefore less susceptible to infection than fish which are artificially confined together in an unnaturally restricted area.

One bacterial disease which can seriously affect both wild and hatchery trout is Furunculosis. Infestation is most likely in warmer waters where temperatures consistently exceed 15°C, which generally confines the disease to the broader, lower reaches of rivers, where it may also attack coarse fish. In its early stages, Furunculosis can be difficult to diagnose as there are then no outward signs of disease but as the infection develops, boils may emerge anywhere on a trout's skin. Sometimes its pectoral fins are also infected and the absence of one or both of these is often a sign that a fish has recovered from Furunculosis. Seriously infected fish may die although it is perfectly possible for others to carry the disease without showing any outward signs of their doing so, continuing to resist its effects unless they become particularly stressed.

Fin rot (coldwater disease), on the other hand, is another bacterial disease only affecting fish in colder waters, usually where the temperature is less than 10°C. It shows by the appearance of pale lines along the fin edges. Sometimes the tissue between fin rays disintegrates causing them to separate and if infection spreads into a fish's body the disease may well prove fatal. It is likely that some form of prior fin damage must first occur, to allow in the bacteria which cause the rot.

Wild trout can die from infection by a single-celled parasite which causes white spot. This disease is also known as 'ich' (Ichthyophterius) after the protozoa that spreads it, and can be carried by minnows or sticklebacks. Individual white spots appear on a fish's skin and fins and, as the infection develops, may merge to form large white patches. These clearly irritate trout which rub the infected area against stones on the stream bed in an effort to gain relief.

Also appearing as large white patches on a trout's body are various fungal infections. Fungi are plants lacking in the chlorophyll required to generate their own food by photosynthesis. They must therefore gain nutrition from other plant or animal tissue. There are fungal spores of the genus *Saprolegnia* in many different freshwater environments which may infect eggs or trout at any age.

Fungi are usually not the primary cause of disease and do not attack healthy hosts directly. Rather, their spores take advantage of an existing injury to penetrate the skin through to the flesh where they anchor themselves with minute threadlike hyphae. The spores then start to multiply, eventually showing as a white mat of infection which may kill the fish if the spread continues. Fungi also attack eggs, initially dead ones, but once established, may infect the whole nest.

The most conspicuous fungal attacks are prompted by the secondary infection of fish with Ulcerative Dermal Necrosis (UDN). This disease affects both salmon and sea trout in salt water, seemingly just as they are about to enter rivers, causing lesions on their skins. These would normally heal up in clean, fresh water but if an infected fish dies, it does so from the secondary attentions of fungi which lodge on the ulcerated areas. The fungi often spread to cover large areas of skin, showing up as distinctive white patches, easily visible on larger fish in still pools. Despite much research the causes of UDN are still unknown. The first reported outbreak of an apparently similar disease came from Scotland at the end of the last century. That lasted fifteen years but it was not until 1961 that UDN appeared again in Ireland, slowly extending its range round most of the British Isles. Since then there have been several outbreaks, each with devastating results, although the affects quickly ease off and for several years after each, only a few fish in isolated rivers continue to be infected.

Stress itself is not a disease but a condition that may affect trout in the wild, occasionally with lethal consequences. Its physiological mechanism is highly complex but at its simplest, involves the release of a particular hormone (cortisol) into the blood (not unlike the discharge of adrenalin into the human blood stream), stimulating a fish to draw on energy reserves never normally available to it. Natural situations of acute stress, such as confrontations with predators or territorial disputes, are usually short-lived but the physiological consequences may last several days and the price for activating this mechanism is to make the fish much more prone to disease. From the continuing stress that may be caused by dangerously high temperatures, oxygen shortages or severe overcrowding, fish cannot escape. If they can adapt to such conditions, cortisol levels will revert to normal, otherwise trout will not feed, gradually losing condition and continuing at much greater risk from disease.

Stress is far more prevalent under hatchery conditions and if affecting wild trout, it is seldom those that have endured the rigours of competition to reach maturity, except during spawning which stresses even the strongest individuals. Then, even these older fish are more at risk from disease although during the rest of the year predation is likely to take a greater toll on their numbers. Any trout that survive to 'grow old' will, in most cases, eventually die of starvation, often brought on by blindness or parasite infestations.

Fish that eat plenty of rooted vegetation rely much less on their eyesight to feed and may be able to sustain themselves almost indefinitely after going completely blind. Carnivorous fish are obviously far more dependent on good eyesight and if this deteriorates, then so will their condition. A trout's sense of smell, or even the receptors in its audio/lateral system, may help it to locate food with limited success. However, an old fish with a large maintenance requirement can seldom sustain itself for long once its eyesight starts to fail.

The compilers of the volume of the Lonsdale Library on River Management gave a full page to a disease of trout they called 'Black Fish' and wrote that

About this disease next to nothing is known. It appears . . . to affect the older fish. The affected fish are blind, black, painfully thin and lethargic. They seek out slack water and lie in the same position day after day . . . The cause of the disease is unknown, whether the fish are thin because they are blind, or whether there is something which causes the  blindness as well as the loss of condition remains to be discovered.

Now, fifty years later, the influences on the colour of fish are better understood. The connection is firmly established between the amount of light entering a trout's eye and its overall colouration, through the activity of the melanophores controlling the supply of dark pigments. Dark fish among a population of lighter-coloured individuals are invariably blind. Such blindness may result from an eye injury or simply from deteriorating eye-sight brought on by increasing age, and will sooner or later be fatal.

The starvation from which most mature trout naturally die is not invariably brought on by blindness. Once in their prime, trout usually breed every year. Then they can regain the strength and weight lost during spawning and throughout the cold winter months that follow, by feeding voraciously in spring and summer. But each year, growing trout need more food to sustain themselves and to recover their condition so as to build up their reserves for the rigours of breeding and survival through the winter; and each year beyond their prime this minimum food requirement becomes harder to obtain. Ferox trout that suddenly become piscivorous, find the change boosts their ability to survive for many more years. Most other trout seem simply to reach a stage where the energy required for living is either no longer recovered from the prey they are able to catch, or else is dissipated in sustaining internal parasites.

And so, very slowly, their condition begins to deteriorate. As trout grow weaker, so their ability to catch prey is diminished and competition from young trout takes a greater toll. The old fish begin to seek out quieter waters where food supplies may be poor but less effort is required to counter the gentler flow. Perhaps these fish visit the spawning grounds one final time, expending more precious energy in a last frantic effort to reproduce themselves. But when winter finally comes it brings with it stronger currents and less food. So the old trout that has survived so much — perhaps the one in ten thousand destined to die a natural death, not in the beak or jaws of a predator or from the internal ravages of parasites, but simply through the weaknesses of age — seeks out a quiet corner of its native stream. And there, alone, the dying fish slowly surrenders its life to the forces of the water that sustained it for so long.

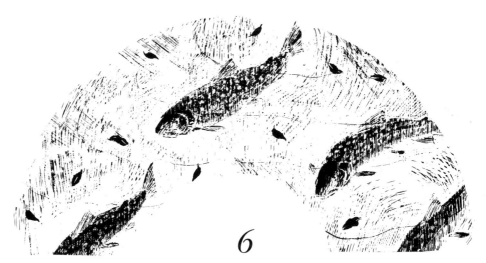

# 6
# Food and Feeding

As if to compensate for the complete absence of any post-natal parental care, Nature endows young trout with their own in-built food supplies. These may last as long as ten weeks but once they are exhausted, and the young trout have swum up to begin feeding for themselves, only instinct guides their efforts to secure nourishment. This instinct stimulates them to seize almost any solid-looking, water-borne morsel passing by them. Competition is intense, and trout snap at anything from midge larvae to minute pieces of vegetation in their efforts to gain in strength, which they can only do at the expense of their siblings. Gradually those that survive begin to temper instinct with experience ignoring air bubbles, vegetable matter and other wasted mouthfuls; perhaps their taste does not conform to the trout's slowly garnered idea of a good feed or some other biological signal indicates their nutritional deficiencies.

With this gradual accumulation of feeding experience grows a heightened sense of prey selectivity and soon the trout's exclusively carnivorous tastes become firmly established. An older fish may still ingest occasional pieces of vegetation but only due to mistaken identity or their being unavoidably swallowed together with fly larvae or other normal prey.

Ultimately, composition of diet depends upon the range of food available in any given environment but, at its widest, includes almost the whole spectrum of invertebrate animal life that crawls, swims, wriggles or floats in the water or on its surface. The contents of a trout's stomach can to some extent serve as a microcosmic indicator of the fauna of its habitat; however, time of year, weather conditions, dietary preferences and the size of prey a trout is physically able to swallow, all influence what it eats which may give a misleading impression of the relative abundance of different animals in an underwater community.

The most fundamental division of trout's food is into prey of either terrestrial or aquatic origin. Of these, the latter are vastly more significant, not least because terrestrial animal life only reaches the alien element of water with the aid of wind or gravity.

The trout's main aquatic prey are insects, molluscs and crustaceans, their respective distributions depending much on type of water and time of year. Insects have been called the 'glue and building blocks of the aquatic community' and without exception, whether merely of underwater origin or permanent water dwellers, they are vital to the nourishment of trout and constitute their most varied and dependable food supplies.

All adult insects have six legs and the class is subdivided into the normal taxonomic groupings of order, family, genus and species. The four particular orders which feature prominently in trout diets are well recognised by their colloquial names. Ephemeroptera is certainly the most conspicuous, even though comprising relatively few species of mayflies, olives and duns. These are often spectacular in their short-lived appearances and attract the attentions of fish and fishermen like no other insects. Trichoptera includes the caddis (sedge) flies, and Plecoptera, the stone-flies. Diptera is a massive order in terms of numbers of species (although few of these are of interest to trout) and includes gnats, smuts, midges and several familiar terrestial insects.

The life histories of aquatic insects are fascinatingly varied. However, the different stages of aquatic insect development are often little known to those who rely on the imitation of those creatures to catch trout, and cannot be better illustrated than by the story of the familiar blue-winged olive *(Ephemerella ignita)*. This is a widely distributed Ephemeropteran of the Ephemerellidae family whose early and prolonged appearances on streams and rivers make it particularly important to trout in British waters.

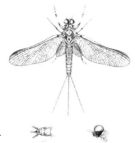

*Blue-winged olive sub-imago.*

Blue-winged olives begin life as they hatch out from eggs attached to underwater vegetation. The incubation period varies greatly, often lasting many months, in contrast to that of most other Ephemeropterans whose eggs hatch after only a few weeks. On emerging the nymphs are barely visible to the naked eye but generally resemble fully formed nymphs in shape. They have strong legs with which they cling to or crawl through thick underwater vegetation. Nymphs grow in a cumbersome and wasteful manner, repeatedly shedding their hard external skeletons to accommodate continuous internal expansion. Each stage between sheddings is called an 'instar' and there are between twenty and thirty in the development of blue-winged olives. Like most other insects, the greater part of their lives are spent in the nymphal stages and as size and conspicuousness increase, so do their chances of falling victims to foraging trout. When newly-hatched, nymphs of all species are minute, but as they grow they range in size right up to the three centimeters of fully-grown mayfly nymphs, thus providing suitable prey for trout of all ages. Insects in their nymphal or larval stages perform a far more crucial role in sustaining trout than the much shorter-lived adults.

During their final instar, mature blue-winged olive nymphs stop feeding and swim up to the surface to emerge from their last protective skin as duns. Sometimes this emergence is referred to as a 'hatch' but true hatching takes place when nymphs first crawl out of their eggs. This journey to the surface from their protective home of weed or moss is a dangerous time for nymphs and once there, duns are especially vulnerable, often struggling in vain to emerge from their nymphal exoskeleton. Until they can fly, duns are also at the mercy of any current that sweeps them down past one hungry trout after another. But for those that emerge successfully to reveal their olive-brown bodies and blue-grey wings there are further dangers: they must still take off from the water and if impurities affect the strength of its surface tension, may find it difficult to launch themselves into the air. Fish and birds lose no time in taking advantage of helpless duns that have capsized or become water-logged in some other way.

Once airborne, blue-winged olive duns fly off to the shelter of riparian trees or other bankside foliage. Their flight is weak and the wind as much as their own efforts, propels them to their resting places. There they seek shelter in preparation for their final moult to a second winged stage — an occurrence unique among insects to Ephemeropterans — and usually up to forty-eight hours later, mature blue-winged olives emerge. Then, as familiar sherry spinners, they are ready to fulfil the only purpose left to them during these last few days of their lives, which is to breed.

The spinners have shiny wings and their three distinctive tails project elegantly from rusty brown bodies. Swarms of darker-coloured male spinners mass together on still evenings at the water's edge luring passing females into pairing with them. Couples then copulate in the air, although their sexual acrobatics often force them to alight on water or land as they mate.

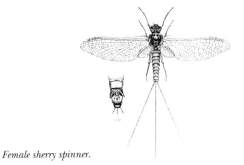

*Female sherry spinner.*

Fertilisation is almost instantaneous and when mating is complete the female is ready to lay her eggs. After uncoupling, she joins other females, flying upstream together in great dipping columns, as the eggs gradually collect in a small cluster near the end of her abdomen. Once the whole clutch has been squeezed out through the oviduct, the female swoops down onto the water, often using the friction of gentle contact with its surface to dislodge her burden.

A sherry spinner usually tries to shed her eggs in fast water. There the cluster quickly disintegrates and the current carries the individual eggs downstream before they come to rest among aquatic vegetation. The eggs then remain secured to their protective plants, which may be thick luxuriant fronds of underwater weed or, in fast upland streams, merely short stubbly growths of moss clinging to rocks. Only in slow muddy rivers and still waters do blue-winged olives fail to find suitable nurseries where their eggs can over-winter until the nymphs' springtime hatch starts the full annual cycle again.

Males find breeding less arduous and after coupling, may return to their swarm and even try to mate again. Despite the release of their burden, females are usually exhausted and collapse onto the water's surface. There, as spent spinners, they float helplessly down with the current, giving one or two valedictory flaps of their wings before expiring. At such times trout are presented with an almost unequalled opportunity for effortless feeding when they determinedly ignore any other food that may come their way.

All of the nearly fifty species of Ephemeropterans are characterised by their distinctive upright forewings. Many of them make vital contributions to the nourishment of trout. As well as blue-winged olives there are several other familiar olives, march browns, all the duns (as a group of flies rather than a stage in their lives) and the tiny, inimitable caenis flies, aptly named the 'angler's curse'. Most conspicuous of all Ephemeropterans are the mayflies, of which there are three species in Britain *(Ephemera danica, E. vulgata* and *E. lineata)*, although the third is very uncommon. Sometimes all species in the order are colloquially referred to as mayflies but this is confusing, not least because adults of one species or another appear in all but the coldest months.

The nymphs of true mayflies live in holes in sand or mud, where their strong mandibles and short legs aid their excavations. This preferred habitat restricts their distribution to slower-flowing and still waters, also frequented by minute caenis nymphs. March brown nymphs are found clinging to rocks in the fastest currents of upland streams by means of a peculiar adaptation of their gill covers; these lie on the underside of their bodies and enable nymphs to stick, through suction, like leeches to the smoothest surfaces.

*Mayfly nymph.*

Olive nymphs are streamlined and can swim strongly. Their gills are less developed and depend on the current to force water through them, thereby effectively confining olives to running water. Nymphs of the blue-winged olive and of its only congener, the yellow evening dun *(Ephemeralla notata)*, are active crawlers and their strong legs propel them easily through the vegetation that is their home.

During their lengthy underwater existence, Ephemeropteran nymphs are almost exclusively vegetarian and need to eat large amounts of food to fuel their growth and regular moults. Nymphal life-span varies greatly between species. Nymphs of mayflies, perhaps not surprisingly as they are the largest members of their order, take two years to mature, blue-winged olives complete a generation within twelve months and the tiny caenis may do so in half that time; however in every case, temperature variations may delay or accelerate the steps to maturity.

Once they are ready to depart their underwater world, nymphs stop feeding and lose the use of their mouth-parts, which slowly degenerate. Final emergence usually takes place on the surface, although some species, such as the late march brown *(Ecdyonurus venosus)*, crawl out of the water onto bankside vegetation to metamorphose; and at least one species, the dusky yellowstreak *(Heptagenia lateralis)*, emerges underwater, rising to the surface encapsulated in a protective bubble of air.

Just as young alevins are vulnerable when they leave the security of their gravelly nest for the open water, so are nymphs during their ascent from the stream bed or its emergent vegetation: as they rise up, the current may carry them past feeding fish which are magnetised by the insects' struggles to shed their last protective skins. Having emerged, duns still cannot leave the water until their wings are dry and their wing muscles have warmed up enough to propel them onto dry land. This pause before they are airborne exposes duns to further danger, but from the fishermen's perspective provides an extra opportunity to compete with the originals for the trout's attentions. Finally, Ephemeropteran duns (sub-imagos) fly off to the security of riverbank vegetation where they rest for up to two days before their final transformation into elegant, sexually mature spinners (imagos).

*Mayfly sub-imago.*

This second, unique moult of winged Ephemeropterans sets the scene for the mating dances which bring the sexes together. Male spinners are initially attracted by sight to the females which hover around the edges of their swarm. At that time a passable imitation of a natural female spinner, dangled on a cast at the edge of a swarm, attracts the attentions of any number of males which are only deterred by actual contact with the artificial object of their desires.

By always facing and flying into the wind at the same speed as it blows against them, the swarms of males remain more or less stationary. When very strong winds are blowing they must seek shelter, but rain deters their mating activities much less than might be expected and certainly less than low temperatures. Just as duns take longer to leave the water's surface in cold weather, many spinners cannot fly well when the temperature drops. When a couple finally mate they do so in the air, the male approaching his mate from below and clasping her thorax with his long jointed forelegs; then, by bending his body upwards into hers, copulation takes place, followed almost immediately by fertilisation of the female's eggs.

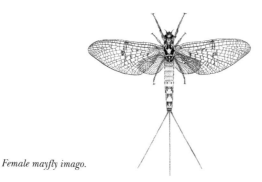

*Female mayfly imago.*

Ephemeropterans lay their eggs in one of two intriguingly different ways. Many of them, like blue-winged olives, oviposit on the water's surface, dropping their burden in one cluster as they fly, with or without the help of friction with the water's surface. Female mayflies also lay their eggs on the surface but actually alight on the water to release some of their clutch and then fly off again before repeating the process until all their eggs have been extruded. In the last scene of this final act, the female usually collapses exhausted onto the water, spent from the efforts of her life's work. Helplessly, she is then borne away by the current, the final waves of her wings so often signalling her ebbing vitality to waiting trout.

Most olives behave very differently when laying their eggs. Large, medium and small dark olives *(Baetis rhodani, B. vernus* and *B. scambus)* and iron blues *(Baetis niger* and *B. muticus)* first cling to rocks, posts, sticks or protruding vegetation. Then they crawl down underwater, often to considerable depths, and lay their eggs on the underside of stones or among weed stems. The forces of surface tension and the bubble of air surrounding each insect keep it alive on its downward journey, even on occasions allowing for a return to the surface and a final feeble flight to a last resting place. More often however, after leaving their eggs in a chosen underwater shelter, spent female spinners are swept downstream before being pushed up by the current into the surface film.

So much happens so quickly in the airborne life of these Ephemeropteran insects that take their name from the Greek word 'ephemeros' which means 'lasting for only one day'. German entomologists call them 'Eintagsfliegen' — 'one day flies' — although for caenis flies, life above the water lasts little more than two hours from emergence to egg laying. After two years underwater, true mayflies live for several days before completing their allotted span, but whether it be a matter of hours or days, this period of their life is critically important to feeding trout. No other food source presents such a short-lived opportunity for such massive piscine over-indulgence as Ephemeropterans do, between emerging from their nymphal exoskeletons and exhausting themselves from their reproductive efforts. The trout's eagerness for these insects has provoked massive human effort to imitate them, whether as nymph, dun or spinner. General patterns such as Grey Wulff, Greenwell's Glory or Pheasant Tail Nymph each endeavour to imitate several different Ephemeropterans. At the same time dozens of specific patterns, all with countless different variations, have evolved on the premise that deception is best achieved by producing the most precise replica of the natural insect.

Adult caddis-flies (sedge-flies) of the order Trichoptera live much longer than Ephemeropterans, partly because in the final stage of their lives they retain the vestiges of a mouth, enabling them to absorb small amounts of moisture. There are nearly 200 species in the order but most are uncommon or only occur very locally. Like all flies with aquatic origins, their distribution is governed by the underwater environment's fitness for the developing larvae; yet there are so many species adapted for such differing habitats that there are caddis-flies wherever there are trout.

Mature caddis-flies have four wings. The front pair is larger than those behind and when at rest folds tent-like over their bodies, like the wings of many different moths. Caddis wings are covered with fine hairs in contrast to the scales which give moths' wings their powdery look. The flies have no tails but display two very prominent antennae which are often much longer than their bodies.

Not all caddis adults lay their eggs in water, and those that deposit them on bankside plants are unlikely at any of the four stages in their development to nourish trout. Species whose larvae develop in water usually lay their eggs on the surface, as do silverhorns *(Athripsodes* and *Mystacides* spp.) and Welshman's buttons *(Sericostoma personatum)*. However, adult brown sedges *(Anabolia nervosa)* crawl down protruding vegetation like Ephemeropteran olives and attach their eggs to underwater stems.

Caddis eggs usually hatch within two weeks. On emerging most larvae start to build their distinctive cases of stones, twigs, sand grains, leaves, mollusc shells or other available debris. These cases are bonded together with a silky secretion produced by the larvae's salivary glands. The construction of the cases, which is as diverse as the nests of birds and often helps identify the occupant, is determined by available building materials. Species like the sandfly *(Rhyacophila dorsalis)* living in fast-flowing upland streams where aquatic plants are scarce, must build their cases out of sand grains and small stones; others, such as the great red sedge *(Phrygania grandis)*, which prefer still waters and sluggish rivers, have no difficulty in collecting up the vegetation required for theirs.

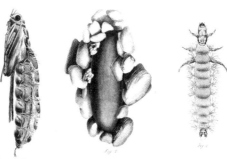

*Sandfly – larva, case and pupa.*

The construction of these cases affects the agility of their builders. Caddis larvae confined within cocoons of pebbles in fast waters are relatively immobile but need the extra weight to prevent the current sweeping them downstream. Those inhabiting quieter waters inside their vegetal cases are much more mobile and can move freely from one source of food to another. Most caddis larvae are vegetarian but some of the larger species feed off larvae and eggs of other insects and even off tiny crustaceans. About fifty British species of caddis-fly do not construct protective cases but instead many of these build web-like protections between stones, serving not only as shelters but also as traps for drifting morsels of food.

Trichopteran larvae (caddis grubs, caddis worms, stick worms or, in Ireland, corbait) are extremely important food for foraging trout which nibble them off the stream bed or from amongst underwater plants. However, trout give almost no visible indication of feeding on them and for fishermen these grubs are impossibly difficult to imitate. Separating larvae from their cases is a virtually hopeless task for fish and bits of grit or vegetation in the stomachs of trout may be the consequence of their having eaten a case along with its inhabitant.

When fully mature, usually several months after hatching, caddis larvae prepare for the third stage of their existence. Both Ephemeropterans and Plecopteran stoneflies emerge from their larval stage into the open air, but caddis-flies undergo a second underwater transformation into pupae, in which form they spend the last days of their aquatic lives.

*Female Welshman's Button.*

The caddis-fly's metamorphosis from larva to pupa is like the butterfly's from caterpillar to chrysalis. Pupation begins with the larva securing its case with silken threads to a firm underwater projection before sealing up the ends with the same material. The free-swimming caddis larva that has not built a case, now does so, preparing one of silk which it also secures firmly to stone, stick or stem. The pupal stage may last several weeks but more often only a few days during which the pupa is unable to feed, remaining immobile in its cocoon. Then, when fully developed, it emerges from its protective housing, using powerful jaws to chew open the ends and fully formed legs to push and paddle its way into open water.

Once out of their cocoons, caddis pupae propel themselves to the surface. There, the adults of most species emerge straight away but some pupae seek out the shelter of riparian plants, where they can complete their transition to maturity in greater safety. They may even find their way onto the boots of a wading fisherman, crawling up his face in an abortive search for protective vegetation. Both struggling pupae and emergent adults are dangerously exposed to the predatory attentions of feeding trout, which can be caught on pupal imitations, although most anglers concentrate more on representing fully-fledged insects.

Adult caddis-flies — at that stage more usually called 'sedge-flies' — vary in size from a few millimeters to nearly three centimeters. Most species are remarkably similar in colour and for this reason less attention is paid to their precise imitation. Body colouring is more variable but the brown, grey or black wings, when at rest, are folded over in such a way that little else of the insect is visible. Many imitations successfully represent several different species which is particularly convenient when more than one emerge together, often contributing to a 'hatch' of almost Ephemeropteran proportions.

*Male Welshman's Button.*

Many fishermen associate the emergence of sedges with late evening, but if they do appear earlier trout avidly seek them out. The grannom *(Brachycentrus subnubilus)* is one of the most familiar species and appears any time after the middle of the day, and the equally familiar Welshman's button may be expected soon afterwards. Nevertheless, early evening is more likely to trigger the emergence of a much wider variety of sedges from both rivers and lakes. Several artificial dry flies, such as Brown, Cinnamon, Mottled, Silver and Little Red Sedges are designed to imitate emerging adults while the Wickham's Fancy and Invicta are better known as wet fly patterns.

Trichopterans live as adult sedge-flies for as long as a month out of their four-stage life span of up to one year. Both temperature and humidity influence their longevity but inevitably the time arrives when they respond to their reproductive urges and couples begin mating in mid-air before completing their union on the ground. Fertilisation is usually immediate but even so, the female often delays before setting off to deposit her eggs on the water, or on emergent vegetation either above or below its surface. Then, spent from her efforts, like nearly all other aquatic insects she slowly expires.

Rocky upland streams where both aquatic vegetation and insect life are in short supply, are the haunt of Plecoptera — the stone-flies. There are only thirty species in Britain but for a trout struggling to survive in these impoverished waters, the stable supply of their nymphs is a vital ingredient of its diet. In the north of England, stone-flies are sometimes confusingly referred to as 'mayflies' and are only of real significance to fishermen as egg-laying adults when, during their brief contact with the water's surface, trout feed on them with reckless enthusiasm. On many streams they emerge from their underwater nursery in early April when there are almost no other airborne insects around, thus further enhancing their appeal in the eyes of hungry fish. The larger members of the order are over three centimeters long with wingspans almost twice that, and few fish can pass over the opportunity of such a meal.

The pedigree of the artificial stone-fly is impeccable, having been first described by Dame Julia Berners, reputed to have been the prioress of St. Alban's, in her *Treetyse on Fysshynge wyth an Angle* nearly five hundred years ago. Now, general patterns like Partridge and Orange, John Storey and Blue Upright may prove successful imitations of most of the natural insects, which include willow-flies *(Leuctra geniculata)*, yellow Sallies *(Isoperla grammatica)*, needle-flies *(Leuctra fusca)* and several different species which pass under the general name of 'large stone-flies'.

The stone-fly's life cycle spans only three stages — egg, nymph and adult. Eggs are laid as the female either swims along the top of the water or lightly touches its surface with her abdomen as she flies. Larger species tend to adopt the first method and the disturbance they cause on the surface is an irresistable attraction to any trout below. Their eggs are equipped with flat little discs which anchor them to the substratum in even the fastest water, while the sticky protective membrane surrounding the eggs of many smaller species serves the same function.

The incubation period varies from a few days to three months. After hatching, stone-fly nymphs are able to grow by shedding their outer skins, as many as thirty times before the adult insect emerges; in this way their growth is like that of Ephemeropterans, from which stone-flies can always be distinguished by their two, rather than three, distinctive tails. Immature stone-flies (creepers) are among trout's favourite foods and although imitations are almost impossible to produce, the natural can be a deadly bait when impaled straight onto a hook. Larvae of the large stone-flies of the Perlidae family are sometimes called 'gadgers' and are much sought by fishermen early in the year, when the adults are beginning to emerge.

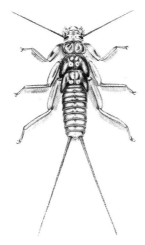

*Stone-fly larva.*

As their vernacular name suggests, stone-fly nymphs crawl rather than swim around in their search for food. All species eat vegetation, but larger ones may attack the larvae or nymphs of other insects in a quite ferocious manner. The stone-fly's nymphal stage may last as long as three years and towards the end of their final instar, by which time the insect's wings are fully developed, mature nymphs crawl across the stones to the shore or up a rock or post protruding from the water. There they rest out in the open, before their last protective skin splits, exposing the adult insect to the air.

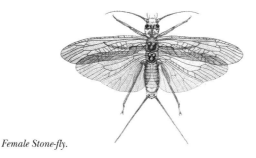

*Female Stone-fly.*

At first, mature stone-flies are lightly shaded but soon darken to their true colours. Despite their large wings, many adults are poor fliers and spend most of their lives hiding under rocks or in vegetation along the banks of the stream or lake from which they emerged. Like sedges, stone-flies can ingest moisture and also some food; yet even these abilities cannot ensure them an adult life much longer than a month, before the efforts of breeding bring on their inevitable end.

The order Diptera is especially interesting on account of its diversity. Each species has only two wings and the order embraces several thousand different insects of both terrestrial and aquatic origin, although no adults are aquatic. The life stages of the terrestrials are less important to fishermen but adult hawthorn and heather flies *(Bibio marci* and *B. pomonae)*, as well as crane flies or daddy-long-legs *(Tipula* spp.*)*, often end up on the water where trout pursue them enthusiastically. Diptera also includes such familiar, mainly land-hatching insects as bluebottles, cow-dung flies, house-flies, horse-flies, gnats and midges most of which only occasionally serve to vary fish's diets. However, there are two families of aquatic origin — Chironomidae and Simuliidae — which are important to trout — often to the intense frustration of fishermen who find the natural flies too small to imitate successfully.

Chironomids are non-biting midges, also called 'buzzers'. Male adults are spindly, long-legged creatures with two transparent wings lying along much of the length of their bodies; they are often also endowed with two large feathery antennae. Females are squatter. Many of the nearly 400 species are brightly coloured green or red and their contribution to the sustenance of trout was long ignored. Now their importance is well appreciated by serious stillwater fishermen and many artificial patterns have been designed to imitate both pupae and adults of the olive, green, brown and red midges *(Chironomus* spp.*)* as well as of the familiar Blae and Black *(Chironomus anthracinus)*.

The larvae of these midges have long worm-like bodies, often even more conspiciously coloured than the adults. Some of the best known are the bright red bloodworms which owe their distinctive colouration to the haemogloblin in their blood, allowing them to survive in thick, poorly oxygenated sediment. Chironomids are short-lived in comparison to most other insects and many species produce two or three generations in a year, helped by the fact that the larvae pass through very few instars before reaching their pupal stage. This seldom lasts more than three days, during which the pupae swim up to the surface of the lake, there to hang suspended, awaiting their call to maturity. Often they have difficulty penetrating the surface film, particularly on calm days; then cruising trout can scoop up hundreds of pupae before these are able to escape into the air. Soon after emerging, adult males form large almost cloud-like swarms by which they seek to attract females ready to mate. Once their union is complete the females swoop down to the water and release their eggs onto its surface.

*Adult male (left) and female Chironomid midge.*

These midges are best known to fishermen on still waters and remain largely ignored by those who fish rivers, despite the larvae being the most conspicuous component of the diet of young fry. These tiny insects are swept through feeding territories by the current and are vitally important to trout at that critical stage in their development. For large fish, the energy obtained from a single chironomid larva is far exceeded by that used up in catching and swallowing it; and perhaps midges can only provide an economic meal for adult trout when the inert pupae can be picked off in large numbers just under the surface. Small trout can make economic use of much smaller prey and for many of them a single midge larva served up by the current is probably their first proper meal.

Generally confined to running waters, reed smuts (or black-flies) of the Simuliidae family are sometimes also called 'angler's curse' and are, like the Ephemeropteran caenis-flies, impossibly difficult to imitate. Despite these insects' tiny size, trout still seem to find feeding on both larvae and adults worthwhile, probably because these are so abundant that a reasonable meal can be obtained with minimum effort from a restricted area. Reed smut eggs are usually laid in the water and hatch after a week. The larvae then moult several times before spinning themselves a protective cocoon in which they pupate. Emergence occurs under water, prompted by the gradual accumulation of small bubbles of gas inside the pupal cases. Eventually the expanding gas splits the cases and the adults drift up to the surface surrounded only by their protective bubbles which then burst, allowing them to fly away almost immediately.

As well as often being called 'black-flies', these reed smuts are also sometimes loosely referred to as 'black gnats'. This name is in fact more correctly given to one of the terrestrial species of Diptera, *Bibio johanis*, which has travelled under the name of 'black gnat' at least since the publication of Alfred Ronalds' famous *Fly-Fisher's Entomology* in 1836. With a good breeze these true black gnats are often blown helplessly onto the water's surface where they are lethally exposed to the attentions of hungry trout.

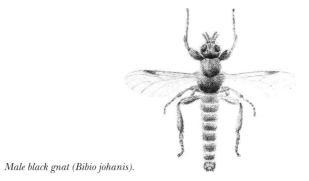

*Male black gnat (Bibio johanis).*

A wide range of other terrestrial invertebrates occasionally also end up in the water. Most of these do so only intermittently and are therefore important neither to fish nor fishermen. Bees, wasps, ants and several species of beetle are all grist to the trout's mill, while coch-y-bondhu beetles (or bracken clocks, *Phyllopertha horticola*) are blown onto the water sufficiently often to merit a familiar imitation. There are also many different beetles whose aquatic habits would theoretically make them tempting targets for trout but which live so securely amongst thick underwater vegetation that they usually remain undetected. Moths, spiders, mites, grasshoppers and lacewings may also inadvertently find themselves on the water's surface where their struggles to escape from that unfamiliar element may attract a fish.

Outside the four main orders there are few flies of aquatic origins of any great interest to trout. Adult alder flies *(Sialis* spp.*)* resemble sedges but have hard glossy wings with conspicuous veins. Their larvae are extraordinarily tough and determined, to such an extent that they are known to have emerged alive after completing the journey through the whole of a trout's digestive system. Trout may be attracted to these larvae as they struggle shorewards to pupate, just as they may by damsel-fly nymphs making similar journeys before their final emergence. Adult damsel-flies lay their eggs underwater and may be attacked in the process. Dragonflies are larger and some species breed underwater too, but for most of their lives these brightly coloured insects stay clear of the surface and avoid the predatory instincts of trout by doing so. Their nymphs are ferocious creatures — up to five centimeters long and quite as fearsome as they look; they may even attack small fish in the course of indulging their exclusively carnivorous tastes, almost as if relishing an opportunity to reverse the usual direction of the food chain.

One other order of insects, Hemiptera, includes several families with differing habits which provide trout with occasional food. These families are often collectively called 'water bugs' (in a stricter biological sense than the word is colloquially used). Water boatmen (Corixidae) keep surfacing to breathe, occasionally attracting fish as they do so. Pond skaters (Gerridae) live on the surface and are distinguished by their two closely spaced pairs of hind legs which are much longer than their antennae-like front ones. They usually inhabit the shallows where trout seldom venture and where also live water measurers (Hydrometridae) which look like stick insects and pierce their food underwater through the surface film. Water crickets (Veliidae) prefer the shallows as well and are more often found along the edge of running water.

The trout's opportunistic diet also includes newts, young frogs, and many different worms. Other fish, and their eggs, also fall into the category of occasional food for trout not yet exclusively dependent on fish for their nourishment. Perch fry and young elvers sustain many stillwater trout through the early summer months when shoals of breeding minnows, oblivious to everything except their reproductive urges, are also easy prey. In upland streams, a single bullhead, stickleback or stone loach can provide a comparatively small trout with the same nourishment as hundreds of midge larvae, although such bounty is exceptional. The territorial feeding habits of trout in running waters preclude them from relying exclusively on one particular prey, unlike ferox trout (Chapter Four) which cast around for other fish over a wide area, becoming almost single-mindedly piscivorous once they have graduated from their more generalised diets.

Molluscs and crustaceans make a far greater contribution to the nourishment of trout than their place at the end of this review suggests. There are many species of aquatic snails found in all but the most acidic conditions where the calcium content of the water is insufficient for their shells to develop effectively. Ideally they prefer thick vegetation in nutrient-rich, slow-flowing or still waters where trout nip them off the weed stalks with great enthusiasm, but in less alkaline lochs they are to be found on stones, grazing algae. On occasions, snails float freely in open water or upside down just under the surface where they are even easier for trout to catch. Some snails are so small that caddis larvae are able to use unbroken shells in the construction of their cases. Of the bivalved molluscs, pea-mussels are common almost everywhere; they are seldom more than one centimeter across but the remains of their little round shells are often found in trout's stomachs.

A wide range of very different crustaceans often feature prominently in trout diets. *Daphnia* are tiny water fleas of the Daphniidae family, living suspended in organically-rich still waters from which they extract nourishment. Once these plankton are sufficiently concentrated to make feeding on their 'blooms' economic in terms of energy expenditure, trout snap them up in rapid succession, perhaps also filtering some through their gill rakers like whales in the sea. These tiny fleas are quite inimitable and when they move up towards the surface which they often do in warm cloudy weather, it is hard to turn the eye of any trout determined to feed on them.

Water slaters (or water hoglice — *Asellus aquaticus*) are crustaceans which resemble aquatic woodlice and, being unable to swim, forage around plant detritus in lakes and reservoirs. Trout may eat them eagerly at the beginning of the year but never with the sustained enthusiasm reserved for freshwater shrimps *(Gammarus pulex* and *G. lacustris)*. These are abundant in still and running waters and are undoubtedly the best all-round source of trout food. Individual sizes vary to accommodate the predatory abilities of trout of all ages, they are present throughout the year and also have a suicidal habit of drawing attention to themselves by suddenly somersaulting off the bottom. Like molluscs though, shrimps require calcium for their shells and are consequently more often to be found in alkaline waters, the carotene in their bodies giving a pinkish tinge to the flesh of their predators. Trout

Different forms of wild brown trout. (*Jonathan Newdick*)

China mark moth
*Cataclysta lemnata*

Arctic charr
*Salvelninus alpinus*

Rainbow trout
*Oncorhynchus mykiss*

Atlantic salmon. *Salmo salar*

Other Salmonids — Arctic charr, rainbow trout and the only other member of the genus *Salmo*, the Atlantic salmon.
(*Jonathan Newdick*)

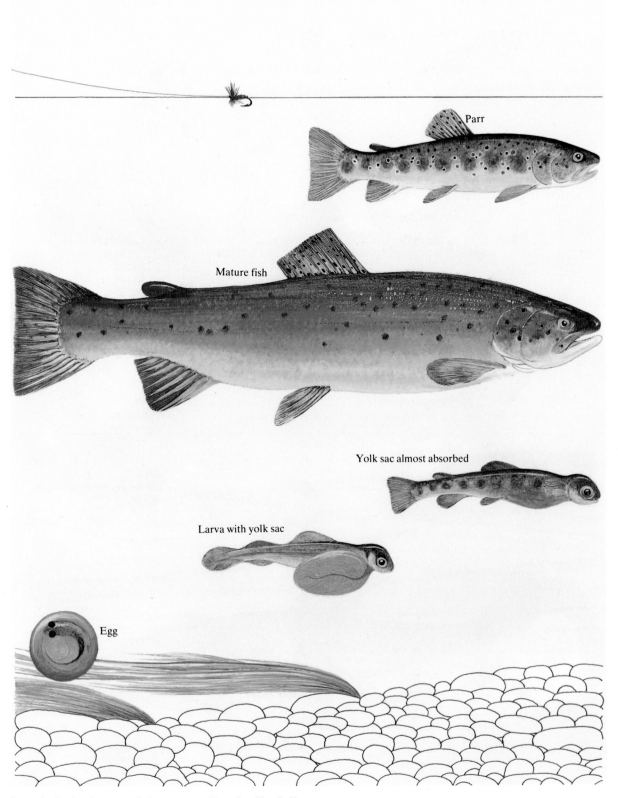

Parr

Mature fish

Yolk sac almost absorbed

Larva with yolk sac

Egg

Stages in the development of a brown trout. (*Jonathan Newdick*)

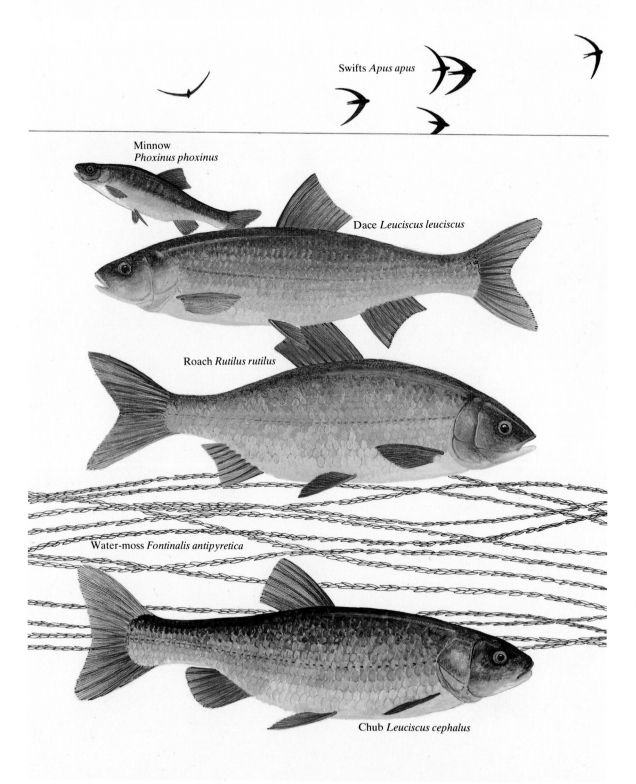

Swifts *Apus apus*

Minnow
*Phoxinus phoxinus*

Dace *Leuciscus leuciscus*

Roach *Rutilus rutilus*

Water-moss *Fontinalis antipyretica*

Chub *Leuciscus cephalus*

Competitors. (*Jonathan Newdick*)

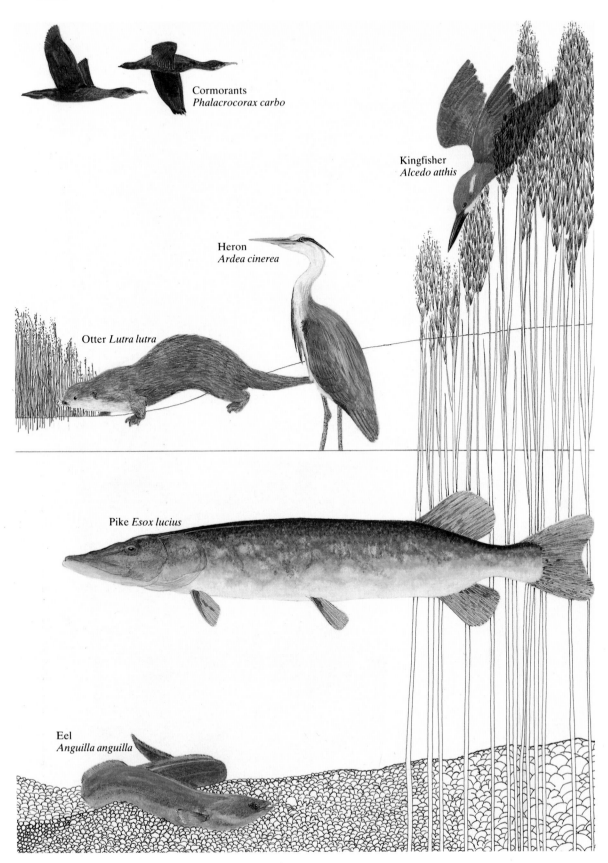

Cormorants
*Phalacrocorax carbo*

Kingfisher
*Alcedo atthis*

Heron
*Ardea cinerea*

Otter *Lutra lutra*

Pike *Esox lucius*

Eel
*Anguilla anguilla*

Predators. (*Jonathan Newdick*)

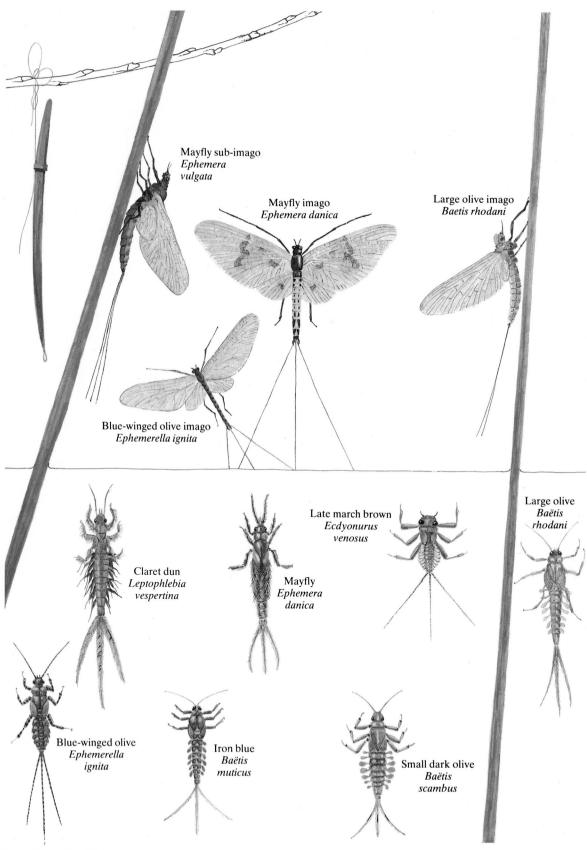

Mayfly sub-imago
*Ephemera*
*vulgata*

Mayfly imago
*Ephemera danica*

Large olive imago
*Baetis rhodani*

Blue-winged olive imago
*Ephemerella ignita*

Claret dun
*Leptophlebia*
*vespertina*

Mayfly
*Ephemera*
*danica*

Late march brown
*Ecdyonurus*
*venosus*

Large olive
*Baëtis*
*rhodani*

Blue-winged olive
*Ephemerella*
*ignita*

Iron blue
*Baëtis*
*muticus*

Small dark olive
*Baëtis*
*scambus*

Stages in the life of Ephemeropteran insects — adults (*above*) and nymphs (*below*). (*Jonathan Newdick*)

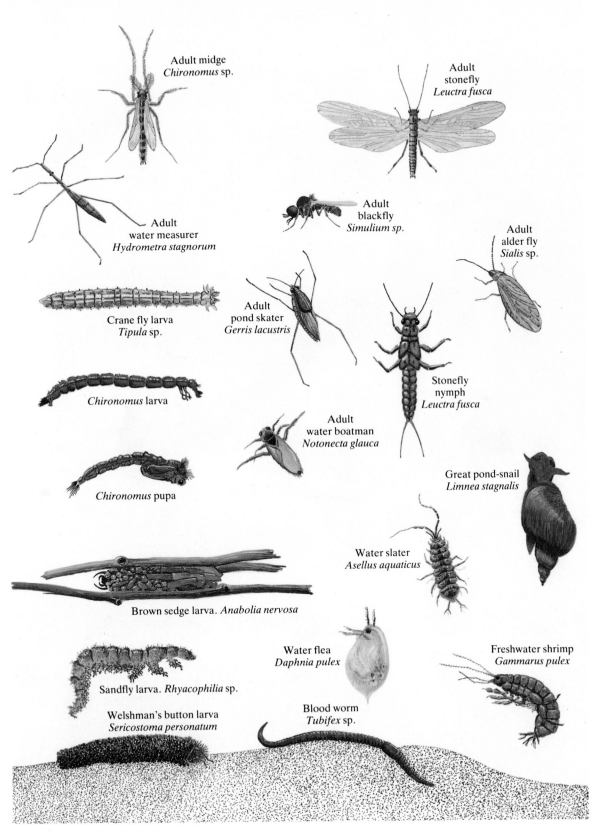

Adult midge
*Chironomus* sp.

Adult
stonefly
*Leuctra fusca*

Adult
water measurer
*Hydrometra stagnorum*

Adult
blackfly
*Simulium sp.*

Adult
alder fly
*Sialis* sp.

Crane fly larva
*Tipula* sp.

Adult
pond skater
*Gerris lacustris*

Stonefly
nymph
*Leuctra fusca*

*Chironomus* larva

Adult
water boatman
*Notonecta glauca*

*Chironomus* pupa

Great pond-snail
*Limnea stagnalis*

Water slater
*Asellus aquaticus*

Brown sedge larva. *Anabolia nervosa*

Water flea
*Daphnia pulex*

Freshwater shrimp
*Gammarus pulex*

Sandfly larva. *Rhyacophilia* sp.

Blood worm
*Tubifex* sp.

Welshman's button larva
*Sericostoma personatum*

Trout food. (*Jonathan Newdick*)

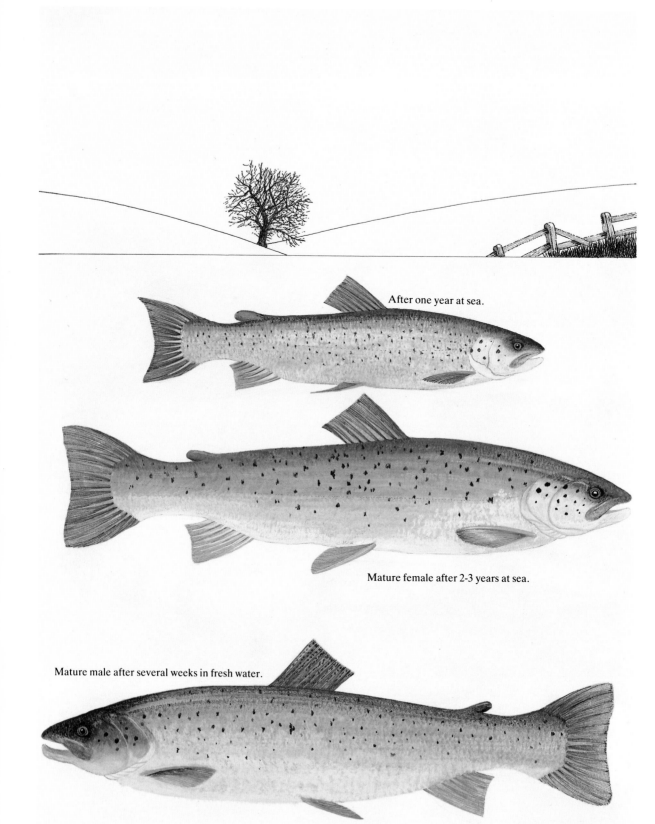

After one year at sea.

Mature female after 2-3 years at sea.

Mature male after several weeks in fresh water.

Sea trout. (*Jonathan Newdick*)

nose them out from among stones, gravel and vegetation and there are a number of imitations designed to deceive a fish feeding intently on shrimps. Crayfish (*Austropotamobius pallipes*) are the largest freshwater crustaceans but can only live in clean, running water where they make a good meal for any trout that encounters them. Being mainly nocturnal, they are actually more common than they seem, but human interference with their habitat and the introduction of crayfish fungus from the USA has seriously reduced their range.

A survey of the trout's food sources is essential to an understanding of its feeding habits. These depend far less on the trout's own inclinations than on the distribution and behaviour of potential prey. From the fisherman's viewpoint, the only legitimate ways to catch trout, other than by stimulating their aggressions or curiosity, are by offering them natural food impaled on a hook, or imitations of particular prey. Therefore ignorance of their diet or at least of their available food supplies, can only impair the chances of catching them.

Trout can only feed on what is available to them. Young fry in saucer-sized territories are restricted in their choice to the organisms brought down by the current. Older fish in running waters forage within their larger domains, and are also more adept at taking food from the surface. Those in still waters cast about much further afield, but nevertheless all trout are unavoidably restricted in their diet to those items that their particular habitat is able to support.

The nature of the substratum is the chief influence on the distribution of water-bred insects. If conditions are unsuitable for nymphs or larvae, they will not survive to maturity. Most stone-fly larvae, which cling to rocks in fast currents, cannot subsist in the sandy river beds so essential for mayfly nymphs; similarly, the distribution of caddis-flies is governed by the availability of the particular building materials that the larvae of each species need to construct their distinctive cases.

Another critical factor in the distribution of aquatic invertebrates is the water's potential for supporting underwater vegetation. Thousands of invertebrate species thrive off the complex community of algae, fungi and other micro-organisms growing round plant matter and without which these invertebrates could not exist. Even the moss of rock-strewn streams may nurture blue-winged olives and black-flies, but more luxuriant underwater plant growth supports a far greater profusion of animal life in terms of both individuals and species.

Most hard alkaline waters are low-lying and their basic topography is conducive to aquatic plant growth. The superior size of their trout once prompted the idea that hard alkaline water itself promoted better fish growth (Chapter Four) but there is no good evidence to support this. There are some distinct differences between the composition of faunal populations of acidic and alkaline waters, especially in terms of the numbers of molluscs and crustaceans which require calcium for their shells. Also, the calcium in nutrient-rich water speeds decomposition, thereby turning plant detritus into food for bottom-dwelling creatures faster than in chemically-impoverished environments. However, the theory that harder water of itself creates a better breeding-ground for aquatic invertebrates and hence has greater potential to promote the growth of the fish feeding on them, has never been proved. Rather, the fact that both invertebrates and fish flourish in hard water is most likely a consequence of a complex mixture of physical factors including higher and more constant temperatures, even substratum and gentle current. Overlaid on this is the crucial component of water, rich in dissolved minerals, promoting luxuriant plant growth.

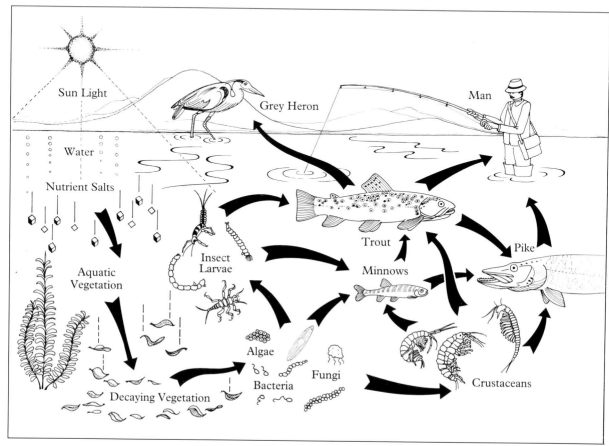

*A food web for a large trout (not ferox).*

There is one very direct consequence of warmer water for the invertebrate population of any aquatic community. Like trout, invertebrates are cold-blooded and less active at lower temperatures: then they mature more slowly and therefore reproduce less often over a given period. So, while the temperatures of northern streams are such that a particular insect may only produce one generation in a year, warmer lowland waters, which are often coincidentally more alkaline, can encourage two generations annually, thereby providing more food for predators.

The trout's feeding habits vary greatly throughout both the year and the day. Much of this variation is associated with annual and diurnal changes in temperature, affecting not only metabolism but also the appearance of prey. As fish are cold-blooded and their metabolic rate is dependent on water temperature, digestion is much slower when this is low. Near the upper limits of their thermal range, trout become sluggish and disinclined to feed. Below about 4°C food takes nearly a week to pass through their alimentary system thus severely restricting consumption, while between 12°C and 15°C digestion may take as little as ten hours. The composition of particular foods also affects digestion rate. Fatty foods, or creatures with hard external skeletons like large snails or crayfish, take longer to digest than protein-rich insects and when protracted, digestion may be much more efficient.

Cold weather inhibits all insect activity which partly explains why it is often associated with poor fishing, although dropping temperatures often trigger the emergence of iron-blue duns and dark olives. Throughout the winter trout feed almost exclusively underwater, only beginning to take food from the surface in the spring when mature insects first appear. Then, during the warmer months when fly life is abundant in all stages of development, trout take advantage of the sudden 'hatches' of a variety of different species.

Many aquatic insects emerge at specific times of the year and often in distinctly localised habitats. Early in the year, march browns and some stone-flies are in evidence in rocky northern streams, and large dark olives on slower, southern rivers. Later, blue-winged olives show themselves over most running waters, often until nearly the end of the summer, and claret duns, (*Leptophlebia vespertina*) with their three tails, appear over English and Irish lakes and reservoirs.. From streams and lakes with soft substrata mayflies emerge in a spectacular, but ephemeral burst of insect life in May and early June, and soon afterwards there are 'hatches' of diminutive small dark olives (or July duns) which sometimes continue through to November. In August, trout often concentrate their attentions on caenis to the exclusion of other seemingly more tempting species and the ensuing frustration of fishermen. Then, towards the end of the season, autumn duns (*Ecdyonurus dispar*) are found round the stony edges of lakes and rivers, closely resembling march browns of which the artificial is a fair imitation.

In early spring, aquatic insects appear in the middle of the day when the water has warmed just enough to stimulate them to emerge and trout to feed. As the afternoon wears on fish decline whatever food is still on offer but when summer approaches, usually feed in early morning and late evening. Later on, during July and August, emerging insects occasionally tempt fish to the surface in the middle of the day. Generally though, feeding is then confined to the cool of the evening when sedges, yellow evening duns and pale evening duns (*Procloeon bifidum*) often emerge in the fading light.

Terrestrial insects are a nutritional bonus for those older trout large enough to catch them. Usually only reaching the surface on a breeze, these are more important to feeding fish than the rather haphazard chances of their falling into the water suggest. Their prominence among the food sources of any particular trout population depends very much on the nature of the riparian vegetation. If there are overhanging branches no more than the simple force of gravity is needed to impel insects into the water, otherwise it takes a strong breeze or heavy rain to blow or wash them off bankside plants.

The seasonal appearances of large numbers of insects of certain species is often spectacular, and the response of the fish equally so. Hatches of mayfly, driving large trout into a frenzy of over-indulgence, are a dramatic sight, but other insect species, less spectacular yet more enduring in their airborne appearances, are ultimately of greater importance to successful trout growth; in particular, Chironomid midges in their larval, pupal and adult stages sustain trout of all ages during almost every month of the year. There are also molluscs and crustaceans, especially Gammarus shrimps, in all but very acidic waters throughout the year and trout feeding on them do so quite unobserved from the bank.

Except in the coldest months, most trout populations are granted the luxury of a choice of food. The reasons why trout discriminate between different prey concern every fisherman and have been the subject of continued speculation through centuries of fishing literature. Initially, trout dart at anything which conforms with their inherited idea of acceptable food but gradually such instinctive behaviour is tempered by experience. Much of this experience is gathered by using their senses of taste and smell which at least partially regulate the exercise of choice between equally available prey. Otherwise, ease of capture, the prey's visual attractions, perhaps enhanced by its flapping wings or struggles on the surface, and the net energy gain from the feeding foray, must all be considerations which trout unconsciously balance before seizing their food.

Young trout in running water are dependent for their food supplies on what is called 'invertebrate drift'. This is the continuous supply of insect larvae and other small animals, swept downstream into a fish's territory and until it begins to forage, is its sole source of food. Older fish continue to make good use of this drift but their increased tendency to forage reduces dependence on current-borne nourishment.

Fish feeding in fast water have less time to evaluate the quality of passing food and their visual abilities are also curtailed. These are distinct disadvantages to trout presented with artificial flies, making them generally easier to catch in fast-flowing rivers or when wind ruffles the surface of a lake. However, even the most cunning trout in still clear water, can occasionally be deceived by insect imitations, only rejecting them if its sense of taste reacts quickly enough to atone for the error of sense of sight.

Whenever trout start feeding, they are at first unlikely to be overly selective; but once they begin to concentrate on a particular type of insect or other prey they become increasingly reluctant to take any other. This is probably because, having evaluated, as well as circumstances allow, the advantages of taking the first insect, trout then continue to take identical ones requiring no further evaluation, so long as these are freely available. Moreover, once established, the feeding movements required to catch one individual of a particular species are easily repeated, making such feeding incomparably economic in terms of energy expenditure.

Emerging or spent insects floating conspicuously on the water can often be identified from the bank. If not, individual insects can be netted off the surface for closer scrutiny or the contents of a fish's stomach analysed. Very often however, the objects of trout's attentions are less easily recognised and the actual movements of feeding fish give key indications of the identity of their prey.

Rises are most simply divided into those which signify the pursuit of prey underwater, and the rest which indicate trout are feeding on the surface. They are all caused by fish displacing water as they feed within it and, except when they are tailing, those feeding underwater hardly ever break the surface.

Trout often betray their presence in clear alkaline waters by rolling over and revealing their paler flanks as they nibble shrimps off the bottom; or they may create the merest hint of a distortion in the regular surface flow by shifting position slightly to catch an ascending nymph. At other times, seizing underwater food such as nymphs, larvae, pupae or shrimps may require more violent feeding movements which make greater disturbances, leaving a wide variety of patterns on the surface. These range from simple concentric rings to what the Lonsdale Library whimsically describes as 'a sort of inflorescence reminiscent of the top view of a cauliflower'. When trout are feeding near the surface, it may be frustratingly difficult to decide whether they are actually rising to insects on, or just underneath the surface, thus immediately provoking the question of whether to fish with a dry fly or nymph. Often the simplest answer is to follow the fortunes of any fully-fledged insects floating near a rising fish; if these escape intact it suggests that trout are feeding on nymphs under the surface.

While bulges, humps and swirls all indicate sub-surface feeding, tailing trout break the surface of the water, sometimes for long periods, as they feed nose down in the weeds on nymphs, shrimps and snails. Gentle movements of their fins and body often keep their tails out of the water quite long enough to give them a misleading resemblance to fronds of protruding vegetation.

Sips, sucks and slashes usually denote surface feeding although the pursuit of insects trapped in the twilight zone of the surface film may still be confusing. The sip is a feeding movement born of confidence that prey is there to be picked off at leisure, and the size of the ring is often no indication of the size of the fish that made it. Sometimes the sip is more of a suck, in that the insect is swallowed without the fish's lips even breaking the surface, as if it could be drawn in from below and ingested without any immediate contact. Often these rises are accompanied by an audible kissing noise created by the intake of air and prey together — an unmistakable sign that it has been taken from the surface. If a fish then retreats to deeper water, it may release tell-tale air bubbles through its gills.

Spectacular slashing rises only repay an energy dividend if the size of the quarry at the very least compensates for the effort of catching it. Prancing mayfly duns, caddis pupae swimming ashore before emerging, or adult sedges laying their eggs in the fading light, may all provoke these apparently desperate lunges.

So it is that life can only continue through the successful capture of food, and the trout's catholic carnivorous tastes and opportunistic feeding behaviour combine to maximise their chances of survival. In impoverished mountain streams and unruffled lowland rivers, in peaty highland lochs or rich man-made reservoirs, there are trout sustaining themselves off the other inhabitants of their underwater communities. Throughout the year trout must feed — indeed for six months they do little else, and it is then that man will fish.

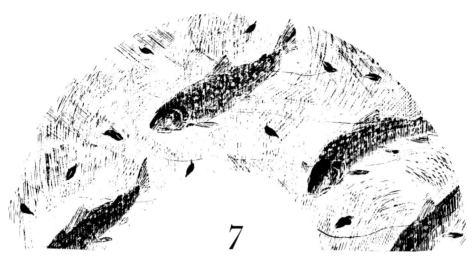

# 7

# *The Freshwater Environment*

'Now for the water, the element that I trade in, the water is the eldest daughter of the creation, the element upon which the spirit of God did first move.' Although inspired more by the influences of Genesis than by any precocious notions of the evolutionary process, Izaak Walton still correctly implied that life on earth first began in the primaeval seas of this planet. From bacterial beginnings over 3,000 million years ago sprang the simple life forms from which all animals are descended. About 2,500 million years later appeared aquatic backboned animals that generally resembled present-day fish — and shortly afterwards some of these clambered onto dry land, the ancestors of modern reptiles, birds and mammals. From those that remained behind in their natural element have evolved the estimated 30,000 species of fish (many of them still unnamed) that now fill almost every aquatic niche. Brown trout are just one of these species and as surely as they are the creation of their element, so water must continue to provide them with food, oxygen, support and shelter.

Compared to many other freshwater fish, trout tolerate a generous range of habitats from cold mountain streams to rich, low-lying still waters. They adapt easily to alien surroundings, and self-sustaining populations have been readily established far beyond their natural range in all continents except Antarctica (Chapter Ten). But despite this apparent tolerance, trout cannot survive unless certain distinct environmental requirements are satisfied; these relate particularly to the temperature, oxygen content and chemical composition of the water and, to a lesser extent, its surrounding geology.

In its purest form, one molecule of colourless, odourless water is made up of one atom of oxygen bound to two of hydrogen. However, in natural circumstances pure water does not exist. One of water's most distinctive characteristics is the ease with which it dissolves other substances which then diffuse evenly throughout its volume.

All water is therefore tainted to a greater or lesser degree by extraneous materials. These include many gases and chemicals which, when dissolved, combine to create such extraordinary variation in the chemical composition of water and in the aquatic communities it sustains.

Water is forever being cleansed and recycled by evaporation into the atmosphere from the sea and large inland lakes, or through the transpiration of green plants. Then, perhaps far from its site of absorption, water falls again to earth as rain, sleet, hail or snow. During this earthward journey or later, on its overland way back to the sea, water dissolves gases and other substances from the atmosphere and also chemicals from the rocks and soil which it touches on its journey. Pure water is sterile, and it is only by accumulating dissolved substances that it becomes sufficiently enriched to support aquatic life.

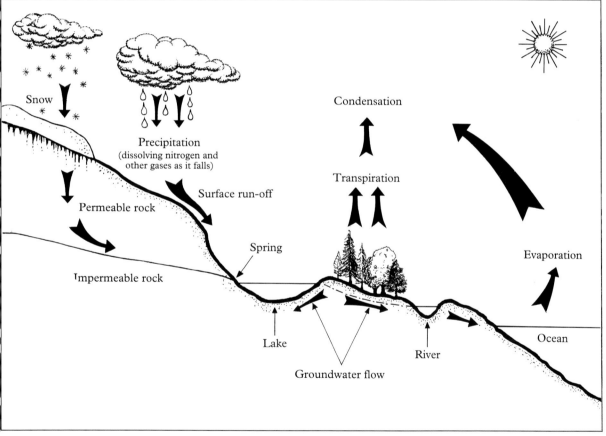

*The water cycle.*

Just above freezing point the density of water is 700 times that of air, allowing organisms that live underwater the ease of existence with a much less rigid structure than they would require for life above it. Water is densest at 4°C. Below this figure density decreases, dropping dramatically at freezing point with the result that ice is much lighter than water and therefore floats. These varying densities cause some still waters to stratify into distinct layers, each with different temperatures.

Water temperature has a critical effect on the incubation of trout ova, 16°C being about the maximum at which they will hatch (Chapter Four). Down at 2°C, incubation is so extended that even if alevins ever emerge it is likely to be too late in the year for them to grow sufficiently to face the rigours of their first winter. Simply to exist, brown trout can tolerate higher temperatures but when these reach 19°C or 20°C they become lethargic and disinclined to feed. Rainbow trout are generally considered to be more tolerant of warmer waters. For this and other reasons, rainbows are more popular stock fish in countries where average daily temperatures are higher than they are throughout the brown trout's native habitat.

This upper survival limit is not absolute in that trout can remain alive in higher temperatures for periods of several days. Under such conditions, perhaps occasioned by midsummer droughts, they become highly stressed, their metabolic rate rises dramatically and death will follow if the water does not eventually cool. At the lower range of the thermometer, neither brown nor rainbow trout will grow much when temperatures drop below 4°C, although their lives are only threatened if the surrounding water actually freezes. When just the surface ices over, trout can easily survive in the water below despite oxygen supplies often becoming seriously depleted, particularly in still waters.

The response of a trout's metabolism to temperature changes also affects its feeding behaviour (Chapter Five), and its bodily systems appear to function at maximum rate between 12°C and 15°C. Respiration, heart beat, feeding, digestion and internal chemical activity are all intrinsically dependant on water temperature. When this is optimum, growth is greatest. Of course more food is required to fuel maximum metabolic activity but the more determined feeding that it stimulates still provides the greatest surplus for growth, after first satisfying the minimum maintenance requirement to sustain a trout in its existing condition.

The temperature of water regulates its capacity to retain dissolved oxygen and this also affects the maximum thermal limit that trout can tolerate. At higher temperatures, the solubility of oxygen in water decreases so that at 18°C fully saturated water contains only two thirds as much oxygen as it does just above freezing point. Because trout metabolise so much more slowly at low temperatures their oxygen requirements are then also lower, even though the supply is more plentiful. As temperatures rise so do their demands for oxygen; and yet there is less available in warmer waters to satisfy these demands. Indeed, if Nature is capable of perversity, then maximising the availability of oxygen when trout least need it and decreasing the supply when their requirements are greatest, would appear to exemplify it.

The geology of the bed of the stream and of the valley it has created can also influence the oxygen content of water. Steep rock-strewn substrata may help to aerate the water so effectively that it becomes super-saturated causing bubbles to well up to the surface. In more sluggish stretches of river the water receives no help in oxygenation from the structure and composition of the bottom. Wind may contribute to the oxygenation of exposed still waters by creating waves from which more protected lakes are less able to benefit.

Normal photosynthesis by aquatic vegetation also boosts oxygen levels as carbon dioxide is exchanged for oxygen through the action of sunlight on the chlorophyll in the tissue of green plants. At night the process is reversed, and oxygen levels in quiet waters, supporting prolific aquatic plant and animal life, drop to their lowest at dawn. Gradually these levels increase again, commensurately with light intensity, until early afternoon when the amount of dissolved oxygen begins a decline which continues right through to the next morning. In natural circumstances there is seldom enough plant nutrition to allow excessive vegetation to threaten trout survival through nocturnal deoxygenation. However, if human influences contribute to unnaturally luxuriant plant growth, the amount of carbon dioxide emitted during the hours of darkness may cause serious oxygen depletion; this can even cause the death of large numbers of fish and invertebrates through what is sometimes called 'summer kill'.

Oxygen shortages can also arise in winter when thick snow covers ice on ponds and lakes in which water flow is minimal. Trout can survive for several days even when oxygen levels are dangerously low, especially if the water is cold and their energy requirements are minimal. But winter days are shorter and if photosynthesis is further restricted by snow preventing light from penetrating below the surface, carbon dioxide builds up and oxygen supply may drop drastically enough to cause 'winter kill'.

Oxygen deficiency in cold or warm weather may also be aggravated by rotting vegetation. As this is broken down by the action of bacteria and fungi, oxygen is used up and carbon dioxide released. Yet while the water's oxygen content may drop, trout also derive benefit from the cycle by the release of nutrients into their food chain during the process of decomposition.

The temperature of water, with which its oxygen content is inseparably connected, is certainly the most important limiting influence on the natural distribution of trout. Their native range is characterised by air temperatures that do not normally exceed 25°C nor fall below –15°C. The climate is generally temperate with plenty of rain and snow in autumn and winter. In natural conditions, the narrower thermal limits required for ova to hatch successfully further restrict the distribution of the species; however, mature fish may move from their nursery areas further downstream, where they are able to live in waters too warm for successful breeding. By continually stocking waters where there are no natural spawning facilities or the temperature is too high for eggs to hatch, man has been able, artificially, to extend the distribution of trout to areas where their inability to breed would naturally have excluded them. Many fishermen are familiar with the large still waters in central and southern England, usually created to satisfy human or industrial thirsts, where repeated stocking is the only way to sustain a trout population.

When superimposed on the topography of the British Isles, the trout's requirements for cool water and a plentiful supply of oxygen still allow for their widespread natural distribution in both still and running waters. Only in flatter parts of England are trout naturally absent and coarse fish, mainly of the carp family, predominate. Even there, trout often thrive in spring-fed streams that well up from far below the surface with constant emergent water temperatures of between 10°C and 12°C throughout the year. In Scandinavia where waters are cooler, brown trout may easily live in the type of lowland habitat that would not support them in Britain, provided there are adequate breeding grounds. Further south, in Mediterranean Europe and north Africa, the appropriate thermal requirements only exist high up mountain ranges and in East Africa where trout were successfully introduced eighty years ago, they are unable to breed below about 2,600 meters.

Rivers, especially in continental Europe, are sometimes divided into four specific regions, each named after one of the species of fish that predominate in them. This division is necessarily based on the concept of the average river which starts in distant highlands where its gradient is steepest and current strongest. Slowly the gradient eases and so does the current, as the river flattens out among rolling lowland hills, becomming sluggish and almost canal-like on its approach to the sea. There are innumerable exceptions to this average river and it is a mistake to be too rigid in the categorization of these different regions, for each river system is a continuum of changing habitats with no precise dividing lines between them. Indeed, Nature abhors rigid demarcations. Nonetheless, despite the indiscriminate translocation of so many species of fish throughout Britain, some form of classification helps to identify potential trout areas and the likely piscine occupants of any particular stretch of running water.

At the head of the river is the trout region (Chapter Five), characterised by swift currents and a stony substratum. Water temperatures seldom rise above 15°C, gradient is often ten per cent or more and the turbulent flow ensures maximum oxygen saturation. Invertebrate animals in this region are specifically adapted to counter the difficulties of life in fast currents and do not generally depend upon rooted plants for food or shelter.

In the rough waters of the trout region, despite the strength of the current, mosses and liverworts can still secure themselves to rocks and stones on the edges of the stream. These tenacious plants provide shelter for blue-winged olive and other Ephemeropteran nymphs as well as for blackfly and midge larvae. Borne down on the current, these latter feature prominently in the diets of young trout until they are old enough to forage for caddis larvae and stone-fly nymphs on the bottom. The vegetation is insufficient to provide actual cover for trout which must seek shelter among the rocks and stones that offer such a wide variety of different lies for them. There they may meet bullheads and loaches which live on the bed of the stream and minnows that congregate round its edges.

The substrata of running waters can be neatly divided into those that are eroding and the rest that are depositing. In the fast upland currents of the trout region, nearly all the stream bed is eroding and there are very few areas where any deposited material can resist the pressures of the current. Perhaps at the bottom of some of the deepest pools large particles of coarse sand may be deposited, but anything smaller would only be swept downstream by the next flood. Trout require an eroding bed in which to breed successfully otherwise their eggs become clogged with sand and silt. The bed of such a stream does not allow underwater plants to take root and the large numbers of young trout that hatch there cannot depend upon rich supplies of food nurtured by thick aquatic vegetation. This eventually encourages many of them to move further down, perhaps into a lake if they were born in a feeder stream, where there may be less competition for more sustenance.

Such rough upland streams are also liable to severe flooding which further discourages aquatic vegetation from taking root. Rainfall is usually greater over high ground increasing the possibility of heavy spates, as does the present tendency to drain upland areas for agriculture or forestry. This results in sudden floods as water is channelled downstream in a massive rush instead of being absorbed, sponge-like, by upland catchment areas, and slowly squeezed out into natural drainage streams throughout the drier months of summer.

At the end of the trout region the gradient levels out to around four per cent and by this time several streams may have been gathered up into a narrow river. Here the bed is still eroding although the less powerful current allows smaller stones to settle on the bottom without risk of being propelled downstream, even in a spate. Areas of sediment in slack backwaters and at the tails of long pools may be sufficient to promote both the growth of some rooted vegetation and also the presence of burrowing nymphs such as those of true mayflies. Faster waters, with their origins in high country, take a more direct course down from the hills than do those that well up from underground; with less haste and a more even flow, these latter meander through broader valleys, still eroding on the outside of bends but depositing more silt and sand in the slack areas opposite.

This is the start of the grayling or minnow region where conditions are still perfectly suitable for trout both to live and breed, but the water is warmer. As well as grayling and various species of smaller fish it may also support chub, dace and roach which all sometimes compete with trout for available food supplies. The more luxuriant growths of water plants nourish large numbers of invertebrates, especially in gravelly spring-fed streams; these are less susceptible to flooding and plants can more easily root here than among the larger stones in the similar reaches of rain-fed rivers. A wider range of Ephemeropteran nymphs, caddis larvae and other insects live in the grayling zone where trout are much better fed than they are higher up the stream.

Further down is the barbel region where the current is lazier, water perhaps travelling at around fifteen meters per minute as it deposits sand and silt on the river bed; there may be shallow gravelly runs between long stretches of smooth deep water. If the water is clear, aquatic vegetation will proliferate and as well as barbel, there may be perch, pike and perhaps rudd, but very few trout. Summer temperatures often reach 20°C for long periods, oxygen levels are low and spawning facilities for trout are usually non-existent. The only trout in the barbel region are likely to be those that have slowly worked their way down from more suitable reaches higher up the river where they were bred. Any that do live in this region are usually larger than those upstream in the trout or grayling regions; there food supplies are less, more energy is expended in countering stronger currents and the detrimental consequences of direct competition from members of the same species are more pronounced.

No trout survive in the sluggish, inhospitable stretches of the bream region where the gradient is minimal, effectively creating a barrier that, except in winter, prevents migratory sea trout either passing down to the sea or if they ever happen to do so, back through to the cooler reaches above. The substratum is muddy and entirely depositing; tench *(Tinca tinca)* and eels also live there as well as sometimes flounders, mullet and other species having edged up from the brackish estuarine waters which are their true home. Along with flat, slow-flowing rivers that have almost reached the sea, many inland waterways of northern Europe are also typical of this region.

Bream can only swim very slowly — less than one meter per second — and therefore cannot counter the effects of any more than a negligible current. Further upstream barbel can reach speeds of up to four meters per second and trout much more than that, depending on their size (Chapter Two). So, along with their specific requirements as to oxygen and temperature, these abilities also effectively confine different fish to waters whose average current is slower than their respective swimming speeds.

Many river systems miss out one or more of these regions, depending on the geology of their surrounding valleys. Sometimes there may be very little of the river which deposits silt, and where its gradient from source to sea is uniformly steep, the whole length of the river may comprise nothing but eroding rocks and stones. On the west coast of Scotland there are rushing rivers whose whole lengths are typical of the trout region. Nearly all depositing material reaches the estuaries, and trout may even live there too (Chapter Eight). More often though, as rivers emerge from hidden valleys or subterranean springs into the broader reaches that prepare them for their final discharge into the sea, so their currents gradually slow to almost minimal speeds. As they do so, the size of the components of the substrata gradually decreases. In the uplands, streams tumble between large boulders; lower down, the river bed is composed of more stones of less disparate size; gradually these eroding stones give way to gravel and sand, then eventually to thick deposits of silt and mud.

All the water that fuels these rivers has fallen from the sky as some form of precipitation. Water dissolves gases on its way through the atmosphere, nearly eighty per cent of which is nitrogen. This is not easily soluble unlike oxygen which, with a small amount of carbon dioxide, makes up the rest of the air in a natural uncontaminated environment. Polluted air contains quantities of other gases, particularly sulphur dioxide and nitrogen oxide which water dissolves into sulphuric and nitric acid. These acidic droplets are often blown many hundreds of miles before eventually falling to earth; for this reason the fact of rain falling on remote areas of northern Europe, far from any source of industrial contamination, is no guarantee of its purity. However, in this chapter the environment is described as if untouched by the lethal hand of mankind and rain must therefore be taken to have dissolved such substances as it naturally encounters on its way down to earth. As well as nitrogen, oxygen and carbon dioxide which are the principal components of the atmosphere, calcium, potassium, nitrates and phosphates are blown naturally around as dust particles by the wind. The sea also contributes to the chemical make-up of still waters even quite far inland; salty wind-blown spray containing sodium chloride, sulphates and potassium greatly enriches coastal lakes which often support more plant life and larger trout than more acidic ones far from the sea.

Water's ability to dissolve other substances also means that immediately on reaching the earth's surface, it begins to absorb, either in suspension or solution, the chemical contents of the surrounding countryside. Freshly fallen rain filters first through the soil, becoming naturally tainted by its chemical make-up. Then, after draining into burns, becks or streams the water passes over the rocks of their higher reaches, slowly accumulating minerals through the actions of erosion and absorption and gradually becoming further enriched on its downstream journey.

Water falling on soft, peaty highlands through which it filters into a network of upland streams, dissolves little in the way of calcium and magnesium carbonates and other salts. Below the peat there may be a layer of hard impermeable granite of which the stream bed is also composed, eroding so slowly that the water is only marginally affected by the rock's chemical composition. These impoverished, surface-fed waters are usually acidic, often because of the organic matter in the peat which, as humic acid, dissolves in water giving it the familiar brown colour. Soap lathers easily in such waters which are described as 'soft'; but their dearth of dissolved salts means that, apart from some mosses, they can support very little aquatic vegetation which is so dependent on water-borne nutrition for its growth.

In obvious contrast to these types of river, are the spring-fed streams of southern and eastern England, fuelled mainly by water which has first seeped through the permeable surface of the catchment area, before reaching a layer of impermeable rock below. These soft upper layers of rock are the aquifers which trap underground water, eventually forcing it out, where the land is lowest, through springs. At least three quarters of the water flow of these spring-fed streams derives from the aquifer, making them far less susceptible to sudden spates than rivers which depend mainly on surface run-off to fill them.

Most of the permeable rock creating these aquifers is chalk. This is soft white limestone made up of the calcareous, fossilised fragments of millions of marine organisms. Chalk is soft in that it is easily eroded and quickly infuses water seeping through it with a distinctive 'hard' alkaline character. Water often filters through aquifers for long distances, dissolving calcium carbonate and sulphate, nitrates and phosphates and other substances on its journey. These dissolved minerals are the basic building blocks in the production of underwater plant life, supporting the diversity of invertebrates which in turn helps trout grow faster and larger.

There is an accurate measure of the relative acidity or alkalinity of water which is known as its 'pH' (potential or *potenz* of hydrogen). Unfortunately this measure is now in far too frequent use as the acidity of so many river systems is raised to dangerously high levels through industrial or agricultural interference. It is now so important as one of the indicators of the water's health that an understanding of its calibration system as well as of the damaging effects of acidity increases is essential.

The scale of pH runs from 1 to 14. At 7.0 water is neutral; as pH drops below that figure water becomes increasingly acidic and a higher pH indicates higher alkalinity. The scale is logarithmic to the base of ten which means that a change of one on either side of 7.0 indicates a tenfold increase in acidity or alkalinity. For example, water with pH 9.0 is 100 times more alkaline than neutral water of 7.0.

There is a slight tendency for the atoms of hydrogen and oxygen which make up molecules of water($H_2O$), to dissociate from one another. When this occurs, one atom of hydrogen splits away from the remaining atom of hydrogen which then combines with the single oxygen atom; the lone hydrogen atoms lose their negative charge of electrons to the other hydrogen atoms, resulting in a number of positively charged hydrogen ions or cations (H+) in any volume of water. The dissociation also produces equal numbers of negatively charged hydroxide ions or anions (OH-). In pure water hydrogen and hydroxide ions exactly balance each other. Acids also dissociate in water; so for example a molecule of hydrochloric acid ($H_2SO_4$) splits into two hydrogen ions and one sulphate ion. All acid molecules contain varying numbers of hydrogen atoms and therefore a measure of these excess hydrogen ions in water is also a measure of its acidity.

This is a great over-simplification of a very technical measuring system. Nonetheless it is such that reasonably accurate pH measurements can be simply obtained by the use of litmus-type paper; when dipped in water its colour changes according to acidity or alkalinity and can then be compared to a colour chart that indicates the appropriate pH. The papers are often sold by gardening shops as part of soil testing apparatus.

The advantages to trout of luxuriant plant growth nourished by richer, more alkaline waters, either as cover or support for their food sources, are abundantly clear. Additionally, trout may benefit directly from calcium intake in the formation of bones and scales, although this remains a point of contention. Pure rain water, fully saturated with a natural supply of carbon dioxide has pH of only 5.6 and trout can live and breed in acidic waters where the pH is down as low as 5.0. Between 6.0 and 9.0 is the optimum range and levels below 5.0, which are increasingly common in areas where the figure was formerly much higher, may prove fatal to fish.

When water becomes too acidic it upsets the processes by which trout maintain their fluid balance and when pH drops below 5.0 trout start to lose sodium and other body salts faster than they can absorb them from their surroundings. Further, the solubility of aluminium is greatest when pH is around 5.0 and an excess of this metallic element also causes sodium loss as well as promoting a build up of mucus on fish's gills which may affect their respiration. If pH drops below 4.5, both breeding and hatching are also adversely affected, although brown trout are much more tolerant of acidic conditions than many coarse fish, and roach eggs, for example, will not hatch if pH is less than 5.5. Rainbow trout are not as tolerant as brown trout but brook charr and eels more so, enduring levels even below 4.0. Young salmon seem less able than brown trout to survive in highly acidic conditions and become stressed at pH levels around 5.5.

The death of trout as a result of pH falling to these lethal levels is usually a consequence of pollution, for if waters are naturally too acidic, as they often are in boggy moorlands, they would never support trout in the first place. Even so, there are sometimes natural surges in acidity which, although they seldom push pH levels above the limits for trout survival, can release lethally toxic quantities of aluminium from the surrounding rocks and soil. In the same way, there is nothing inherently unnatural about acid rain since pure rainwater combines with small quantities of carbon dioxide in the atmosphere to produce a weak solution of carbonic acid — just like soda water. It is only when abnormal quantities of acid, emitted during industrial or agricultural activity, become dissolved in rain or stream water that catastrophe can threaten the trout's element.

Apart from regulating the distribution of insect-sustaining plant growth, water chemistry appears to have little direct effect on the composition of invertebrate populations, unless pH falls to dangerously low levels. If it does, aquatic insects may eventually die from physiological disturbances similar to those affecting trout. The amount of calcium in the water, which acts as a buffer against excess acidity, definitely regulates the distribution of freshwater shrimps (not usually found where pH is less than 6) and also of the larger crustaceans and molluscs that are even more dependent on calcium for their shells. Conversely, water boatmen and some species of pond skaters are particularly tolerant of highly acidic conditions and live happily in small moorland tarns.

The effect of differing quantities of dissolved nutrients on aquatic life has been well illustrated by controlled experiments with the artificial fertilisation of lakes and ponds. By adding lime to the water, either in feeder streams or directly into a lake, pH can be significantly raised, but this on its own is of little direct benefit to fish unless it raises pH above otherwise critical levels. More beneficial is the addition of phosphate or nitrate fertilisers which quickly encourage plant growth and thus the presence of invertebrates. Ideally, fertilisation should be accompanied by the introduction of other aquatic invertebrates such as shrimps and water slaters which are better able to take advantage of the improved conditions and provide more nourishing food for trout than the existing species. How quickly the beneficial effects of such enrichment wear off depends on the speed at which the lake replaces its water content. This may vary from six months to a year. Therefore, unless the fertilisation programme is sustained its advantages are likely to be short-lived and any improvement in trout fishing does not usually justify the expense.

Electrical conductivity is a simple measure of the quantity of dissolved substances in any particular sample of water. In theory, distilled water simply cannot conduct an electric current although completely pure water is almost impossible to obtain, even artificially. Accordingly, water with lower conductivity contains less dissolved substances and is therefore less conducive to sustained plant growth. It is not surprising that the conductivity of chalk streams is perhaps four times as great as that of small highland lochs and that while a river is still eroding, conductivity invariably increases the further downstream it is tested.

Dissolved nutrients, particularly phosphates and nitrates, are the final link in all underwater food chains. Above them are aquatic plants, life-giving oxygenators of many freshwater environments, particularly still waters. Indeed, green plants, through their ability to harness energy from sunlight and to utilise water-borne nutrition, are the primary source of all energy below the water's surface. Planktonic algae and the many more complex underwater plants all act to make energy available, directly or indirectly, to the whole of the aquatic animal kingdom.

The simplest of all water plants are blue-green algae which may be familiar to most fishermen only in the context of their 'bloom'. These algae are actually more closely related to bacteria than to other species of algae and are among the earliest known life forms on earth. They provide both a taxonomic and evolutionary link between bacteria and plants and occur in almost all aquatic habitats. Along with other algae, all deriving their nutrition from sunlight and dissolved minerals, they make up much of the free-floating plankton community of still waters.

Blooms of blue-green algae usually occur from mid-summer onwards. Natural circumstances may combine to promote these unwelcome population explosions but they more often result from the water's enrichment by accidental seepage of nitrogen-based fertilisers. These filamentous algae float on the surface or create a slimy blue or brown blanket over rocks and stones as well as over other vegetation, and at night can cause oxygen depletion which may have dangerous consequences for the whole underwater community. Some blue-green algae, like certain leguminous plants such as beans or clover, also act as fixers of nitrogen. This they extract from the atmosphere and release into the water, often in the form of highly toxic nitrogenous compounds.

True algae range from tiny single-celled diatoms to fairly complex plants such as stoneworts, most of which are particular to alkaline still waters and grow as long as sixty centimeters. Seaweeds are also algae, right through to the giant kelp whose fronds are often over fifty meters in length. The most familiar varieties are those which form slimy, green filaments and sometimes pass under the colloquial name of blanket-weed or flannel-weed *(Cladophora* spp.*)*. In summer these take immediate advantage of low water, when flow is gentle and light can easily penetrate into the river, to cover the bed with waving tentacles of vegetation. Low summer levels are seldom conducive to good fly fishing in any event and blankets of algae which continuously foul up wet flies or nymphs only add to fishermen's frustrations.

Like all other green plants, algae photosynthesize, absorbing carbon dioxide and then emitting waste oxygen into the water. In running waters, natural excesses of algae may be an inconvenience and can even choke young trout, but on balance the oxygen they add to the water and the food and shelter they furnish for insect larvae and crustaceans benefit the whole aquatic community — trout included. Only in quieter flowing rivers and still waters, usually aided by the unnatural process of over-enrichment (eutrophication), do algal populations sometimes reach danger levels. When this happens, they begin to compete with other plant life for available nutrients and algal blooms threaten to starve rooted underwater plants of crucial sunlight either by carpeting the water's surface or by actually colonising their leaves.

More complex plants are less ephemeral and their dependability makes them more fundamental to the ecology of their environment. In rocky upland streams nymphs and larvae rely entirely on the presence of mosses and liverworts which are able to cling to the stones in all but the fiercest currents. Without the algae and detritus which depend on or derive from these resilient plants, the tiny insects, particularly midge larvae, that provide crucial food supplies for young trout, would themselves starve.

Larger plants require a more stable substratum in order to root effectively and therefore usually spread their considerable benefits around stiller stretches of rivers and the edges of ponds and lakes. There they act as life-sustaining oxygenators as well as both refuges and generators of food supplies for much of the invertebrate population. They also serve to level out the flow of the current and to filter out impurities from the water, as well as helping to bind together the bed and banks of the river. The fronds of large water plants also provide trout with a place to hide from the potentially fatal attentions of pike and other predators.

The distribution of plant life in still waters is largely regulated by the depth to which light is able to penetrate. Clean water therefore encourages growth at greater depths than is possible in more turbid conditions. Spring-fed chalk-stream water is nearly always clearer than that from peaty highland catchment areas. This contributes significantly to the former's more luxuriant plant life although less so than the amount of dissolved nutrients in the water and the suitability of the substratum for rooting plants. In the sluggish bream zones of lowland rivers the penetration of light below the surface is also a critical factor in the growth of aquatic plants. Here the water is often dirty and vegetation much sparser than further upstream where the river is both shallower and cleaner.

Water absorbs light, much of which is also reflected back into the atmosphere, with the result that even in the clearest lakes little plant life can flourish below ten meters. At this depth some species of water starworts *(Callitriche* spp.*)* and also algal stoneworts may grow, but taller plants cannot establish themselves. These small plants contribute very little to the oxygen supply but in running waters they may help to consolidate the river bed with the webs of their root systems.

As oxygenators, the most efficient plants are those that grow tall but remain totally submerged. Water buttercups (or crowfoots — *Ranunculus* spp.) with only their distinctive white flowers protruding above the surface, are a common feature of nearly all clean streams and root easily even in stony river beds. Real watercress *(Nasturtium officinale)*, like water buttercups, remains green throughout the year growing half-submerged in shallow water; fools watercress (or water celery — *Apium nodiflorum*) is also a very effective oxygenator in similar conditions. All three species of water milfoils *(Myriophyllum* spp.*)* grow up to four meters long showing only red or yellow flowers above the surface while their long green stems are gently waved from side to side by the current; they also stay green in winter although photosynthesis is then inevitably curtailed by the shorter days.

Round the edges of lakes and ponds more than in running waters, grow species of protruding vegetation which root underwater but grow stiffly up above its surface. Such plants effectively link the elements of water and air and are able to absorb water-borne nutrients, as well as carbon dioxide from the atmosphere. Under the water, like truly aquatic plants, they may support numbers of invertebrates and make their contribution to its oxygen content. For many insects these plants are of special importance in providing a suitable stem for adult females to clamber down before laying their eggs. They also allow emerging nymphs or pupae to crawl out of their aquatic nursery into the open air that is their element during the final stages of their lives. Most Ephemeropteran olives (although not blue-winged olives), as well as brown sedges, crawl down emergent stems to lay their eggs while late march brown nymphs and pupae of other sedge species rest up on protruding vegetation before they fly away.

Because of the relative densities of water and air as well as to counter the effects of wind and waves, emergent plants need much stiffer stems to support them than do those that are totally aquatic. Marestail *(Huppuris vulgaris)* grows either completely submerged or partly protruding above the surface. It can tolerate darker conditions than many other plants but requires slightly alkaline conditions. Bulrushes *(Typha latifolia)*, yellow irises *(Iris pseudacorus)* and various species of sedges, grasses, water plantains and reeds are all to be found emerging from the edges of still and running waters; there they may be invaluable in holding the banks together as well as providing aquatic insects with paths into or out of the water. Arrowhead *(Sagittaria sagittifolia)* is very distinctive and like many emergent plants, dies down in the winter. Its protruding leaves are shaped as its name suggests;

however, to adapt to the different densities of air and water, its leaves are oval where the plant emerges into the air allowing them to float easily on the surface, while underwater near the roots they are thin and linear, presenting minimal resistence to the water. Common water crowfoot *(R. aquatilis)* is not an emergent plant but also has diversely shaped leaves — broad and floating to support its flower above the surface and delicately divided, underwater ones which act to prevent the current from pushing the rest of the plant upwards. Many species of pondweed *(Potamogeton* and *Elodea* spp.) are similarly adapted.

Still other plants float on the surface, sometimes forming rafts of matted vegetation, their thin spindly roots extracting food direct from the water. These are of course more common in still waters than in streams, because it is only in sluggish canal-type environments that they are not susceptible to being swept downstream. Some species, like hornworts *(Ceratophyllum* spp.) are subaqueous but most float on the surface. Duckweeds *(Lemna* spp.) are the smallest flowering plants in Europe and may form thick carpets over parts of ponds and lakes. Frogbit *(Hydrocharis morsus-ranae)* is also free-floating but the water soldier *(Stratiotes aloides)* of the same family remains on the bottom of its pond, only rising up to flower on the surface in late spring. Bladderworts *(Utricularia* spp.) are rootless, floating plants that survive on a diet of insects and water fleas; it is intriguingly tempting to regard them as competitors of trout for available insects but their respective distributions are only likely to coincide in lowland still waters where the continued presence of trout usually depends on regular stockings.

While some plants are carefully adapted to life in still or running waters or to growth in particular substrata or depths, others can only tolerate water of a specific chemical make-up. The quantity of phosphates, nitrates and other nutrients in the water obviously has a direct affect on the proliferation of aquatic plants. However, different species of the same genus, perhaps having evolved from a common ancestor that flourished in all types of water, often now occupy different ecological niches created by variations in the water's chemical composition. The river water crowfoot *(R. fluitans)* grows best in slightly acidic water while stream water crowfoot *(R. penicillatus)* thrives in an alkaline environment. Spiked water milfoil *(M. spicatum)* is also at home in hard water but its counterpart, alternate flowered water milfoil *(M. alternifolium)*, is only found in soft water. Quillwort *(Isoetes lacustris)* is strictly confined to acidic tarns and lochs in highland areas. It is a flowerless plant whose underwater presence is often revealed by piles of dead leaves, detatched and tossed up along the high water mark by waves. Stoneworts on the other hand can only survive in highly calcareous water, to such an extent that these complex algae often become so coated in lime deposits as to merit their alternative name of 'brittleworts'.

All these plants, from minute algae through to protruding bulrushes, from carpets of moss clinging to rocks beside waterfalls to the feathery fronds of water crowfoot or floating rafts of duckweed, play their part in the creation of a highly complex, interwoven aquatic community. In upland streams where there are often very few species of vegetation, the disappearance of one of these might have a devastating effect on the insects relying upon it, and in turn on the trout that eat them. In the more hospitable surrounds of rich spring-fed rivers there is a whole mosaic of less specialised plant life. Here the environment is less fragile and perhaps more forgiving of ill-treatment and abuse; but indeed it must be, for here far more than in highland country, are man's influences more directly felt.

Vital though water plants are to the health of all underwater life, as any fisherman who has been privileged to fish chalk streams knows, excess growth not only hinders fishing but can also affect the well-being of the river itself. Left unchecked, weed (as it is suddenly referred to when damned for causing a problem rather than valued for conferring a benefit) can grow so thick by the end of June that fishing becomes quite impossible. Furthermore, the weed's bulk may be such as to accelerate the current and raise the water level, with the ensuing possibilities of flooding and bank erosion. Then some form of control becomes essential, usually taking the form of selective cutting along the length of the river to ease the flow and open up spaces between rafts of weed.

Like most interference with nature's patterns, weed cutting is not without its dangers and difficulties. Many insects may be killed in the process although it is conveniently argued that weed drifting downstream may repopulate more barren areas with invertebrates. Weed that is not taken out, being allowed to rot in the water, uses up precious oxygen from more sluggish parts of the river as it does so; and if too much is cut it can no longer act to filter out silt and organic debris from the current. Cutting also denies trout of all ages feeding territories in open spaces between areas of weed and refuges from danger amongst its growth.

At the end of the season cutting is usually less discriminate, allowing winter floods to scour accumulated mud and silt from the river bed. It is then also easier to net out or electrocute unwanted species of fish. Nonetheless, if the river bed is cleaned too thoroughly, the next summer's plant growth may be poor: it is far easier to get rid of water plants than to establish them from nothing.

Where the river's state encourages the growth of aquatic plants, the effect of excluding light from the water is often apparent in the shadow of large overhanging trees. There the bed is usually bare, providing little shelter for trout or their food (although it may as a result be suitable for spawning). These shading trees may compensate for checking underwater plant growth by delivering a supply of accident-prone terrestial insects from overhanging branches; and on hot sunny days their shadows look as if they would be refreshingly beneficial to any trout lurking among the roots below. Riparian vegetation is essential to many Ephemeropterans in the course of their final metamorphosis from dun to spinner; and beside the banks of fast-flowing hill streams that support little in the way of plant life anyway, overhanging trees may be of real benefit. There, alder *(Alnus glutinosa)* or mountain ash *(Sorbus aucuparia)* can provide shady refuges as well as a supply of terrestial insects, helped onto the water by the stronger breezes that usually blow at higher altitudes. Lower down, occasional large, deciduous trees promote welcome variety in the riverine landscape. However, in general, underwater plant life confers greater benefit to fish than do rows of closely planted trees which from the fisherman's point of view hinder casting anyway. Aquatic vegetation also provides a more consistent supply of plant detritus, so crucial to the production of the bacteria and algae which support the river's invertebrate population. Only if plants cannot root in the substratum may the river benefit more from overhanging deciduous trees which shed their leaves into the water in the autumn.

Much of this chapter has concerned the characteristics of running waters as a habitat for trout, but they are equally at home in many still waters. Natural still waters are simply depressions in the earth's surface where quantities of fresh water are restrained by geological accident, on their way to the sea. This delay in the water's journey immediately highlights the fundamental distinction between still and running waters and between the habits of the trout that live in them. This is their comparative rate of flow and the different feeding behaviour necessarily adopted by trout in each of these environments.

Water in highland streams at the head of the trout region may flow at around one meter per second and much faster through stretches of rapids. Trout expend considerable energy countering the effect of this flow and may have to shelter behind stones or in slack backwaters on the edge of the current. However, fast flow serves up food as if on a rapid conveyor belt and acts to compress what may actually be a fairly impoverished food supply into one of apparent plenty. Trout in fast water are given little time to size up their prey and may use more energy in its capture, but the current at least ensures a regular supply. In lakes and ponds water may have a turn-over time of six months or a year and is for all practical purposes static. This simply means that trout must go and forage for their food, rather than remaining stationary in the expectation that it will be brought to them by the current; and the energy which river-dwelling fish use up in countering the effects of the current, stillwater trout expend in searching for prey.

Windlanes along the surface of a lake occasionally channel huge numbers of insects into a small area of water but trout usually find the richest hunting grounds round lake edges. Here light penetrates easily and aquatic vegetation may range from emergent plants right beside the bank, out through a band of those with floating leaves to others growing totally submerged in deeper water. The abundance and diversity of plant life depends on the formation of the lake bed and the supply of phosphates, nitrates and other plant food in the water.

Lakes with little in the way of dissolved food substances and which therefore sustain only poor plant growth are said to be 'oligotrophic' (*oligoi* is Greek for 'few' and *trophia* means 'nourishment'). Often such waters are newly created in the measure of the vast geological clock, being strewn with boulders which have yet to erode. Because of their immaturity, these lakes are often short of both underwater sediment to support rooted vegetation as well as dissolved nutrients to encourage its growth. They may also have steep sides and a very narrow littoral zone which gives opportunities for none but the narrowest fringes of aquatic plants to grow round the edges. Such waters are usually cold and well oxygenated and often support prolific numbers of small trout and also perhaps relict populations of Arctic charr. Only if there are no good breeding facilities in feeder streams, and fish must rely on haphazard and often unsuccessful efforts to lay their eggs in the lake shallows are there likely to be trout of any reasonable size, although in such circumstances obviously far fewer of them.

Eutrophic (well fed) still waters are usually older in geological terms — often evident from their gentler, more rounded contours. The erosions of age have also endowed them with more silt and therefore less depth, both of which combine with the wealth of dissolved minerals to encourage plant growth and a rich stock of invertebrate trout food. Charr cannot live in such conditions but trout may, although if feeder streams are also silted or temperatures too high they will not be able to breed. Generally, eutrophication tends to encourage the emergence of a different fish fauna, more vegetarian in diet and better suited by warmer, less oxygenated water which may result from the decomposition of much rotting vegetation. Because eutrophic lakes are normally low lying the streams that fill them have often travelled further and in the process have become greatly enriched during their journey, so passing on such benefit to their stillwater destinations.

Unnatural over-enrichment can literally feed a lake to death (Chapter Eleven) but eutrophication is also a natural process that follows from erosion; and the process does not end there. It is the inevitable destiny of natural depositing lakes, supporting prolific vegetation, to fill up, first becoming boggy wetlands and eventually flat dry areas, split by what were originally their feeder streams. But as some lakes die, so others are born by the eroding activities of glaciers and rivers, and occasionally by more dramatic upheavals in the earth's crust. Thus new aquatic habitats are gradually created in which underwater communities will slowly evolve and flourish.

One important feature of still waters — usually more apparent in deep oligotrophic lakes than in warmer, shallow ones where wind action keeps the water well mixed — is their thermal stratification at varying depths. With the onset of summer the lake surface is heated up by the sun. Cold water is denser than warm, down to its maximum density at 4°C, and therefore tends to remain at deeper levels. The whole process is accentuated during the summer as the surface warms further and the difference in temperature between the upper and lower layers widens.

This upper layer of water (epilimnion) may extend for ten meters or more before merging with the middle layer (thermocline) that separates it from the cold depths of the hypolimnion. The depth of the epilimnion increases through the summer and may also be affected by the clarity of the water in that, under turbid conditions, radiated heat is quickly absorbed near the surface. The difference in temperature between the upper and lower edges of the central thermocline may be considerable, dropping by more than one degree per meter through a distance of anything between two and ten meters. During summer, water in the epilimnion can be thoroughly and frequently mixed by wind and waves but still remain distinctly separated from the thermocline.

Even though it is warmer than the water below, the epilimnion is better oxygenated. To some extent the hypolimnion at the bottom of the lake circulates within itself, but it is too far down to support plant life and is effectively insulated from the surface. Any oxygen used up in the process of decomposition is not replaced and the water becomes very stale. Neither trout nor their prey are usually found in such conditions although they may live in the middle reaches of deeper oligotrophic lakes where the oxygen is never fully exhausted. Normally however, they seek out the better supplies of oxygen and food in the epilimnion, only retreating down to the cooler but less oxygenated waters of the thermocline if conditions near the surface begin to stress them.

At the end of the summer, air temperatures drop and still waters start to cool. Slowly the temperature of the three layers equalises and a gradual mixing begins. As the surface cools further it becomes colder and therefore denser than the water at the bottom, causing a complete turnover of the lake's contents. The same process may occur in spring when ice melts; then the resulting cold water, which is just above freezing and heavier than the warmer water below, sinks to the bottom forcing the stale deoxygenated water slowly up to the surface.

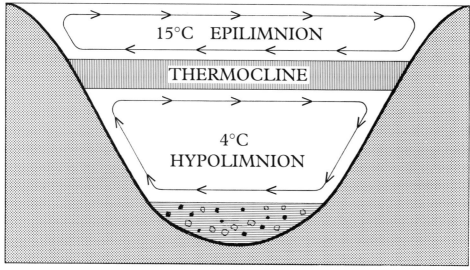

*The summer stratification of water in a lake.*

Lakes and ponds are the creations of their surrounding geology. Absorbing nutrients from their substrata and nourished by inflowing streams, the chemical composition of the water and topography of their basin's shape the aquatic communities that flourish in them. If particular environmental conditions are satisfied, into the intricate web of plant and animal life that go to make up an individual aquatic community may fit a population of trout.

Rivers and streams form the gorges and valleys through which they flow and which surrender life-giving nutrition to the water, by the gradual processes of absorbtion and erosion. At the same time, the actions of this interchange may also create the environmental conditions for trout to flourish. As surely as trout are the product of their food supply, so the underwater communities of still and running waters are the product of the land that cradles these waters or through which they flow. And in this way, with the help of the sun, water eventually conducts the goodness of the surrounding land and of the air above, through plants and smaller animals, up to the fish that live in it.

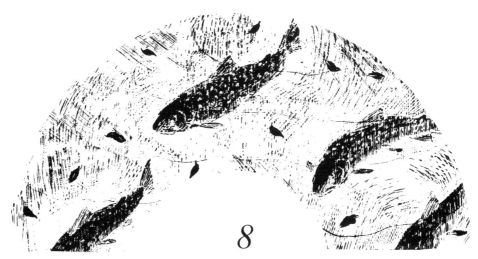

# 8
# The Urge to Migrate

Tiny red-spotted brown trout that will never weigh more than 200 grams and salmon-like sea trout of over five kilograms both belong to the same species, *Salmo trutta*; they could have been born on the same redds and may even be siblings. Given the vastly different behaviour and physiology of the adult fish it would have been strange, at least when the science of taxonomy was in its infancy, if sea trout had not been classified as a species quite separate from brown trout. And so they were. Carl Linnaeus named sea trout '*Salmo eriox*' differentiating them from two species of non-migratory brown trout, *Salmo trutta* and *Salmo fario*, and 100 years later Dr. Albert Gunther of the British Museum christened brown trout '*Salmo fario*' and sea trout '*Salmo trutta*'; he also recognised four other distinct species of migratory trout. Francis Day was the first real protagonist of the single species argument in his *British and Irish Salmonidae* published in 1887. Twenty years later this view was endorsed by the much respected ichthyologist Tate Regan and from then onwards, the sea trout's place as a form of the species *trutta* in the genus *Salmo* was firmly established.

In order to ascribe a specimen to a particular taxonomic niche, early naturalists relied upon visual appraisal together with any available knowledge of its behaviour. Linnaeus could differentiate sea trout from Atlantic salmon but did not know enough to include sea trout and brown trout within the same species. Much later, Day and his contemporaries were able to study trout in captivity and this must have helped them reach the tentative conclusion that brown and sea trout sprang from the same origins. Now, researchers have a wealth of technical apparatus to assist them in the study of fish in their element, as well as access to highly sophisticated protein testing equipment which can build up a detailed genetic profile. Still the scientific consensus remains the same; sea trout and brown trout are one and the same species.

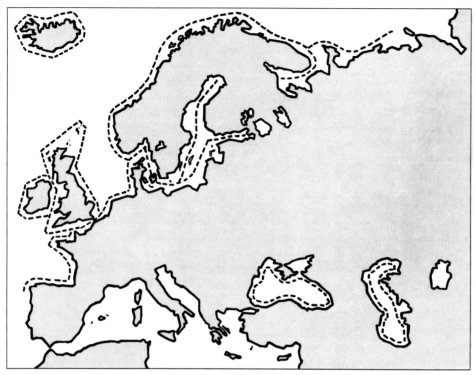

*The present natural range of sea trout.*

Within their native range, brown trout are migratory from the Biscay shores of northern Spain, along the length of the whole north European and Scandinavian coast up to the White Sea in western Russia. Many British, Irish and Icelandic rivers have prolific runs of sea trout as do those of some of the smaller outlying Atlantic islands. There are also migratory populations of trout in rivers flowing into the Black and Caspian Seas. Accurate information from Russia is difficult to obtain but the parlous state of the Aral Sea makes it quite certain that trout no longer reach its waters to feed. The migratory urges of many other brown trout populations are satisfied by less dramatic journeys down to the large freshwater lakes into which their natal streams discharge.

Wherever they occur, brown trout's migratory capabilities are greatly limited by the temperature in the lower reaches of their stream of birth. To migrate successfully, the whole length of the river, from redd to estuary, must conform with their thermal requirements. Before reaching the sea, a river may flatten out into long stretches of sluggish, poorly oxygenated water where temperatures often exceed 20°C for long periods; under such circumstances trout will not be able to reach the estuary from the upper reaches of the river, no matter how suitable these are for their survival, and the sea itself may also be too warm.

In the southern hemisphere, brown trout introduced into New Zealand and South America have often shown a tendency to migrate, but mainly within the cooler, more southerly limits of their range. There, richer food supplies in the cold sub-Antarctic seas may be a powerful inducement to migrate, or at least to repeat a migration after the trial and error of the first journey. However, the higher temperature of more northerly rivers is likely to deter movement downstream even though it may lead to better feeding grounds.

There may well be several distinct races or forms of sea trout, some of which perhaps correspond quite closely to those described by Gunther as separate species — Orkney, Galway, Welsh and Eastern sea trout (*S. orcadensis*, *S. gallivensis*, *S. cambricus* and *S. brachypoma*). Regan also appreciated this, noting that sewen (which he called *S. cambricus* even though he had no intention of describing a separate species) of Wales, Ireland and the west coast of England often differed from the sea trout (*S. albus*) of the east coast. Fish from the Galway area of western Ireland very seldom weigh more than two kilograms, and are usually less than half that size. In some Welsh rivers, sea trout may average nearly two kilograms, and fish twice that weight are not uncommon. On the west coast of Scotland, sea trout tend to grow more slowly and survive longer than on the east coast where they are often larger but shorter-lived.

*Sea trout.*

It may be tempting simply to attribute better growth rates to richer offshore feeding, but early taxonomists relied heavily on differences in size to support their conclusions. In many respects their findings have been substantiated by later researchers using modern protein analysis techniques. Distinct variations in the genetic make-up of sea trout from different parts of British and Irish coasts support the view that diet alone does not account for variation in size. And while sea trout from one river system may intermingle with those from another when they are feeding at sea, the great majority return to breed in their natal stream. By so doing they still remain reproductively isolated from neighbouring populations. Therefore the gradual evolution of distinct races remains a real possibility even within a single river system closely adjoined by others.

Trout appear to have colonised British and Irish waters in two distinct phases (Chapter Three), as the ice gradually retreated at the end of the last glacial period. The first influx moved up from southern Europe and is genetically quite distinct from the later invasion less than 10,000 years ago. Many of these earlier arrivals were isolated by the final erosions of melting ice in remote highland lochs. Others found themselves in streams above impassable waterfalls where any tendency to migrate soon proved incompatible with the urge to return to their place of birth. So by force of geographical circumstance these populations are strictly non-migratory. Later arrivals occupied stretches of river where passage to and from the sea was and remains perfectly possible. These fish lost nothing in retaining their migratory instincts to a greater or lesser degree. By doing so they increased their behavioural options and therefore their chances of survival, and today many of their descendants still go to sea to feed.

If gradual invasions from the sea spread trout throughout British and Irish waters it lends great strength to the argument that brown trout have their earliest origins in the sea. In 1911, Tate Regan wrote that

'The distribution of the Trout is sufficient evidence that the migratory and non-migratory fish are not distinct species, nor even races; there are no true freshwater fishes — Roach, Perch, etc. in the Hebrides, Orkneys or Shetlands; yet in these islands every river and loch is full of Brown Trout, which is only to be explained by the supposition that the latter have been derived from the sea-trout, which have lost their migratory instincts and at different times.'

By contrast, most 'true freshwater fishes' or coarse fish are extremely intolerant of high levels of salinity and only spread to Britain when it was joined to Europe and huge rivers drained both westwards down the English Channel and up today's North Sea. During the Ice Age the climate in south-east England probably allowed for the survival of some species of freshwater fish which slowly moved north and west as the glaciation receded. Others may have spread from the continent down the great rivers of melted ice which accompanied the ending of the Ice Age. Not surprisingly, there are fewer species of freshwater fish in Britain than in northern Europe and far fewer in the north and west of this island than in the south-east. When Ireland left Britain, which was after the latter's split from the rest of Europe, no bream, tench, perch, pike, rudd, dace, gudgeon or minnows had reached its rivers and no snakes or moles had colonised its land.

Some scientists still argue that all Salmonids evolved from freshwater origins (Chapter One) chiefly on account of the fact that none of them spawn in the sea. But whatever their beginnings, brown trout have retained the ability to adapt to life in both fresh and sea water. That trout use this ability with such success is only too apparent from their prodigious growth at sea — almost spectacular in comparison to that achieved by those that never leave fresh water.

Fish that routinely migrate between salt and fresh water as part of their regular life cycle are often referred to as 'diadromous'. They include those species that breed in fresh water but otherwise spend most of their lives in the sea (anadromous, from the Greek 'ana' meaning upwards and 'dromous' running) and others like eels and, to a lesser extent, mullets that, more unusually, live chiefly in fresh water but migrate to sea to breed (catadromous). Brown trout are so elastic in their migratory behaviour that it may be imprecise to describe them as truly anadromous. They exercise the widest possible range of migratory options and if deprived of the ability to reach the sea, are perfectly able to complete their lives in the streams where they were hatched.

*European sturgeon.*

In normal circumstances, Atlantic and all six species of Pacific salmon must migrate to sea to grow sufficiently to contend with the rigours of successful spawning. Like Atlantic shortnosed, European and Arctic sturgeons *(Acipenser brevirostrum, A. sturio* and *A. baieri)* and the parasitic sea lampreys they can be described as truly anadromous; so too can twaite shad *(Alosa fallax)* which are sea-dwelling members of the herring family, common round European coasts, that run up rivers in early summer to spawn — in England especially up the Severn. Yet in exceptional circumstances every one of these species is able to feed and breed successfully without going to sea. Their young and indeed those of all other Salmonid species, feed in fresh water and if confined by geological upheavals or behavioural changes, to their streams of origin, may establish landlocked populations. Sometimes temperature changes or serious pollution in the lower reaches of a river can also deter the downstream migrations of young fish, barring access to and from the sea quite as effectively as any landslide.

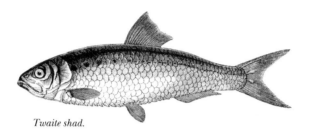

*Twaite shad.*

There are also many examples of anadromous species remaining in fresh water without any obvious environmental coercion. In Sweden's Lake Wener live stocks of non-migratory Atlantic salmon, quite able to reach the sea but which could not negotiate waterfalls on their return. There are other 'volunteer' populations of non-migratory Atlantic salmon in eastern Canada and America, and in the west, of nearly all species of Pacific salmon. Chinook salmon introduced to New Zealand established a non-migratory population even though access to the sea was and remains perfectly possible. Sea lampreys now live permanently in all the North American Great Lakes, and there are freshwater populations of twaite shad in lakes of south-west Ireland and the Italian Alps. In all these cases, fish find the environment of a large lake an acceptable salt-free substitute for the sea, satisfying their migratory urges with journeys down and up inflowing feeder streams.

From salmon's ability to grow and breed without visiting the sea, even if they do not reach nearly the size that they otherwise would, there is obviously no physiological necessity for them to migrate to salt water. On the simple assumption that all Nature's aids to survival are designed to ensure the continuation of the species, migration merely appears to be a strategy which is likely to enhance the chances of successful spawning — so much so that under normal circumstances salmon always try to migrate. For rainbow and cutthroat trout as well as all the charrs, the advantages of migrating are less clear cut. However, like brown trout these species seem able to select from a choice of life patterns the one which will best promote the interests of their species. Some populations of each species find it beneficial to feed in salt water while others remain all their lives in fresh water although perfectly able to reach the sea if they choose to.

Many rainbow trout migrate to sea. They are called steelheads on their return to fresh water and are probably the most sought-after game fish in North America. There is as little certainty over their migratory behaviour as there is over that of brown trout. In short streams where food is scarce, almost all the rainbow trout travel to sea. In longer rivers some migrate while others remain behind to extract what nourishment they can from freshwater food supplies. Once at sea many steelheads range far offshore in their search for food — much further than most sea-run brown trout. Others forage closer to the coast spending less time at sea before they return to spawn, often feeding in fresh water on their way up to do so. There are also migratory populations of the closely related cut-throat trout, but these seldom travel further afield than the river mouth. There they spend the summer months pursuing sticklebacks and other estuarine prey before moving back upstream to breed in the autumn.

There are migratory runs of all species of Salvelinus (charr) except probably lake charr which are intolerant of strong salt water. Sea-running Arctic charr occur along the north coast of Canada, Alaska, Russia and Scandinavia as well as round the shores of Iceland and many Arctic islands. They are long-lived fish which remain in fresh water for up to five years before moving down to sea where they feed throughout the summer. All sea-going charr seem to return to their natal streams in early autumn and with the short Arctic summer therefore have little time to search very far offshore for food. None of the charr in Britain or Ireland migrate to sea although some leave their lakes and travel up inflowing streams to spawn.

Less migratory, but even more adaptable, are three-spined sticklebacks. In the northern limits of their range, through both Atlantic and Pacific oceans, they are mainly sea-dwellers with only a few populations living either wholly or partly in fresh water. In Britain they occur both in rivers and along the coast, while around the Mediterranean most sticklebacks live exclusively in fresh water. As a species, brown trout show less versatility in their life style, but much more as individuals in their selection of migratory options. For many of them there seems to be an element of discretion in a choice of life pattern so fundamental, so much researched and yet still so obscure.

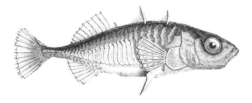

*Three-spined stickleback.*

The most obvious benefit to be gained from migrating is the ability to exploit the greater food resources of the sea. At the same time, sea-running trout can avoid the pressures of competition for food and territory from other members of their species and also escape from the whole variety of freshwater predators. On returning to spawn, their size leads them to lay significantly greater numbers of larger eggs; these are buried deeper, in more secure nests than smaller fish are able to excavate. Nonetheless, the journeys both down and up river are potentially hazardous, as is life at sea. On their way downstream, parr are faced with continual changes in temperature, current, diet and eventually salinity; once in the estuary, the need to reverse the osmotic process is particularly stressful to the system of any fish just down from the river. Out at sea young sea trout must contend with a whole new range of predators, they need to adjust quickly to an entirely different diet and there is always the risk of losing their way back to their home stream. Yet some subconscious set of scales appears able to weigh these advantages and dangers and so often they are tipped in favour of migration.

Experience gathered particularly in the course of propagating trout beyond their natural limits, shows clearly that non-migratory fish retain both the physical ability and latent inclination to migrate to sea; all that is required is for some aspect of their new environment to press an internal trigger that stimulates them to do so. In New Zealand and southern South America there are migratory populations of brown trout descended from non-migratory stock, while in the Falkland Islands descendants from common ancestors adopt both migratory and non-migratory life patterns. Conversely, within the brown trout's native range it has been repeatedly demonstrated that many offspring of migratory parents never leave fresh water.

Into this whole question of alternative behaviour patterns must be introduced the comparative effects of genetic influence and environmental pressures. Before they enter the sea, migrating brown trout parr that have moved downstream go through an additional stage in their development which resident fish do not. This is the smolt stage and entails the gradual acquisition of a silvery-blue colour brought on by the secretion of guanin in the epidermis; this silvering is prompted, at least in part, by thyroid activity. As it occurs while the fish is still in fresh water the process cannot be a reaction to contact with the different environment of salt water. Therefore it seems that the same process which initially induces a trout to choose the migratory option must then also be responsible for inducing the smolt stage in its life, usually some time after downstream migration has begun. This points to genes rather than environment as the primary influence over migratory behaviour, as do the results of experiments with the translocation of offspring of migratory parents into landlocked Scottish hill lochs. Many of these parr began to show obvious silvering after one or two years, contrasting distinctly with non-migratory brown trout reared in parallel.

Among certain populations of brown trout there is a noticeable tendency for females to migrate while most males remain behind in fresh water all their lives. Examination of smolts and returning adult sea trout has repeatedly shown that a great majority of migrating fish are females. This is not a universal pattern and the migratory tendencies of the sexes vary between stocks of sea trout in different rivers. Still, there may be distinctly less advantage to males in risking the hazards of going to sea when their function in the spawning act is confined simply to the fertilisation of eggs; the benefits of migration to females, in laying larger eggs and being able to excavate deeper nests, are far more apparent. This behaviour is to some extent parallelled in that of Atlantic salmon. Male salmon parr often remain behind in their natal stream, becoming sexually mature and even fertilising the eggs of returning females, before they too eventually head for the sea.

Research into possible genetic differences between migratory and non-migratory trout has done little to uncloud the picture. Some studies have revealed that these are considerable. Others have found both forms of trout to be identical in their genetic profiles. In all events, the likelihood of identifying dissimilarities is greatly enhanced if the fish compared come from separate river systems whose populations of trout may have evolved distinctive genetic differences anyway. In some instances, environmental pressures may spur the urge to migrate. Food shortages, overpopulation or the sudden onset of unsuitable water conditions may all trigger some intuitive realisation that life downstream may be preferable. When unchecked, this search for better conditions may end in the sea. All the same, it seems quite unrealistic to suggest that trout have any inherited preconception of the existence of some great marine cornucopia at the end of their river, otherwise they would all wish to take advantage of it. The silvering of smolts is clearly a process that prepares brown trout for life in the sea. However, parr sometimes reach the estuary without passing through the smolt stage thereby undermining some of the more categorical explanations as to why sea trout migrate; so too does the abundant evidence that siblings, even of the same sex, may select different (some migratory and some non-migratory) life options.

The early life of migratory and non-migratory brown trout is identical. This is only to be expected of members of the same species whose behaviour does not differ until the urge to go to sea takes hold. The larger eggs of sea trout produce larger alevins. After swimming up into open water these will have a distinct advantage over the smaller offspring of non-migratory females in the same nursery area. Thereafter, life through their first summer and winter and for much of the second summer continues just like that of resident fish. It is usually only towards the end of the second summer that differences in colour and behaviour begin to emerge — perhaps only formulated shortly before they occur or somehow predisposed at birth to enhance the trout's prospects of survival.

During their second summer those trout that are touched by the urge to migrate usually begin to show outward signs of this being so. Slowly they drift downstream, feeding as they go on prey similar to that consumed by the trout left behind. Gradually they form shoals, collecting other migrants on the way. By autumn their silvery smolt colouring starts to show and they are readily distinguished from resident fish. During the winter months smolts remain in the lower reaches of the river taking any food that is available in preparation for their final move to sea. When spring comes, measuring between fifteen and twenty-five centimeters and brightly silvered, they are ready to face the hazards of life beyond fresh water. Some may wait a further year or even two before making their move and there is a distinct tendency for this to be delayed in more northerly latitudes; however, usually just over two years after hatching, sea trout move into the estuaries and experience their first contact with salt water.

When in streams and rivers, the trout's blood and other body fluids are more chemically concentrated than the surrounding fresh water (Chapter Two). There osmosis causes fish to absorb water through the membranes lining their gills and mouths, any surplus being expelled as urine by way of their kidneys. The chemical strength of brackish estuarine water is much closer to that of sea trout's body fluids and water absorption slows down. Trout blood is about one third as saline as average sea water; therefore when the proportion of diffused sea water in the estuary exceeds one third, fish gradually begin to lose water through the surface of their gills. Then, spurred by pituitary activity, the kidney slowly begins to reverse its function and sea trout start to swallow extra water, secreting the surplus salt as small quantities of concentrated urine and through cells in their gills, specialised for the purpose.

This reversal of the normal direction of osmotic flow places great strain on a trout's metabolism. It is therefore important for them to spend time in the estuary, gradually adapting to its increased salinity. Fish suddenly transplanted from fresh to salt water without time to acclimatise become highly stressed and may even die. Larger fish seem better able to withstand the shock, perhaps because they have less surface area in relation to body volume than smaller ones. The oxygen content of salt water is markedly less than that of fresh water and this also adds to the importance of a stay in the half-way habitat of the estuary.

Some smolts remain in the estuary for two months or more before moving out into the open sea. Others may linger there for the summer, in the river mouth or just beyond, feeding on the richer diet of estuarine aquatic life before returning to fresh water in the autumn weighing usually less than half a kilogram. Then, known by a variety of local names as 'finnock' (*fionnag* in Gaelic from *fionn* meaning 'white'), 'peal', 'whitling' or 'herling', these post-smolts move upstream in large shoals (schools). Occasionally they seem to edge down the coast into neighbouring estuaries and even move up the alien rivers that flow into them. Finnock may overwinter in the river or otherwise return to sea, sometimes even going back up river again shortly afterwards. Some finnock breed, depending on their size, but they lay smaller eggs which disadvantages their parr, and their upstream journey is not specifically undertaken in order to spawn.

It is tempting to compare finnock, as a stage in the life of sea trout, to small salmon returning to their natal streams as grilse. This is however, a confusing comparison because grilse have spent at least a whole year in the sea (although always less than two) and are returning specifically to spawn. They are fully mature fish and having spawned there is no evidence to suggest that their survival rate is any greater than that of larger salmon; if grilse were still on their way to maturity when they first spawned, they would be expected to stand a much better chance than larger fish of surviving to spawn again.

The most apparent advantage gained by migratory fish, which benefits even those that go no further than the estuary, is access to the richer feeding in salt water. Post-smolts that go straight to sea and finnock that return to spend a few months in fresh water before doing so, all show clear evidence of the benefits of a marine diet, growing up to twice as much in one year at sea as they did in their first two or three years in fresh water.

Some migratory brown trout go no further than the estuary in their search for more varied and abundant food supplies. These are 'slob' trout (or bull trout — *Salmo eriox* to many early taxonomists) which make their limited migrations without passing through any smolt stage, seemingly adapting to life in the estuary without undergoing any dramatic physiological changes. They are sandy coloured and thick set, and like true sea trout migrate upstream to spawn in the autumn. Slob trout are highly susceptible to estuarine pollution and are much less common than during the last century when several rivers experienced quite distinct runs of breeding fish.

Sea trout and slob trout are opportunistic feeders and can easily adapt to the availability of different species of prey. At the river mouth they continue to devour any familiar freshwater food reaching them from upstream and insects still make up a large proportion of their diet. Lower down the estuary, where the sea's influence is more apparent, crustaceans and small fish are more important to them. Sprats *(Sprattus sprattus)*, sand eels *(Ammodytes* spp.), sand smelts *(Atherina presbyter)*, young herrings *(Clupea harengus)* and sticklebacks are eventually the most essential dietary ingredients but in their first months at sea, post-smolts may not be large enough to catch other fish. When they are, small species of shoaling fish provide energy-efficient prey both in terms of ease of capture and nutritional benefit.

Sea birds, as well as many other species of fish, rely heavily on sand eels as a vital component in their diets. Of the five different species of sand eel found around British coasts, the most important is *Ammodytes marinus* which is also commercially exploited as a source of fish meal and oil. At one time the oil was even used to fuel Danish power stations. Arctic terns, kittiwakes and puffins are particularly dependent on sand eels and sometimes suffer disastrous collapses in their numbers, almost certainly following the depletion of stocks of their staple food. Periodic crashes in sea trout populations, particularly from the west coasts of Scotland and Ireland, have been even more catastrophic. Inevitably, it is no more certain that these are a consequence of vanishing sand eels than it is that there are no sand eels because they have been overfished. But whatever the connection, the parallel between the decline in numbers of fish and birds is likely to be more than simple coincidence.

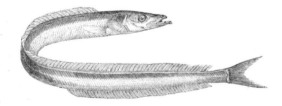

*Sand eel.*

Sprats usually occur closer inshore than sand eels and are also exploited commercially for fish meal. The methods used to catch both species can indiscriminately sweep up all but the smallest marine organisms, almost denuding great expanses of sea of all animal life in the process. Feeding sea trout may also be netted at the same time.

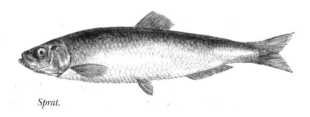

*Sprat.*

*Pollack.*

If there are no shoals of small fish, sea trout must become more selective in their pursuit of prey, singling out individuals of species with more solitary habits. Then they may search for young pollack *(Pollachius pollachius)*, and even bottom-dwelling plaice *(Pleuronectes platessa)* and flounders *(Platichthys flesus)* in shallow water. Marine molluscs, small crabs and young lobsters are also picked off individually. These and smaller crustaceans like shrimps and prawns, which may be more plentiful, all contribute from the carotene in their shells to the pink colour of sea trout flesh. However, fish forced to adopt this discriminatory feeding behaviour use more energy in pursuit of their prey, growing more slowly as a result; and the sparser food supplies also sustain far fewer of them.

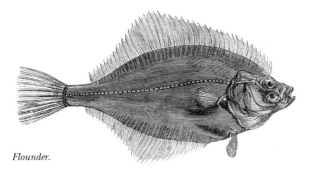

*Flounder.*

Once out at sea, the availability of food largely influences the trout's travels. If food is prolific there is little compulsion to migrate beyond the borders of plenty. Sea trout in general remain closer inshore than Atlantic salmon and most probably never stray further than thirty kilometers from the estuary of their native river, although this is a generalisation for there are many records of tagged sea trout being recaptured several hundred kilometers from where they were first caught. Fish from the coasts of eastern Scotland and northern England have often turned up around the shores of Denmark and Holland where sea trout are often caught, despite the dearth of suitable streams in these countries where they can spawn. Interesting too, are the successful sea trout fisheries off the Wash and East Anglian coast. There are no sea trout rivers in these parts of England and yet drift netsmen make good catches, probably of fish from further north. A few adult fish tagged in Northumbrian rivers have been recovered as far afield as the Norwegian coast and occasionally sea trout from rivers on one side of Britain are recaptured off the other. Rainbow trout are equally unpredictable in their migratory behaviour at sea and although most steelheads remain fairly close inshore, some shoals have been reported feeding far out into the Pacific.

Sea trout that have not gone back up river as finnock usually spend more than a full year in the sea before their reproductive urges turn them homewards. The vast majority of fish return unerringly to their natal stream guided, so it seems, by their olfactory powers which sense out its distinctive chemical make-up. Once there, sea trout are also able to return with ease to their particular tributary of origin. It has even been suggested that small trout remaining behind in fresh water, give off a particular odour that guides their siblings back to the pool where they were spawned. While at sea, trout must rely upon different navigational aids to guide them round its featureless waters, perhaps using the sun and moon to help them. Sea trout found far from their native river may have lost their way and such distant recoveries do not necessarily provide good evidence of their navigational abilities.

Despite an undoubted ability to return to their place of birth, there is clear evidence that sea trout of all ages, not only finnock, enter 'foreign' estuaries, even travelling some way up the inflowing river. Still, this does not necessarily demonstrate an intention to breed in it. Perhaps it is part of a trial and error process which requires sea trout to sample more than one river by way of comparison before being able to identify that of their origin. On the other hand they may just be fulfilling an urge to rest up in the nearest fresh water for a time, before returning to a more rigorous existence at sea.

It is difficult to extrapolate firm conclusions from much of the research into migratory behaviour. Unless fish are first tagged as parr or smolts there is no certainty that they were hatched in their river of capture nor that adult sea trout, caught in an estuary or on an adjoining coast, were spawned in the nearest river. Furthermore, movements of mature fish up a particular river do not necessarily indicate an intention to spawn there; only by actually watching fish spawn or recovering spent adults near redds can proof of breeding be inferred. If these limitations are imposed on the evidence accumulated so far, there are no certain records of sea trout ever spawning in streams other than those in which they were hatched.

Most sea trout return to fresh water after just over a year at sea. Having migrated down to the estuary in February or March, those that did not return as finnock will have moved out to sea and spent a full summer and much of the following winter there. Some fish remain at sea for a further year or even more and the timing of their return to fresh water varies around the coast of Britain. In south-west England and Wales, runs are early and fish may enter estuaries in March or April. Elsewhere sea trout usually move up in mid-summer and many rivers have an autumn run as well.

Sea trout are less dependent than salmon on a spate of fresh water to help them upstream. Usually, being smaller, they can negotiate shallows more easily, although when they arrive in the upper reaches of their chosen stream further progress may be checked by low water, especially during summer. Likewise, ascending fish may only be able to negotiate high waterfalls with the help of an increase in water volume. Once sea trout have begun to congregate at the mouth of the river it seems clear that they then respond positively to even a small rise in its level.

Just as they must linger in estuaries on their way out to sea, sea trout returning to fresh water need time to reverse the osmotic process, so that excess water attracted by the higher chemical concentration of their bodies is safely expelled. Time spent in the estuary may vary and is difficult to monitor but while there, sea trout seem to move up and back with the tide before finally making their first run into pure fresh water.

Upstream migrations are also difficult to observe but in the course of researches sea trout have been fitted with acoustic or radio tags allowing their progress to be followed, provided conditions are suitable. Most movement appears to be at night unless there is a spate in which case, perhaps exploiting the cover afforded by dirtier water, they seem prepared to swim upstream during the day. Normal swimming speed is around two kilometers per hour but since larger fish swim faster it often makes more sense to relate speed to size; one half of body length per second is a good average rate.

How long their journey upstream takes obviously depends on how far the fish must travel, but usually they do not stay for long in the river's lower reaches. Instead they prefer to swim steadily upwards, perhaps until reaching a large holding pool near the confluence of their spawning tributary with the main river, where they remain for most of the summer. If there is a loch fed by smaller spawning streams at the head of the river, sea trout usually move quickly up to this more peaceful stillwater environment and wait there until urged up these streams in autumn to breed.

On their way upstream, sea trout normally lie up in deep pools during the day, only becoming active towards dusk. Those fresh out of the sea, perhaps still fortified by recent feeding, are more lively during the day but they too seem to be further stimulated by the approach of darkness. When light starts to fail, fish leave the depths of their daylight refuges and begin to cruise around the shallows, particularly at the tail of a pool. Some then move further upstream, conspicuous by the bow waves that precede them as they go. Occasionally, sea trout continue to splash around after darkness but usually stop doing so once night has fallen, perhaps showing themselves again with the first light of dawn.

It is well appreciated that salmon returning to spawn do not feed in fresh water, probably ceasing long before they even reach the river mouth. In contrast, the behaviour of sea trout is much less consistent. They undoubtedly still feed in estuaries, and finnock continue to do so as they move upstream, often taking flies off the surface. However, the stomachs of adult sea trout seem to contract in fresh water and analyses of the contents very seldom show remains of much freshwater prey. In some Scottish lochs fish are lured to the surface by the attractions of large, fuzzy dry flies dapped along the waves but the reasons for the success of such tactics are still uncertain. In Ireland, fishermen impale crane flies (daddy-long-legs) on a bare hook and these can prove equally successful at attracting sea trout 'on the dap'. This may provide evidence of sea trout's muted inclinations to feed in fresh waters but they are often large fish and if all those in a river fed as avidly there as they do in the sea, the freshwater food supplies would soon be decimated, to the obvious detriment of resident fish. Sea trout do not need to eat while in fresh water and are well able to live off their sea-gathered reserves. Despite this, the stomachs of larger fish are often found to contain a few small insects and there is no doubt that they do occasionally feed, perhaps out of some opportunistic reflex prompting them to seize easy prey without actively seeking it out.

Sea trout fresh into the river are easily confused with small salmon. In their parr stage, all brown trout are difficult to differentiate from salmon of the same age although there are distinct characteristics that help to distinguish them when young (Chapter Five), some of which continue to mark the adults of the species. Salmon retain both their distinctive forked tail and the thinner wrist that allows them to be tailed by hand; large sea trout with much thicker wrists are almost impossible to grasp behind their tails. However, long gone are any distinctive fingerprint marks which may have identified young parr, as are the orange edges of young trout's adipose fins. Instead, the spots on mature fish can aid identification. A sea trout is often heavily spotted above the lateral line and sometimes even below it; salmon have far fewer spots and very rarely any on the lower part of their bodies. When hooked, the two species respond very differently and the frenzied runs and leaps of sea trout contrast strongly with the slower more measured struggles of salmon.

Scale counts provide the surest means of distinguishing the two species although even these may need to be substantiated by actual scale analysis. With mature fish it is simple to count the number of scales in a line angled forwards from the rear of the adipose fin to the lateral line. On salmon the number ranges from ten to thirteen although eleven is normal. There are usually between thirteen and sixteen on sea trout, most often fourteen. In the event of a fish having a count of thirteen or if for any other reason the evidence is inconclusive, a detailed examination of individual scales may be called for. The actual make-up of scales of both species is identical, but few salmon spawn twice while sea trout may return to do so year after year, especially those from the longer-lived populations of the west coasts of Scotland and Ireland. Therefore if a scale shows more than one spawning mark, especially if taken from a fish which would rank as small for a salmon, it is most likely to have come from a sea trout. Conversely, only one spawning mark on a scale from a fish weighing several kilograms would almost certainly point to its having been taken from a salmon.

As sea trout reach the headwaters of their natal river they begin to lose the silvery sheen that earlier in their journey identified them as migratory fish. Now in colouration they are more like brown trout from which they can usually still be distinguished by their larger size. Scale analysis can also show clearly whether a trout has benefited from a prolonged spell of rich feeding in the sea. In such cases the ridged circuli are thicker and spaced widely apart. From red, torpid salmon that are also about to breed it is easy to differentiate sea trout by their heavy spotting and browner colour.

Before spawning, sea trout usually hold up in a deep pool some distance downstream of their final destination, awaiting the usual autumn floods which will help them up to the redds. If they run up river early in the year they may have to wait several months, becoming gradually staler and less active. Slowly their reproductive organs enlarge. Freshwater food intake is minimal in comparison to the amount needed to maintain sea trout in the condition in which they left the sea and they start to lose weight as their flesh becomes soft and flaccid. Then towards the end of summer, as days shorten and the water cools, some hormone-induced catalysis prepares the fish for spawning.

In Britain, most sea trout breed in cold upland streams so their eggs usually take several weeks to hatch, although not as long as they do in Scandinavian rivers where water temperatures are only just above freezing. Eggs are therefore laid comparatively early, in October or November, which also usually coincides with higher water levels.

A good flow eases the way to the redds, ensuring they are adequately covered with water and providing protection for spawning fish which are then particularly vulnerable. Sea trout build nests and spawn in exactly the same way as non-migratory trout (Chapter Three) although sea trout can displace much larger stones in the course of their excavations and are therefore able to make use of a wider range of nesting sites. Large sea trout and small salmon often select similar or even the same redds for spawning, and hybridisation is not uncommon. Despite this, Nature's intricate patterns limit the chances of this happening, as salmon usually spawn at the end of the year by which time nearly all sea trout have already left their redds.

When a female has prepared her nest and shows signs of readiness to spawn a male attaches himself to her, perhaps having fought off other males for the privilege. Once both have spawned, small non-migratory males may dash in and also fertilise the eggs before these are covered over with stones. This must increase the chances of successful hatching and as migratory females often outnumber migratory males it may even be a crucial component in the reproductive behaviour of sea trout. It also serves to compound the mystery surrounding the acquisition of sea-going tendencies by providing that young trout may sometimes be the product of migratory females and non-migratory males.

Another strategy sometimes adopted by sea trout, perhaps also in response to the shortage of large migratory males, is to construct a communal nest which two or three females share. When this happens, a male can fertilise the eggs of several females. Moreover, the construction of one large nest may also provide greater security for eggs than the shallow depressions of several smaller ones.

The spawning process is an exhausting one for all Salmonids, especially those that stopped feeding when they left the sea, perhaps several months earlier. For all species of Pacific salmon it inevitably culminates in death. Most Atlantic salmon also only spawn once but between five and thirty per cent return to breed again; the proportion varies greatly between rivers but always it seems that far fewer males than females make the journey a second time. Scale analysis has shown that very occasionally Atlantic salmon return to breed for a third and even a fourth time.

Somehow sea trout seem better able to survive the combined stresses of breeding and the return journey to the sea. Like salmon, they are at their weakest after spawning and then least able to resist the pressures of the current or infection by disease. However, sea trout appear to regain their strength much faster than salmon, so much so that it may be quite possible to confuse kelts returning to sea with clean incoming spring fish, at least in shape if not in colouring. Sea trout that breed in short rivers headed by a network of small spawning streams may quickly return to salt water, reaching the estuaries by Christmas. In contrast, if there are large still waters in which the fish can lie up on their downstream journey, they may not reach the sea until springtime; by then they may have begun to feed in fresh water and much improved their condition by doing so.

So it is that sea trout frequently spawn several times in their life and having bred once, will usually return each year to do so again until they die. The smallest multiple spawners are those which first spawned as finnock. These may weigh no more than a kilogram on return to the river but fish that first spawned as adults will be heavier. Those that have bred three or four times might weigh up to five kilograms and from scale analysis the highest recorded number of spawnings is twelve. Two fish from Scottish rivers were each found to have spawned eleven times; both weighed 5.5 kilograms and one was in its sixteenth year, the other in its nineteenth. However if the upstream journey is particularly long and arduous, this may reduce the likelihood of sea trout spawning more than once. Before a dam barred their way, sea trout used to run up the Vistula river in Poland which flows through Cracow, Warsaw and out into the Baltic Sea at Gdansk. The great journey to the redds made such claims on their energies that no fish was ever known to return to spawn a second time. To fortify themselves for their ascent these sea trout often spent four years at sea, growing up to 15 kilograms, before setting off upstream on a journey of at least 1000 kilometers.

While genetic make-up may have some influence on their size, the weights sea trout attain depend largely upon their age and the food supplies in their offshore feeding areas. These latter are particularly rich in the Irish Sea but less so off the Atlantic coast where sea trout may be noticably slighter in build. Better feeding in the Baltic Sea probably accounts for the heavier sea trout in Poland and Sweden. There fish run to much greater weights than they do even in the Tweed which probably has the largest fish round British and Irish coasts even though these are comparatively short-lived; the heaviest recorded sea trout is one of thirteen kilograms caught in the nets at the mouth of that river and one of nine kilograms taken some distance upstream is almost a rod-caught record.

Now, throughout much of their native range sea trout are threatened, both at sea and in fresh water. In rivers they are relatively conspicuous and the pressures of sport fishing, inspired more by economic than aesthetic considerations, at least ensure the most careful husbandry of both fish and their environment. This is in sad contrast to their fate in the 'no man's water' of the sea where migratory trout pass unseen, only apparent in death, caught up in the nets of fishermen.

The ecologies of sea and estuary are immensely intricate. Overlaid on their intricacies is a web of competing economic and political interests, with the result that the responsibility for the welfare of sea trout in their marine environment assumes all the attractions of a ticking parcel. So far, Nature has shown an ability to heal human-inflicted wounds that mankind little deserves. How long such beneficence can continue is up to mankind not Nature. But the interests of sea trout could not be better served than by finding the answer to one tantalising question. What urges them to sea?

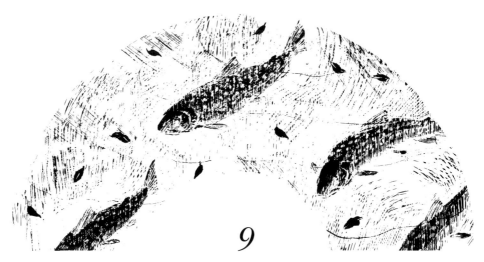

# 9
# *Farming and Stocking*

Mediaeval monks introduced fish culture into Britain, concentrating their early efforts on breeding carp which they cropped throughout the winter. Monasteries were almost always built on river banks, so ensuring a permanent flow of water through an often labyrinthine system of interconnected ponds where fish were both bred and fattened for the table. Common carp were brought to Britain from their native eastern Europe, probably in the early Middle Ages. Certainly they had reached England by 1486 when Dame Juliana Berners wrote that the carp was a 'daynteous fusshe, but there ben but few in Englonde and therefore I wryte the lesse of hym'.

As long as water is warm enough in summer, carp breed easily among the weeds in their pond, and the monks needed little skill to propagate them. By contrast, successful trout cultivation requires much technical expertise as well as sensitive handling of fish and eggs, and no large-scale hatcheries appeared until the middle of the nineteenth century. As far back as 1420 Dom Pinchon, a French monk, described the natural spawning behaviour of trout in an unpublished manuscript, but there is no evidence that he ever attempted to breed them artificially. The first person to succeed in doing so was probably a German named Ludwig Jacobi in 1765, but no-one continued his work after he died, even though the British Government considered it important enough to grant him a pension in recognition of his efforts. Not until eighty years later did two Frenchmen, Remy and Gehin, both unaware of any earlier efforts to do so, set up what was almost certainly the first successful trout hatchery.

In 1843 Remy had written to the Prefect at Vosges describing his experiments and observations.

'At the season of spawning, in November, when the eggs appear at the vent of the trout, by passing the thumb and pressing gently against the vent of the female without doing her any injury, I cause the eggs to fall into a basin of water; after this I seize the male and by operating in the same manner cause the milt to flow over the eggs until they have become opaque. As soon as the operation is completed, and the eggs have become clear, I dispose them between coarse grains of sand in the bottom of an iron box, pierced with a thousand holes. I place one of these boxes in a spring of fresh water . . . towards the middle of February the eggs . . . begin to hatch . . . it appears to me that a discovery of this nature, especially at a time when the rivers are nearly deprived of fish . . . is worthy of the attentions of the government.'

Remy's researches did not pass unnoticed and earned him a grant of 100 Francs and a bronze medal from the Society of Vosges. They culminated in 1852 in the establishment of a huge fish hatchery at Huningue near the Rhone-Rhine canal in south-east France. This operated on a vast scale, covering eighty acres, but appears to have been more successful in breeding coarse fish, probably because the water was too warm for trout eggs to hatch.

Just as the shrinking fish populations in France had encouraged Remy's researches, so the Industrial Revolution provided much of the impetus for the development of trout farming in England, however noxious to the natural environment the dark satanic mills may otherwise have been. Wholesale pollution of air and water, as well as the construction of dams, weirs and mills, all took a heavy toll of indigenous fish and with the need to repopulate streams and rivers, there slowly began to emerge sufficient expertise to do so. Increased prosperity attracted many new enthusiasts to trout fishing and once large scale trout farming was firmly under way, fish to stock man-made ponds and other troutless waters for sport fishing were soon in great demand. Almost simultaneously, the advent of refrigerated transport stimulated orders from the most distant destinations for fertilised ova from Britain (Chapter Ten).

One of the first to appreciate the fish farming possibilities in Britain was Frank Buckland, who was largely responsible for the successful exportation of brown trout ova to Australia from his own hatchery in the south of England. By 1863 he had already published the first detailed work on the subject — *Fish Hatching* — in which he reflected that

'Man has dominion given him over both land and water. Of the former he has taken every advantage . . . however the human race seem to have entirely forgotten the second item . . . they take no pains to cultivate the largest portion of their earth . . . we have been asleep, we have had gold nuggets under our noses and have not stopped to pick them up.'

Apart from Buckland's, most early British fish farms were in Scotland, where water conditions were most obviously suitable. The first was a salmon hatchery opened near Perth in 1853. Slowly others followed, perhaps the best known being one at Howietoun near Stirling which started in 1874 with 25,205 brown trout ova and ten years later was raising nearly 300,000 young fish annually; it is still in operation and with the help of nearly a million gallons of water per day, continues to rear young fish as well as producing ova for export all over the world. Now there are over 200 trout farms throughout Britain; most of these concentrate on farming rainbow trout for the table but many also raise the much slower growing brown trout for stocking purposes. Italy, Denmark and France are the major producers of trout in Europe, each rearing almost twice as many as Britain whose output is comparable to that of Spain and Germany.

Trout farming splits into two main activities. First is the production and hatching of eggs and the care of young fish, at least until they are no longer dependent on their yolk sacs; this is done at a hatchery. Then there is the work of rearing trout up to their full size either as stock fish or for the table. Some farms both hatch and rear trout but others specialise in one or other of these operations.

The essential requirements for setting up a successful trout farm have not changed since Buckland's time, although they are now more precisely and scientifically appreciated. First, and by far the most important, is a steady supply of fresh, clean water which must be completely free from pollution. Preferably the water should be slightly alkaline with a pH of just over 7.0. Some silt is almost unavoidable in water taken from a river liable to occasional flooding. It will do little harm to adult fish but there is a risk of it clogging the gills of fry or parr, and even small amounts can prove fatal to eggs.

Provided its chemical composition is suitable, spring water has many advantages as a source of supply for both hatcheries and rearing ponds. It is invariably cleaner than river water and maintains a more constant temperature. Spring water usually emerges out of the ground at consistent temperatures of between 8°C and 12°C throughout the year. This may be just too cool to promote maximum growth of young brown trout which metabolise best at around 15°C, but there is less likelihood of flow falling to dangerously low levels in summer, and of icing in winter. The spring is also usually controlled by the fish farm's owner, so reducing the possibility of contamination between the water's source and its use.

Temperature has a critical effect on the oxygen content of water (Chapter Seven). If it rises too high and oxygen levels fall, rearing ponds support fewer trout than they otherwise would. A good flow of water can partially compensate for oxygen shortages and also helps flush out excreta, uneaten food and other waste products from ponds. Too strong a flow causes trout to dissipate energy just holding themselves in the current and if there is a danger of flooding, bypasses are often built to take off surplus water. If flow falls dangerously low, water may be artificially oxygenated, and in extreme conditions even recycled; but these are expensive operations and impossible to set up quickly.

The best way to supply a trout farm with water is by gravity, which means situating the farm below the inflow level. At the inflow there must be some form of screening system to keep wild fish, as well as leaves and branches, out of ponds. These screens need to be cleared at least twice a day to ensure they do not become clogged and so block the flow of water. The layout and construction of the ponds control the course the water then takes through the farm. One of the most simple and efficient layouts was developed in Denmark and comprises rows of excavated ponds supplied individually from one large communal feeder channel; all the ponds discharge together into a back channel which then empties into the river again or, if the water comes from a spring, simply continues on its downstream journey. All water discharging from a fish farm should pass through at least one settling tank where waste is given time to sink down to the bottom, leaving the water clean and fit to sustain healthy aquatic life below the farm. If the surrounding soil is impervious, as it will be if consisting largely of clay, ponds need not be lined, otherwise they are often faced with imported clay or covered with sheets of artificial material. They usually slope in depth from one meter at the inflow to double that at the outflow, which is often through an exit system called a 'monk', being similar in design to those used in monasteries to prevent carp escaping. Sometimes electrified exit gates deter fish from even approaching them.

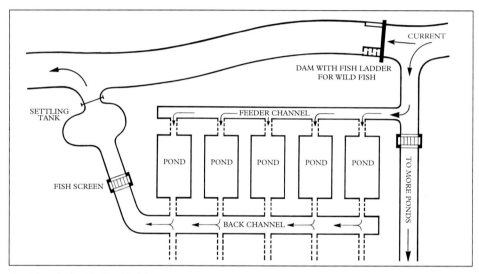

*Trout farm laid out in Danish style.*

Intensive fish farms producing trout for the table — invariably rainbows — often use round tanks of concrete or corrugated iron. These are cheap to sink into the ground and easy to scrub out. Each has its own inflow and the outflow is either through a simple plug hole in the bottom or over the lip of a central pipe protruding nearly to the surface and surrounded by a screen of wire mesh to retain the fish; this latter type of outflow creates a vortex round its edges that also helps keep the tank clean. These more portable tanks allow for a much more flexible operation than the permanent arrangement of the larger Danish ponds.

A third type of design is the raceway, where holding areas are laid out in series rather than parallel. Each raceway comprises a narrow channel up to 100 meters long, divided up by screens above steps down which water falls into the next section. The flow speed is much greater and for this reason, trout reared in raceways are more suited for stocking rivers where they must continually strive against the pressures of the current. Trout bred for the table are better left to divert their energies into faster growth. The continual movement in raceways creates a natural self-cleansing mechanism by keeping waste matter in suspension. However, this is also the cause of this design's main disadvantage which is one of hygiene in that fish at the end of the raceway must contend with all the excreta expelled by those higher up.

Whatever type of layout is used, open water often needs to be netted over to protect fish from avian predators, particularly herons. Netting is costly both to erect and maintain, but unless fish are kept in large round ponds, where they can take refuge away from the bank, or in steep sided concrete or metal tanks, preventing predation frequently justifies the expense. Eggs and fry are also highly susceptible to predation by small mammals and by almost any bird that finds its way into the hatching sheds.

Trout farms producing eggs and fry, either for their own rearing or to sell to other farms which for one reason or another do not breed their own fish, rely on a brood stock of trout from which ova and milt are stripped. This brood stock is treated with a degree of respect not normally accorded to farmed trout, but perhaps equal to the importance of its role. The chosen fish are given plenty of space in their ponds, which are usually deep and shaded, and are often fed a special fat-free diet until they are three years old. Females may sometimes be stripped of their eggs at two but it is more usual to wait another year.

When the female is ripe, which means that her eggs are loose in her body cavity, she may be anaesthetised before stripping to reduce the chances of injury during the process. If they are not anaesthetised, large struggling female fish aged four or five may require two people to strip them. An experienced operator should not take more than half a minute to strip a smaller trout. This is done by grasping the fish firmly with one hand just in front of its tail, while the other hand holds its head up and gently starts to squeeze the abdomen from just behind the pectoral fins. Gradually this hand moves downwards while exerting an even pressure all round the fish's underside with fingers, palm and thumb. Slowly the eggs should squirt out into a bowl, although not with too much force in case they break against its sides. To strip large fish, a rubber ring like that of a blood-pressure meter is sometimes used, ova being squeezed out by its gradual inflation.

After the female has been carefully returned to the pond, her eggs need to be quickly fertilised by a male's milt before their micropyles close up. Males are stripped in the same way, but only a little milt is needed to fertilise all the ova from one female. The milt from one male is usually enough to fertilise ova from at least three females; otherwise a male can be partially stripped more than once provided there is a break of a day or two in between.

In the early days of trout farming, eggs were squeezed from female fish directly into water in the bottom of a container. This was called the 'wet' method and stripping is still sometimes done this way. Damage to eggs during their actual extrusion is minimised, but it means both male and female being stripped and milt mixed with eggs within little more than a minute; otherwise either the eggs swell and the micropyles close up preventing sperm from entering, or the sperm, which only remain active for about a minute in water, die before they reach the eggs. Now the 'dry' method is more common in which males are usually stripped first into a container, which must be completely dry. Eggs from several females can then be added, since both semen and eggs remain alive and fertile for up to four minutes without water. Milt from more than one male should be used in case one of them is sterile and also to broaden the genetic base of the offspring. Males are usually only used for one season's breeding but females may be kept for at least three.

When newly fertilised, eggs are sometimes described as 'green' and are not damaged by careful handling. They must quickly be transferred to baskets rather like office filing trays, which are then put into incubating troughs. There the eggs remain until ready to hatch. Incubators vary considerably in design but the one basic requirement is for water to percolate continuously up through the bottom of each basket, thereby keeping the eggs permanently supplied with oxygen. Unless the water is chemically treated, baskets need to be checked as often as every two hours for signs of eggs infected with fungus. This can spread to healthy eggs at almost visible speed and infected ones must be removed immediately. Any showing signs of infertility are also removed; these are distinctive either in their early stages as being white and opaque or later, through the absence of the two black dots of the developing retina that first show in all fertile eggs half-way through their incubation.

Once they are 'eyed', usually two or three weeks before hatching, ova can be handled with minimal risk of damage and if they are to be sold, are then packed up and transported. Sometimes even eyed eggs are infertile and to identify these the whole tray is usually shocked in some way, either simply by stirring the eggs or by tipping them from one container to another. Shocking in this manner breaks the yolk sacs of infertile eggs which can then be removed with the help of a siphon, or by putting all the eggs into a saline solution in which only infertile ones float. Once sorted, eggs are then packed in insulated containers to which ice is added if delivery is likely to take several days or is to a hot destination.

The length of the incubation period depends on water temperature. Ideally this should be around 10°C, when brown trout eggs hatch in about forty days — considerably longer than those of rainbow trout which, at that temperature, do so in little over thirty. When eggs are ready to hatch, their shells break open and the alevins emerge, in some systems then dropping down through the mesh of the basket into a trough below, and in others remaining where they were hatched. Whichever design is in use, it is important that the basket is cleared of unhatched eggs, empty shells and dead fish.

Alevins remain in their hatchery until they have used up their yolk sacs; in warm water this takes less time than in cold and in the wild, varies from three to twelve weeks. At 10°C it is about five weeks before brown trout alevins have fully exhausted their in-built food supplies but again, rainbows are able to feed for themselves appreciably sooner. Once alevins have swum up, feeding begins almost immediately; and some farmers even start them off before their yolk sacs are exhausted. Once they have begun feeding, or shortly afterwards, the young fish are usually transferred to special fry tanks where water flow, temperature and chemistry are regularly checked.

These fry tanks are kept free of uneaten food and fish waste and fry remain there for at least twelve weeks if they are eventually to be transferred to unlined mud ponds. By then their cartilaginous skeleton has hardened into bone and they are no longer susceptible to attacks of 'whirling' disease (*Myxosoma cerebralis*). The parasite which causes this acutely damaging infection lives in mud and feeds off the cartilage of young fish. When this has hardened it becomes impossible for the parasite to penetrate and the fish is then effectively immune.

Having outgrown their tanks, then being about eight centimeters long, fry are graded into batches of similar size before being transferred to earth or other ponds. There they spend the rest of their time in the farm, either remaining to be fattened for the table or being transported elsewhere to stock fishing waters. The chosen few may be kept aside for breeding purposes but there are always dangers of in-breeding; to avert these, eggs or older fish from different sources are imported to vary the broodstock.

Grading is important for fish of all ages. In the company of larger fish, small ones in the crowded, artificial conditions of a farm are severely disadvantaged and will continue to want for food unless given the chance to grow among fish of their own size. To ensure equality, batches of trout are continually graded. Sometimes this is done by hand and eye, first netting out the fish before simply separating the smaller ones. Trout in raceways can be graded through a grill in the water acting as a sieve to retain bigger fish behind it, and on large farms several different mechanical methods are in use. There is no fixed rule as to the frequency of the operation. Fish are usually graded first as fry but from then on some farmers find that the advantages of grading are often offset by the stress fish suffer in the process. Grading only becomes unavoidable shortly before trout are to be sold, purchasers usually requiring a particular size either for the table or for stocking.

The density of young fish in a farm is governed by the size of the pond or tank and the oxygen supply in the water. Oxygen content depends upon temperature, flow and whether artificial aeration machines are in use. Generally, larger fish can be stocked more densely than smaller ones which both metabolise and grow more quickly and require far more oxygen per unit of weight. In optimum conditions forty kilograms of fish can be kept in one cubic meter of fully oxygen-saturated water and this figure may be doubled by using artificial aerators. If oxygen levels fall dangerously low they can be boosted with the help of cylinders of compressed oxygen, released through special valves into the water, but this can only be regarded as an emergency measure.

Trout transferred from their fry tanks to larger ponds are often called 'growers' and the aim of the fish farmer must then be to maximise their growth at minimum cost. This must be achieved through diet. In the wild, young fry which have just begun feeding can take only the smallest morsels of food, most commonly midge larvae. Under artificial conditions fry are usually fed tiny crumbs of a pellet mixture, high in protein content and also particularly palatable so as to encourage them to take food whenever it is offered. Fry must be fed small quantities frequently, as often as fifteen times a day, which usually means using automatic feeders. As they grow older and metabolise more slowly, the need for frequent feeding decreases; bigger fish can be given more food less often until they may only need feeding twice daily. If water temperature nears the upper limits for trout survival, rations should be cut drastically as there may be insufficient oxygen to fuel both digestion and respiration. In extreme cases food supplies are cut off altogether.

Larger trout require less protein and the composition of most artificial foods reflects this. Small quantities of vegetable protein are often added to make up the total protein content. About fifteen per cent of diet should comprise digestible carbohydrates and fats. Minerals are an important additive to fish foods, especially if the water is naturally deficient, and certain vitamins are also essential. Towards the end of their lives, trout being farmed for the table are usually fed crab shells, shrimp meal or krill which all contain carotene to colour their flesh pink; or they may be given the synthetic pigments astaxanthin or canthaxanthin which have the same effect.

Food is usually made up into pellet form and fed to trout either manually or, more often, by a variety of mechanical devices or sometimes a combination of the two. Over-reliance on automatic feeding tends to discourage the farmer from keeping a close personal watch on the condition of his fish. In Denmark, where the sea is never far away, a system of 'wet' feeding has been developed to make good use of the large numbers of fish, too small for human consumption, that are netted by boats out to catch other species. Whiting *(Micromesistius merlangus)* and sand eels in particular, as well as waste from fish processing plants, are delivered fresh to trout farms where their low cost goes some way towards offsetting the considerable difficulties of storage.

The amount of food required to promote a specific weight gain depends on the type of food, water temperature and the age of the fish. Young fry usually grow better on any given quantity of food than older fish; in fact their conversion ratio may even be less than 1:1 meaning that, as a result of water intake, their weight gain is more than the weight of their dried food. In earth ponds, where wastage is greater than in concrete or corrugated iron tanks, a dry food conversion ratio of 2:1 is normal. With a wet natural food diet the high percentage of water in fish flesh might push the figure as high as 5:1, closer to the average conversion ratio of trout in the wild. There, under less hospitable conditions, the basic maintenance requirement to sustain fish in their existing condition is usually much higher, averaging around 7:1.

Farmed trout are selectively bred to produce fish which grow quickly and show a range of other qualities appropriate either to fish reared for eating or stocking. The quickest-growing fish, which are usually also the best converters of food, may be kept as brood stock and, in order to spread hatching over as long a period as possible, this stock usually comprises some fish that mature early in the year and others that do so later. Disease resistance is another important consideration and if trout are being bred to stock running waters, fast growth may be less important than the strength to withstand the pressures of a natural life beyond the benign confines of the trout farm.

But modern reproductive techniques have now advanced far beyond the relative simplicity of selective breeding. Some years ago trout farmers and fishery biologists began to appreciate the potential benefits to be derived from being able to produce large numbers of either exclusively female, or sterile trout. In a hatchery, milt from one male fish can fertilise the eggs of several females so the energy expended by surplus males in the development of their reproductive organs is largely wasted. If this energy is channelled into the continuation of normal body growth, trout can go on improving in condition throughout the year. Further, sterile fish of either sex whose reproductive organs never develop, have far greater potential for growth and longevity and are therefore more suitable for many fisheries, especially those without any natural breeding facilities where attempts at reproduction are wasted. And perhaps most important of all for the future of the species, sterile trout introduced into waters where there are already wild fish cannot make unwanted contributions to the gene pool of the indigenous stock.

The result of much scientific research and practical experimentation culminated in the perfection of techniques both to alter the sex of trout and manipulate their chromosome composition. Until recently these practices would have sounded like excerpts from futuristic fiction, yet now they are commonplace in hatcheries throughout Europe.

The sex of trout, like that of humans, is governed by their chromosomes, of which those responsible for sex determination are termed X and Y. Brown trout have forty pairs of chromosomes (their haploid number). During the normal process of cell division, the chromosome composition of each new cell is identical to that of each other cell but this is not the case when sex cells divide; then the number of chromosomes must halve; otherwise, when a sperm fused with an egg the resulting cells would have double their quota. All female body cells carry two X chromosomes so when ovarian cells divide, each resulting cell has only one X chromosome. All cells in the body of a male trout have one X and one Y chromosome so when sperm cells split into two, one has an X and another a Y. Then, when sperms meet eggs, equal numbers of fertilised eggs end up with the female XX combination as with the male XY.

Sex chromosomes signal the production of specific sex hormones so that where the Y chromosome is present a preponderance of the male hormone, testosterone, is produced. However, the balance in the production of different hormones is extremely delicate since trout of each sex also produce small amounts of the other sex's principal hormone. If this delicate equilibrium is disturbed it may result, as with humans, in an upset of the fish's sexuality. By giving female fry doses of testosterone for over two months from the moment they begin to feed, it is now possible to transform them into functional males without altering their XX chromosome identity. When they are then old enough to breed, these masculinised females can successfully fertilise normal female fish but, because they contribute only X chromosomes, all their offspring will be female. To compound this bizarre practice, in order to extract their milt these fish have to be killed first, as they appear to develop imperfect sperm ducts. In the same way, all-female stock can be directly produced by feeding fry with female hormones but this may eventually mean hormonally treated fish being offered for sale which is often illegal as well as offensive to consumers. So there are now fish hatcheries where all the fish are female and all that is required to produce the next generation, which itself is exclusively female, is a supply of male hormones to generate some sperm.

The abnormality of this manipulation of the reproductive process has been taken one step further through the development of a practice called triploidy to produce sterile females whose reproductive organs never develop.

Although females lose less condition than males during the development of their reproductive organs, spawning still sets their normal growth rates back considerably. So, if their efforts to spawn are completely wasteful, the resources otherwise expended in ova development are much more effectively exploited by being diverted to growth. Spawning also depresses fish's appetites and avoiding it helps them to grow much faster.

Triploidy is a method of providing a trout with three instead of two sets of chromosomes. In the course of normal fertilisation, one set of chromosomes from the egg combines with another set from the sperm to give the full diploid number for the particular species — eighty for brown and sixty for rainbow trout. During the first stages of fertilisation, the egg is actually still in the diploid state; only after nearly an hour does the female's chromosomal contribution split to the haploid number which, when added to those from the male, make up the full diploid number in the offspring. During the split, the chromosomes not contributed by the female to the developing ova, are lost. To induce triploidy, this split is prevented so that successfully fertilised eggs contain two sets of chromosomes from the female and one from the male — a triploid rather than diploid number. As the sperm has been provided by masculinised females, the fish now have XXX sex chromosomes. This means they are both female and sterile.

In order to suppress the natural split in the diploid number, eggs are shocked shortly after they have been fertilised, usually by means of a sudden increase in temperature from the average 10°C up to 28°C; this is then maintained for ten minutes before the eggs are allowed to cool. Hydrostatic pressure can also be used to suppress chromosome division and thus induce triploidy. As eggs are themselves largely made up of water they can withstand considerable pressure without rupturing; 630 kilograms per square centimeter applied for five minutes appears to give as good results as those achieved by heat treatment.

It is just as easy to produce male triploid trout through the same procedure, but they still seem to develop testes when two years old even though these do not produce milt, and also display other characteristics associated with breeding. For these reasons they are far less suitable for stocking or rearing than females whose ovaries never develop at all. Outside normal spawning times triploids grow no better than ordinary diploid fish — if a population of all-female trout bred of masculinised females can in any way be described as 'ordinary'. However, their ability to continue growing in autumn and winter, while other trout spawn, gives them an enormous advantage over naturally bred fish, and even allows some still waters to offer year-round fishing.

Genetic engineering as a technique for improving strains of trout is still in its infancy, and perhaps mercifully so. The isolation of individual genes within any one chromosome may ultimately result in trout eggs being treated by the injection of particular genes that promote abnormally fast growth or confer resistence to certain diseases. The cloning of millions of genetically identical trout may have some future but they should be sterile and confined to rearing ponds. The release among populations of native trout, of fertile fish whose genes have been artificially manipulated, could result in the most unimaginable genetic chaos.

When introduced into the wild, sterile fish, advantaged as they are by their potential for better growth, pressurise native fish relentlessly. Feeding throughout the year, sometimes even on the eggs of these wild fish, larger stocked trout secure the best feeding stations, growing stronger and faster than their resident competitors. Often the end result is both fewer wild fish and fewer reared ones, yet stocking waters holding native populations with sterile fish may still be preferable to the introduction of breeding stock from different strains of trout. The genetic composition of each wild population of trout has evolved over thousands of years — in the case of most of Britain and other parts of northern Europe, at least since the end of the last Ice Age 10,000 years ago. Mountain ranges and other natural geographical barriers which have kept different stocks of trout apart, have also served to keep these stocks reproductively isolated from one another. Where mankind has never adulterated these pristine populations, this isolation has caused each separate one to evolve distinct characteristics particularly suited to their specific environment (Chapter Three). Trout may breed for the first time after their third summer, but more often not until a year later and a generation of trout might span four years, compared to about thirty years for humans and two weeks for fruit flies. Evolutionary change marches to the slowest of tunes but for all this, 250 generations in a thousand years and ten times that many since the end of the last Ice Age, give the processes of natural selection time at least to show the drift of their influence.

Trout bred under hatchery conditions, for whatever purpose, are artificially selected for different strengths than those required for life in the wild. Fast growth on a concentrated diet, resistance to diseases more prevalent under unnatural conditions, a tendency to feed throughout the year and aesthetically pleasing colouration, are all traits fish farmers promote in the course of selecting parent stock for the production of further generations. Yet such traits may not encourage survival under natural, more oppressive conditions, and by introducing genetically distant fish where there are already native trout, the gene pool which confers such advantages on the existing stock is dissipated by the addition of unwelcome genes from hatchery-bred fish. It may well be argued that in the course of future generations, many of these alien genes, unsuitable as they are to help trout bred in the wild to survive, will eventually be suppressed by more favourable ones and the gene pool will slowly revert to its original state. This may indeed prove to be true but each stocking represents a dangerous trial with the ever-present possibility of it turning out to have been an irreversible error.

The genetic make-up of each reproductively isolated population of brown trout differs to a greater or lesser extent from that of neighbouring populations, and geographical proximity is no certain indicator of genetic proximity. What is certain is that, given time and environmental stability, many of these populations would eventually differ so much from others that they might even come to be regarded as separate species. Today the extinction of any species is rightly regarded as ecologically calamitous, yet is the extinction of a potential species not equally so? For the introduction of large numbers of fertile non-native trout amongst a population of indigenous fish is as likely a method of exterminating a potential species as the comprehensive destruction of all its members.

Nevertheless, fishing pressure is often such that replacement of native trout stocks by natural breeding cannot match the expectations of fishermen in terms of the numbers of fish they want to keep. At present, throughout much of the trout's original range, there are too many fishermen casting for too few fish (although in the highlands and islands of Scotland it is often the other way round). In such cases, stocking may be one of the ways of bringing catches up to expectations. Where there are already native trout in the water to be stocked, if at all possible reared fish derived from that native population should be used to supplement it rather than importing an alien strain of trout. If this cannot be done, stock fish are theoretically best taken from another river similar in character, where natural selection may already have equipped them for life in an environment like their new one. If both these alternatives fail, there may be no alternative but to bring in hatchery-bred fish from elsewhere.

In all events, stocking must be used as a policy of last resort and if it is deemed essential, for whatever reason, all other ways of increasing natural stocks of fish should have been exhausted. Perhaps most obviously, efforts can be made to control competitors and predators. It is difficult to justify the total eradication of a fish from a particular stretch of water, ostensibly to improve the sport of mankind. Indeed, both the water and those who fish it would be the poorer for any decrease in its diversity of species. However, any reduction in numbers of grayling, chub, dace and roach in the warmer downstream reaches of trout rivers and of perch in large still waters, lessens some competition for trout food, although their different breeding season ensures that these species do not compete with trout for spawning territory. Control of predators, particularly pike, also enhances trout stocks and is soon likely to bring apparent benefits.

More food means better growth and any measure that increases the population of invertebrates will directly benefit the fish that prey upon them. Detailed descriptions of fishery management are beyond the scope of this book but there are many different ways of encouraging insects and other food animals to breed successfully. The introduction of new species which have never frequented a particular water is unlikely to be successful in the long run; if it were, then natural forces would almost certainly have induced their presence long before. This is especially true of free-flying insects but less so of animals like shrimps and snails which find it difficult to expand their range naturally. These a helping human hand may introduce successfully to a fresh environment, perhaps a newly created reservoir or otherwise a remote loch which had previously proved beyond their reach.

Generally more fruitful is likely to be the improvement of the aquatic habitat to increase its production of food. This may be done by directly encouraging plant life which in turn will support more invertebrates or through the creation of better breeding facilities for them by using devices like fly boards. Adding limestone or phosphates and nitrates to the water may boost vegetation and provide calcium for the shells of any molluscs and crustaceans already there. The only difficulty with this approach is that unless fertilisation is regularly repeated its benefits quickly wear off and the water soon reverts to is original impoverished state.

Trout can also be encouraged to grow and breed by improving their physical habitat. Removing surplus underwater vegetation where growth is too prolific and providing better shelter and more oxygen by constructing pools and small waterfalls, all help to do this. The current may be diverted to shift silt from the river bed or to conserve the banks which can be supported by planting shrubs and trees to give limited shade over the best lies. Most important is to encourage spawning by the provision and maintenance of good gravelly redds; this will help to ensure natural regeneration of trout stocks although there is always a danger of over-population with small fish if breeding facilities are too good.

If after improvements to the trout's natural habitat the expectations of fishermen are still unfulfilled, it may be worth trying to lower those expectations by imposing bag or size limits on numbers of fish caught or kept. Longer close seasons, access to the water for limited numbers of fishermen or only on certain days, and restrictions on fishing methods are other means of controlling the depletion of natural stocks and are mentioned later. Theoretically these all help to reduce the number of fish taken from the water, thereby saving more for the fishermen that follow. However, either in conjunction with other measures or because these have no noticeable effect, there are times when stocking may be the only way of satisfying the demands imposed upon a particular water. The questions which then remain to be answered are what kind, what size, how many and when?

The choice of species invariably narrows down to either brown or rainbow trout. Fish breeders have experimented with almost all possible crosses between brown and rainbow trout and brook and lake charr in the hope of producing hybrids which combine the best characteristics of both parent species. Tiger, zebra and cheetah trout, brownbows, sunbeams, splakes and more have all emerged from experimental interbreeding but only the splake (male brook charr and female lake charr) is reasonably fertile. Before the production of all-female fish or triploids, the sterility of hybrids was a point in their favour but now it is no longer, and there is therefore little advantage in breeding them.

Rainbow trout can grow almost twice as fast as brown trout which is why rainbow trout are invariably produced for the table. Their fast growth also makes them popular as stock fish but the biological price for fast growth is a short life. Where food supplies are rich and able to sustain the full growth potential of rainbow trout, they are probably a better choice for stocking than slower growing browns. When hooked, rainbows offer stronger resistance to capture and often jump spectacularly in the course of their struggles. These qualities together with their free feeding habits and tolerance of higher water temperatures make them the favoured choice for most lowland still waters although brown trout, being generally harder to catch may actually survive to grow bigger than rainbows. In upland lakes and reservoirs with poor food supplies there are often indigenous brown trout and good spawning facilities for them. The introduction of rainbow trout to such waters has little to recommend it, although rainbows are unlikely to breed and if they do, will not adulterate the gene pool of existing stocks of wild brown trout.

Running waters pose entirely different problems and rainbows are often less popular because they tend to move quickly downstream, sometimes for long distances, immediately after stocking. If there are already native browns in the water, the introduction of large ready-to-catch rainbow trout can have disastrous consequences for resident fish which often find themselves being edged out of their feeding territories and even chased round their redds by large rainbow trout hungry for brown trout eggs. Fortunately, fertile rainbow trout seldom manage to breed in European rivers, and while in England there are self-sustaining populations in the Derbyshire Wye and Blagdon reservoir near Bristol, elsewhere successful breeding is only intermittent. The demand for fishing may indeed be so intense that no matter how successful its efforts at natural regeneration, the resident brown trout population will never be large enough to satisfy the expectations of fishermen. But if this is so, ideally it is preferable in one way or another to reduce fishing pressure, even at the price of less fishing for fewer people and less revenue for the fishery owner, than continually to stock rainbow trout already large enough to keep.

Trout can be introduced into new waters at all stages of their development, from eyed ova upwards. When virgin waters without native trout are first stocked, planting out ova may be successful. This can be done either by putting fertilised eggs straight into redds excavated by hand or by using hatching boxes which are themselves put into the river wherever conditions appear suitable. These boxes are designed so as to allow fish to hatch inside them and then to swim out into the open water when they are ready to feed. If trout are already breeding in the river, the addition of extra ova seldom pays dividends and is unlikely to make any noticeable contribution to eventual numbers of mature fish. Trout lay a massive surplus of eggs and the mortality of young fry is so great that in most cases there are already far more fry than territories available for their occupation. All the same, if building up a stock of trout in this way seems appropriate, every effort should be made to obtain ova of fish from the same river system. Such fish will already have evolved those particular qualities that should help their offspring adapt readily to similar conditions. If stock has to be obtained from elsewhere, from the genetic aspect there is much to recommend planting ova or unfed fry upon which the forces of natural selection will have maximum time to work before the few survivors reach maturity.

Fry can be stocked either before or after they have begun feeding. The introduction of unfed fry still dependent on their yolk sacs, and which have not yet felt the urge to establish their own feeding territories, is beset by the same problems as affect the planting of ova; it is therefore only fitting for streams that are troutless or almost so. As most wild trout are hatched in running water, very young fry are unlikely to thrive if introduced straight into still waters where they must immediately forage for all their food. They are also sometimes reluctant to leave the apparent protection of their shoal which makes them easier prey for predators.

Older, larger parr can contend better with the pressures of life in the wild but still need to be planted out with care and, particularly in running water, well spaced throughout the area to be stocked. They can be conveniently introduced in this way with the help of a simple garden watering can. If young fish are all introduced into one short length of river, there will be nowhere near enough feeding territories to support them and as any tendency to migrate even short distances has yet to take hold, most will die. It is also important to place them in parts of the river with suitable backwaters and calm places along the edge of the current. Unless they can be evenly spaced in this way, stocking with young fish is likely to be needlessly wasteful and is best avoided in favour of the introduction of older fish that are at least able to distribute themselves around a wide area.

Larger trout obviously stand a better chance of survival but are harder to transport and more expensive. Unless they are ready to catch fish still need to survive at least until they are large enough to keep; how long this is depends upon their size at stocking and the size limit of the fishery. During that period they are inevitably at risk from predators or from being caught before they are keepable and injured in the process. Where fishing pressure is relatively light, or where transport difficulties militate against the purchase of larger fish, stocking with trout below keepable size may be preferable. Many fishermen also gain much greater aesthetic satisfaction from catching trout that have been introduced into the water at a comparatively young stage in their lives and which are largely the product of their environment, than from the capture of fish only a few days out of their rearing ponds. In heavily fished waters however, especially those where there are no breeding facilities, the introduction of keepable trout under a 'put and take' system has, perhaps sadly, most to recommend it.

The amount of trout flesh that any water can sustain permanently in good condition, either by way of many small fish or fewer larger ones or a combination of all sizes, is known as its 'carrying capacity' (Chapter Four). If in natural circumstances this is exceeded, fish deteriorate in condition and continue to die or be killed until the optimum balance is regained. Fishermen are however, as a group, highly successful predators and by quickly taking out a proportion of the fish soon after they are put in, but before their condition has begun to deteriorate, stockings far in excess of the water's natural carrying capacity are possible. The introduction of catchable fish at regular intervals throughout the fishing season, rather than just once at the beginning, allows carrying capacity to be repeatedly exceeded on the assumption that excess fish will soon be removed. Although disconcertingly unnatural, this is by far the best strategy for heavily fished waters and may even be combined with a degree of supplemental feeding, especially in concrete-lined reservoirs with little or no aquatic vegetation to sustain a good stock of invertebrates.

If there is to be a single annual stocking at the start of the fishing season, which exceeds the carrying capacity of the water, the excess should soon be taken out to allow the remaining fish at least to maintain their existing condition. In heavily fished waters this usually means good fishing during the weeks immediately after stocking and comparatively poor sport for the rest of the season. So, if the fish remaining after the excess have been caught are to satisfy the expectations of fishermen for the rest of the season, either numbers of fishermen or their expectations must somehow be curtailed.

It is impossible to generalise on the carrying capacity of running waters, such is their variety. The width of a river or stream is the most important factor, but depth, chemical composition and food supplies are also critical. The quantity of fish which any particular stretch of water can support is best ascertained by trial and error backed up by detailed records of numbers and sizes of fish caught.

The carrying capacity of an area of still water is easier to establish although it varies greatly with depth and food availability. Rich lowland lakes and reservoirs may be able to sustain up to 100 kilograms of trout flesh per hectare, representing perhaps 200 keepable fish. In acidic highland lochs the figure may be less than a quarter of this and with such a low carrying capacity, the decision to stock should not be taken lightly. In upland waters there are also usually more feeder streams and trout may be able to breed successfully enough to keep their numbers up to fishermen's expectations. Often these waters are remoter and less fished than lowland ones in more populated areas and this may actually lead to their becoming over-populated with small fish. In such cases, stocking with larger fish is wrong and either plenty of these small trout should be fished out or, often more effective, access to breeding areas can be restricted to reduce natural regeneration. As a general rule, whatever the water and however heavily fished it may be, fishing is likely to be poor if the trout population falls below forty or fifty fish per hectare.

The annual catch from a fishery may be limited in a number of ways including instituting size or bag limits. Size limits impose their own problems, particularly with the need to put back undersized fish. Opinions still differ over the degree of harm suffered by fish returned to the water without any visible injury, and even over the best way to handle them in the process. Wet hands do less damage to the protective layer of mucus, secreted by glands in the epidermis, but make the fish more difficult to hold; dry hands have the opposite effect and are often recommended by fishing authorities in America. In any case, if there are undersized trout in a fishery that operates a size limit, there is much to be said for making the use of barbless hooks compulsory: surprisingly few fish are lost before landing, through lack of a barb.

The imposition of appropriate bag limits is a question of juggling fishing pressure with fish stocks. If limits are too high, too many fish may be taken early in the period between stockings, to the detriment of later fishermen. If too low, they may deter fishermen from visiting the fishery at all. Another difficulty with the imposition of bag restrictions is that catching the limit figure tends to become regarded as a contractual right following from the purchase of a ticket, rather than as a rare privilege.

The ultimate in bag limitation is to impose a complete 'catch and release' policy whereby all fish caught are returned to the water. For this to succeed the use of barbless hooks is essential but one disadvantage is that it may encourage fishermen to catch too many fish, confident that they can release any excess relatively unharmed. The idea is popular on many American rivers where fishing pressure is intense, and generally fish seem to recover remarkably quickly from the trauma of capture. Waters in Europe seldom operate a catch and release policy but may soon need to if more and more fishermen persist in their pursuit of fewer and fewer trout. A variation on this theme is to charge fishermen an additional fee for any trout they keep and to hold the charge for actual fishing down to a reasonable level.

As well as, or instead of, fixing size or bag limits, restrictions can be imposed on the actual amount of fishing allowed on the water. These can take the form of controlling numbers of fishermen with access to it, perhaps by establishing a private club with restricted membership, or by imposing a limit on the number of tickets issued on any given day or week. Sometimes fishing may be stopped completely to rest the water and allow native stocks to regenerate and grow.

Numbers of trout killed in any stretch of water may also be limited by the imposition of closed seasons. Throughout their native range there are distinct seasons of the year and fishing is prohibited to protect trout while they are breeding and thereby to secure replacement stock for future years. In any case, after spawning trout are weak and flaccid and of little use to fishermen until spring brings an improvement in their condition. On the equator, where there are no definite seasons, fishing is never usually closed altogether. There, trout tend to breed during the rains when the dirty, turbulent water affords them protection from predators and also makes fishing futile.

Another way to control the catch is to regulate fishing methods, usually by confining fishermen to the use of less successful baits, artificial or not, thought to give the fish a greater chance of evading capture and therefore perhaps to be 'more sporting'. This is a concept so subjective as to be almost indefinable and seems ill at ease with the fisherman's eternal quest for more successful flies and lures. Trout fishing regulations often ban all baits or lures other than artificial flies and on chalk streams it may be 'dry fly only' with even the use of nymphs disallowed. Perhaps such restrictions do make catching fish harder and therefore their pursuit more sporting. Even so, the motives for these restrictions transcend any perverse altruistic wish to help fish survive by making their capture more difficult: making them harder to catch today simply ensures that there are still plenty for the fishermen of tomorrow and spreads the total take from the fishery more evenly throughout the season.

The best time to put trout into a water depends on frequency of stocking and size of fish. Annual stockings of keepable fish are usually made either a month or so before, or to coincide with the start of the fishing season. In a short stretch of river early stockings may give fish the undesirable opportunity to move beyond its boundaries. Nevertheless, early stocking does give trout time to recover from the initial stresses of their introduction to natural conditions and to become reasonably acclimatised to their new environment, before the predatory attentions of mankind are focused upon them. If there is a natural stock of trout it may be appropriate to introduce fish in late April or May when the previous year's spawners have fully recovered and are strong enough to compete with the new arrivals. Sometimes small trout are even put in at the end of the season when, apart from other considerations, they are usually cheaper. In September and October there is still plenty of natural food about and if not yet old enough to breed, the small newcomers can continue growing while the energies of older residents are concentrated on spawning.

Newly stocked fish that until their introduction were regularly supplied with an artificial diet, must make swift and significant changes to their feeding habits and seem well able to do so. Almost immediately after stocking, trout may be seen feeding but during these first few days still usually lose condition. This may indicate that they take time to learn to take full advantage of the natural food supply. Alternatively, the initial stresses of the change from an artificial to a wild environment may exert a greater toll on the fish's resources than is made up for by normal feeding. However, within a week of stocking, artificially bred trout are usually feeding as effectively as their native neighbours. The ease with which trout adjust to new surroundings and their wide-ranging diets are the main reasons for the success with which they have been spread around the world (Chapter Ten). The behaviour of hatchery-reared brown trout, newly introduced to natural habitats, is further evidence of the remarkable adaptability of the species.

Fry remain close to where they were stocked until old enough to leave their feeding territories. Bigger trout may quickly move long distances. In still waters this allows large numbers of fish to be stocked in one place in the knowledge that they will soon spread evenly over a wide area. Yet in streams and rivers these migratory tendencies are an important consideration in deciding where and when to stock.

The inclinations of rainbow trout to move away from where they were introduced are stronger than those of brown trout and the local migrations of brook charr are so pronounced that, whatever their other merits, they are not really a viable fish with which to stock running waters. The longer trout spend in the river, the more likely they are to move away from their stocking point. If this is in a small stream where water levels are low and food supplies poor, movement is most likely to be downstream. Low water temperatures below about 8°C at the time of stocking, may also encourage a gradual drift downstream in search of warmer water. But, if the water quality, temperature and food supply of their new environment are favourable, and if there is enough space for most of them to find good feeding stations, hatchery-bred brown trout are unlikely to stray more than two or three kilometers during their first year. Individual trout may move long distances and while in the absence of any more direct influences their general direction of migration is more often downstream, this is certainly not always so.

Stocking streams, rivers, ponds and lakes with brown trout reared specifically for the purpose is a practice which has endured for at least 130 years. Now to supplement existing farmed stocks, eyed trout ova are freely despatched by air freight from one country to another, but the ease with which they travel is not without its dangers. During long sea journeys to distant countries diseased eggs died *en route*, leaving those alive on arrival free from infection. Now disease accompanies eggs to their destination with potentially disastrous consequences for importers' existing stocks. To stagger breeding programmes, summer hatching ova are imported to Europe from Tasmania and South Africa and even for stocks of normal winter-hatching fish, Britain continues to rely heavily on Denmark. So thoroughly levelled are the genetic identities of many hatchery stocks that there is every chance of creating one amorphous, nondescript breed of trout fit for nothing but the table. Boosted by the enthusiasms and expectations of fishermen which fishery owners are only too happy to exploit for their own commercial ends, stocking is now more prevalent than ever. Hundreds of races, forms, strains, varieties and perhaps even sub-species of brown trout may have disappeared through the indiscriminate introduction of hatchery-bred fish. Yet, along with the burgeoning numbers of fishermen seems to be emerging a far greater general awareness of the complexity of Nature's patterns and the processes of evolution. From this awareness may develop a sense of responsibility to future generations of fishermen and naturalists, for the preservation of the genetic identity of existing stocks of wild fish. Already there are indications that the advantages of restocking with reared offspring of native trout are now more fully appreciated. Nevertheless, fishing pressures are such that fishermen are seeking ever remoter streams and lakes in pursuit of their pleasures and, as numbers of native trout are depleted, the temptation to respond by random stocking often proves irresistible.

(*Above*) Sea trout jumping up the falls in Glen Almond, Scotland (*Ardea*). (*Below*) A fish pass to help migrating fish up a weir on the River Kent in Kendal, Cumbria. (*I.F.E.*)

Simple earth ponds on a trout farm in Swaledale, North Yorkshire (*above*) and raceways on a Norfolk trout farm (*below*). (*Author*)

A trout farm in Denmark (*above*) and one of the spectacularly-coloured brown trout it produces (*below*). (*Hans Hansen*)

Beyond their native range (*above*) the Hunter River in New South Wales (*Christine Osborne*) and the Chania River in Kenya's Aberdare Mountains (*below*). (*Author*)

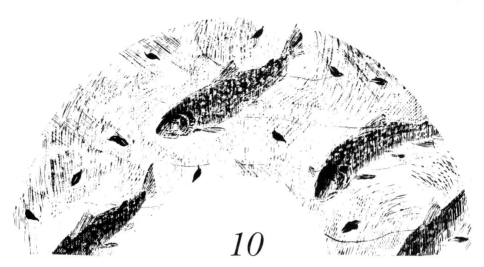

# 10
# *Beyond their Native Range*

A modern map of the brown trout's range shows it established on every continent except Antarctica and more widely distributed than any other species of freshwater fish except rainbow trout. This distribution of both species, so far beyond the geographical limits imposed upon them by Nature, is the direct result of the migration of Europeans beyond their own natural boundaries. For many of these early colonists, the traumas of their translocation were considerably alleviated by attempts to duplicate in their new country the ambience of the one left behind. One significant aspect of this process was the urge to indulge in long-established recreations, so far as new locales allowed. Settlers relied heavily on myriad imports from their country of birth and if trout fishing was impossible because there were no trout, only the impracticability of transporting them could prevent their eventual introduction.

Given the British passion for fishing, it was inevitable that the first efforts to establish trout beyond their natural range would begin in a British colony. In Australia and New Zealand, many of the rivers were almost devoid of indigenous fish, or at least hosted nothing of fishable size, and seemed ripe for the introduction of trout or salmon if this was possible. Typical of the longings experienced by colonial administrators starved of their accustomed leisure activities were those expressed by J.C. Bidwell who in 1852, when Commissioner of Crown Lands for New South Wales, wrote to Sir W. Denison, Governor of Van Diemen's Land (Tasmania) that

> 'When formerly travelling in New Zealand and admiring its noble rivers, I could not help lamenting that they should be so scantily stocked with fish and I was gradually led to speculate on the best means of supplying the deficiency by the introduction of the Salmon and other valuable fish from the rivers of Europe.'

As Mr. Bidwell and many of his fellow settlers and administrators continued to lament the lack of any good fishing in Australia, the country was becoming touched by a near mania for the importation of exotic fauna and flora from Britain and elsewhere. Camels, rabbits, blackbirds, sparrows, starlings and goldfish were all soon firmly established. The Acclimatisation Society of Victoria, founded in 1857 to 'encourage the introduction of foreign animals and to domesticate the indigenous mammals and birds of the colony', attempted to introduce nightingales while other similar societies experimented with Egyptian geese, Angora goats, moose and Californian quail. In April 1864 the editor of the *Melbourne Argus* imputed an unlikely puritanical motive to the efforts of Australian Acclimatisation Societies,

'. . . in seeking to stock this country with new and beautiful things, to add to our national wealth, to suggest new forms for our colonial industries, to provide for manly sports which will lead Australian youth to seek their recreation on the river's bank and mountain side rather than in the cafe and casino . . .'

Against this background of colonial yearnings for good trout fishing and a determination to impose foreign plants and animals on the hapless Australian landscape, it was not long before enterprising individuals began trying to surmount the difficulties impeding the introduction of brown trout into the antipodes of its natural range. To begin with the only known method of naturalising trout in countries far removed from their native habitat was to transport live fish in large freshwater tanks. In 1850, Britain's Secretary of State also wrote to the Governor of Van Diemen's Land on the subject of fish transport, to say that

'. . .the obstacle to the proposed plan has been the apparent impracticability of carrying the fish in the mode you suggested, namely in tanks placed in the poop of the convict ships. . . . under the circumstances, therefore, it has not been considered advisable to take any further steps in the matter until I shall be in possession of any additional suggestions which you may have to offer upon it.'

'Apparent impracticability' was an understatement. With the technology then in existence, sustaining the trout's basic requirements of cool fresh water, sufficient oxygen and minimal stress throughout a three-month journey by sailing ship, which also entailed an equator crossing, was impossible. Soon after the middle of the nineteenth century, fish breeders in Europe, particularly in Germany and Scotland, began to perfect the science of fertilising ova artificially, and hatching and rearing young trout. Having done so, all subsequent efforts were directed towards packing and transporting fertilised ova — physically a much simpler task, even if biologically far more complex.

At first, ova were optimistically consigned to their ocean voyage without any artificial refrigeration, hatching and dying about thirty days later — long before their transport even reached the equator. After several failures for similar reasons the early shippers realised that a way must be found to defer hatching until the eggs were safely settled at their destinations.

If maintained at a temperature of 5°C, brown trout eggs hatch about ninety days after fertilisation (Chapter Four) which was ten days longer than the journey to Australia usually took. At lower temperatures, fewer eggs hatch but the incubation period is greatly extended, so that at 3°C it may be as long as 130 days. This less successful hatching rate was a price well worth paying for even limited success and an efficient system of refrigeration was therefore crucial if trout transportation was ever to succeed.

In the middle of the nineteenth century, the only way to maintain low temperatures over long distances was by using lots of ice. If properly packed, it could easily last the length of a normal journey from England to Australia, but the technology required to pack both ova and ice was then very much in its infancy. Fertilised ova of carp, perch and tench had been successfully exported to Australia, and perch even reached there alive in an aquarium mounted on gimbals, but both eggs and adults of these species can withstand much warmer temperatures than those of trout.

The trout importation project aroused great enthusiasm, much of it generated by James Youl, a wealthy and energetic Tasmanian sheep farmer. His efforts began with three expensive failures when either the ice melted, killing the ova or they hatched prematurely. Youl's fourth attempt succeeded: on 21 January 1864 the English clipper *Norfolk*, loaded with 181 pine-wood boxes of freshly-fertilised salmon ova — but also containing 2,700 trout eggs from the rivers Itchen and Wey — sailed for Australia, arriving in Melbourne eighty-four days later. The size of large shoe boxes, each was packed with 550 ova sandwiched between layers of moss and ice, all on a bed of charcoal. The boxes were perforated and themselves surrounded by blocks of ice provided by the Lake Wenham Ice Company; this ran a thriving business cutting ice at Lake Wenham in Massachusetts and exporting it to Europe for use as a refrigerant on long sea journeys.

On arrival at Melbourne, both salmon and trout eggs were found to be generally healthy and several days off hatching. Some of the boxes, including those containing the trout ova, were quickly transshipped to Hobart in Tasmania, and thence to a hatchery twenty-five miles from the town. The first alevin emerged on 4 May and after hatching was over it became apparent that ten per cent of the original consignment had survived the journey. Nearly half of these were to die over the next two years and at the beginning of 1866 most of the survivors were released into the River Plenty where they began to breed in the wild.

The breeding stock kept back in the rearing ponds was soon augmented from England by a further consignment comprising 15,000 sea trout eggs from the river Tweed and 500 brown trout eggs from Worcestershire, as well as a large quantity of salmon ova. The shipment was carried by the clipper *Lincolnshire* which sailed on 8 February 1866. The mortality rate was again disappointingly high: no brown trout eggs survived but over 500 sea trout eventually hatched out successfully.

By the middle of 1866, hen fish from the first consignment were being successfully stripped and their eggs artificially fertilised, although this eventually proved less successful than allowing fish to breed in specially designed ponds with gravel beds, and then collecting up the naturally fertilised ova.

Fry from the breeding stock founded by these first two shipments to Tasmania were soon introduced to the Australian mainland, first into rivers in Victoria. Today they are firmly established both there, in New South Wales and in western Australia. Efforts were also made to establish populations elsewhere, particularly in South Australia, but in these lower-lying areas, as in so many other marginally suitable parts of the world, the freer-feeding rainbow trout with its tolerance of slightly warmer waters eventually thrived much better.

From the Tasmanian stock were also bred the first brown trout to reach New Zealand where the Canterbury Acclimatisation Society imported 800 ova in 1867. They derived from the initial Itchen/Wey shipment to Tasmania but only three eggs hatched, from which two fish survived to maturity. Meanwhile, other acclimatisation societies in New Zealand were busy wreaking irreparable havoc on the native fauna of their adopted country (which had no indigenous mammals except bats) and the following year those in Southland, Canterbury, Nelson and Otago all successfully imported ova from Tasmania. Most of the imports after 1870 were descended from the Tweed sea trout stock and not until 1883 was the first consignment of trout ova successfully brought in direct from England. That same year — and before they had reached Australia — rainbow trout ova were also imported, and by the turn of the century naturalised populations of both species of trout were firmly established in almost every suitable location in both North and South Islands of New Zealand. Average temperatures being higher in the North Island, rainbows thrived better there than the brown trout which still predominate throughout most of South Island.

As the indefatigable Youl strove to establish trout in Tasmania, Francis Day, author of the splendid volume, *British and Irish Salmonidae*, was all set to exploit the lack of indigenous fish in the highlands above Madras in India:

> 'When at Ootacamund on the Neilgherry Hills in the Madras Presidency in 1863, I observed a deficiency of fish in the waters of the upper plateau . . . I proposed to the Governor of Madras attempting to introduce fresh-water trout from England by means of their eggs.'

Day was unsuccessful, hampered mainly by the difficulty of refrigerating the ova during the long overland journey that unavoidably preceded the ascent to cooler, higher ground. A second attempt in 1868 resulted in the tenuous foundation of a breeding population but this success was short-lived. Twenty years later, with the benefit of considerably improved overland refrigeration, a shipment of European brown trout ova was hatched successfully in the colder waters of Kashmir. These trout readily established themselves, providing the breeding stock for subsequent propagation throughout much of northern India. Towards the end of the nineteenth century efforts were also made to introduce brown trout into the highlands of Ceylon but, once mature, they only bred there in exceptionally cold years and were gradually replaced by rainbow trout which reproduced freely and continue to do so.

Spurred by the success of the Tasmanian importations, South African settlers first tried to introduce trout in 1875. All the ova in the first shipment were dead on arrival and it was not until 1890 that John Parker successfully hatched a consignment in Natal, there releasing fry into three separate streams flowing eastwards off the

Drakensberg mountains. Parker's first attempt failed for the same reason as Day's: by the end of a thirty mile journey from the nearest railway station in a horse-drawn cart, either the eggs had died or, if they had hatched, the alevins had failed to survive. To surmount the difficulty of keeping the ova cold enough on their overland journey, Parker eventually established his hatchery beside a main railway line. This ensured not only refrigerated transport right to the hatchery but also daily deliveries of ice until the eggs hatched.

Elsewhere in South Africa, the government of Cape Province agreed to allot funds for the importation of both trout and a professional aquaculturist to supervise the development of hatcheries and breeding. One, Ernest Latour, established the infrastructure for the successful breeding of brown trout but it was left to his successor John Scott, in 1895, to strip the first home-bred fish of their ova and milt. Scott then devised a system of sending fertilised eggs through the post which soon spread trout throughout Cape Province and eventually to suitable areas in the Orange Free State and Transvaal.

Southern Africa was the first part of the Dark Continent to experience the dubious benefits of European colonisation, and with lower average temperatures than more northerly latitudes was patently suitable for the introduction of trout. Further north, Europeans were slower to establish a presence and suitable habitats for the introduction of trout only sparsely dotted the map. However, there is permanent equatorial snow on the 6000 meter summit of Tanzania's Mount Kilimanjaro and there are several isolated mountain ranges reaching well over half that height. The topographical upheavals which formed the Great Rift Valley in eastern Africa created most of these areas of high ground from which eventually flowed streams quite cool enough for trout.

Rhodesia, Nyasaland and Basutoland (Zimbabwe, Malawi and Lesotho) all imported trout from South African hatcheries between 1900 and 1930. East Africa relied at first on direct imports from England. In 1904 Lord Delamere wrote to Ewart Grogan to say that what Kenya's settlers wanted was wheat in their fields and trout in their rivers and that he, Delamere, would see to the wheat if Grogan would organise the trout. True to his word and spurred by an almost altruistic wish to enhance Kenya's attractions for potential settlers, Grogan brought the first consignment of brown and rainbow ova to East Africa the following year. Unlike early stockings elsewhere, it was planned to plant these eggs straight into a chosen stream without any prior attempt to hatch them. After unloading at the railhead the eggs were taken on horses to an altitude of 3,200 meters and placed carefully into the gravelly headwaters of the Gura river on the Aberdare mountains. There they were left to their own devices until several years later when reports of fish spawning lower down the river encouraged the first fishermen into the forest, to be rewarded with spectacular catches.

From then on, several consignments of brown and rainbow trout ova were brought to Kenya, both from England and South Africa, and a hatchery was set up on the Kinangop plateau from which to stock rivers rising in the highlands throughout East Africa. Ova of both species were sent to Uganda, and in the early 1930s to Tanganyika (Tanzania) where isolated breeding populations still survive, as they do in the Ruwenzori mountains of western Uganda. Less than thirty years ago brown trout from Kenya were also introduced into the Bale Mountains in southern Ethiopia where several rivers now have thriving naturalised stocks.

That America was not in the vanguard of attempts to import brown trout is not as surprising as it may seem. It is true that the sea journey from England was relatively short with none of the difficulties imposed by the heat of an equator crossing. In addition, the climate along much of America's east coast is very similar to northern Europe's. This meant that even at sea level many rivers were cold enough for the direct introduction of brown trout and there was no need for long hot overland journeys first. However, much of north America was already well-populated with native Salmonids. Brook charr were common in many of the continent's north-eastern rivers, and lake charr occurred throughout most of Canada. Along the Rocky mountains there were rainbow and cutthroat trout as well as five species of Pacific salmon, and this range of indigenous fish was more than enough to satisfy the needs of early settlers for both food and sport.

Perhaps inevitably, those Americans familiar with European brown trout eventually felt that sport might be improved by their introduction into local rivers. So from Germany Baron Friedrich von Behr despatched trout ova to New York in the winter of 1883 on the steamship *Werra*. The eggs hatched successfully and fry were released in Pennsylvania with no attendant publicity. Further shipments followed from Germany, and from Howietoun and Hampshire in Britain, which stocked Michigan's Pere Marquette river. Hatcheries began to spring up on the east coast, and by the turn of the century brown trout were being farmed right across America. Subsequently, there was something of a reaction against their indiscriminate introduction into waters already stocked with indigenous Salmonids. Nevertheless, only Alaska, Mississippi, Alabama, Louisiana and Texas never attempted to introduce brown trout, and today naturalised populations of this exotic species are firmly established in thirty-four of the United States of America.

Loch Leven brown trout from Howietoun were the first to reach Canada in 1884, but subsequent introductions nearly all derived from neighbouring American states. The spread of exotic trout through Canada was slow, again because the country's prolific population of indigenous Salmonids meant there was no urgent incentive to experiment with introduced species. Eventually only the Yukon, Northwest Territories and Prince Edward Island resisted the temptation to stock with brown trout, and today there are established populations in all the remaining provinces except Manitoba.

In South America the naturalisation of brown trout has been a spectacular success. Importation of English ova began in Argentina in 1904, and on hatching, fry were planted into streams in the Santa Cruz area of Patagonia. A year later German ova were shipped to Chile and from then on trout stocking slowly spread both north and south. Now nearly all suitable lakes and rivers on both sides of the Andes, from the Tropic of Capricorn down to Tierra del Fuego, have at some time been stocked with brown trout, which have since continued to breed freely.

During the Second World War, Chile sent a consignment of brown trout ova to the Falkland Islands which was augmented by importations from England when the war was over. The fry were stocked into the flat, shallow rivers of both East and West Falkland but the initial results looked disappointing. The first fish caught showed only the minimal growth that was to be expected from these barren waters with such scarce food supplies. Yet perhaps it was this dearth of nourishment that stirred the migratory instincts in some of the trout because before long large sea trout began to appear. These fish were returning to breed in fresh water after feasting out at sea on the vast shoals of krill which form the base of a food web supporting such a prolific diversity of wildlife in the cold waters of the south Atlantic. Now small resident brown trout and, at specific times of the year, large migratory sea trout are found together in many of the rivers on both Islands.

These are the most significant propagations of brown trout beyond their natural range but there are also naturalised populations as far apart as Japan, New Guinea, Peru and Pakistan. Many other more marginal countries sustain small, rather tenuous stocks but in these less perfect habitats populations may come and go, perhaps to be replaced by rainbow trout or otherwise simply disappearing through lack of enthusiasm for their preservation.

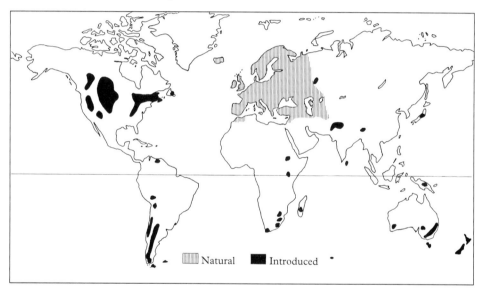

*World distribution of brown trout*

The rainbow trout's native range runs down the west coast of North America from Alaska to California and into parts of Mexico. Rainbows were first exported beyond their natural boundaries in 1874 and are now established in thirty-nine of the forty-two states of the USA to which they are not native. Their ability to breed and thrive in marginally warmer waters has resulted in their now being even more widely distributed than brown trout, with self-sustaining naturalised populations in such unlikely areas as Hawaii, Venezuela, Israel, Sudan and Madagascar.

With the exception of the Asian continent there remains little suitable habitat in the world where no attempt has been made to introduce brown trout. There are thousands of rivers and lakes in the Himalayas and in other mountain ranges of China and what was the USSR where brown trout could flourish, but difficulties of access have so far hindered attempts to introduce them. Otherwise, in almost all other suitable environments if they are not established it is because either stocking with rainbow trout has been preferred, or the presence of indigenous Salmonids has made the introduction of exotic species superfluous.

Migration to sea by some brown trout while others from the same population remain behind in fresh water is one of the most intriguing characteristics of the species. These alternative behaviour patterns are made even more mysterious by the fact that whether the ancestral stock was migratory or not appears to make only minimal difference to the habits of their offspring. Anadromy has been discussed earlier (Chapter Eight) but the behaviour of certain naturalised stocks of brown trout can often illustrate these differing life options more succinctly than any study of sea trout in their native habitat. Of course, if ova from both brown and sea trout were used in an initial stocking it would subsequently be virtually impossible to identify the precise parentage of any particular fish, as would also be the case if the origins of those original ova had become obscured. Nonetheless, introductions to Tasmania, New Zealand, North and South America and the Falkland Islands have all founded sea-going populations of brown trout, many of which are undoubtedly descended from non-migratory ancestors. Similarly, in many of the Falkland Islands rivers, non-migratory parent stock has produced both migratory and resident descendants.

By way of contrast, one related subject which bears consideration is the intriguing failure of the Atlantic salmon to establish itself anywhere outside its natural range. Because there are six species of Pacific salmon freely distributed round the northern rim of the Pacific basin, and the Atlantic salmon is widespread on both sides of the ocean from which it derives its name, efforts to introduce Atlantic salmon elsewhere have been understandably confined to the southern hemisphere, but they have all been total failures.

Early attempts to transport fish ova concentrated on salmon rather than trout. Youl's first successful shipment in 1864 contained over 100,000 salmon but only 2,700 trout eggs. However, this and every subsequent attempt to introduce salmon, both to Tasmania and alsewhere in Australia, met with complete lack of success and there is no evidence that salmon ever returned to breed once they had migrated out to sea. In 1868 the *Celestial Queen* brought 100,000 British salmon eggs to New Zealand, the first of an estimated five million to be imported during the next fifty years. These were introduced as egg, fry or parr into every conceivable type of stream, river, pond or lake, throughout North and South Island. Despite this massive effort, the only naturalised populations that established themselves were in small land-locked South Island lakes. As late as 1960 attempts were made to introduce salmon to Falkland Islands rivers, but even extensive electric fishing failed to find any evidence of salmon returning from the sea.

New Zealand also tried to introduce sockeye salmon from Canada but again only succeeded in establishing a land-locked population. Only after repeated efforts to stock Chinook (king) salmon from California's Mcleod river in the early years of this century, were salmon finally established in the Waitaki river on the east coast of South Island. These fish have spread to neighbouring rivers and constitute the only truly migratory salmon population in the southern hemisphere.

Why migratory brown trout should have established themselves so successfully while there is not a single recorded instance of their closest relative ever having returned to its stream of introduction, remains an unanswered question. There is no doubt that food supplies in the surrounding seas are more than adequate. The south Atlantic in particular is extraordinarily rich in potentially suitable food for salmon, and wherever abortive efforts have been made to establish them there are thriving populations of migratory trout making impressive use of these same food resources. Similarly, there is no suggestion of mass predation or that introduced Atlantic salmon may die through some chemical unsuitability of the sea. But without exception the fish have thrived in the fresh waters where they were introduced, migrated to sea and quite simply disappeared.

The most likely explanations for their disappearance centre round the difference between the behaviour of sea trout and salmon once they reach the sea. While sea trout tend to remain relatively close to shore, feeding opportunistically on whatever food is available, salmon in the Atlantic ocean undertake more definite and much longer migrations to distant and distinct feeding areas. And, for salmon newly introduced into southern hemisphere rivers, these migrations must be to destinations unknown and from which, mysteriously, they never return.

So, sea trout continue to flourish far outside their natural range in many parts of coastal South America and Australasia. Yet the Atlantic salmon, physiologically so similar and with an ability to navigate round its native seas in truly spectacular style, appears to become lethally disorientated when introduced elsewhere and thus remains stubbornly confined to its own ocean and the rivers which feed it.

It is axiomatic that the extraordinary success in propagating brown trout throughout so many alien environments, once the transportation difficulties had been surmounted, was a direct result of the suitability of those environments for its introduction. Where brown trout flourish, the water clearly satisfies the basic thermal and chemical requirements to sustain a breeding population (Chapter Three) and there are also suitable gravel beds on which they can spawn. In addition, the aboriginal fauna must include prey which is attractive to trout, and the environment must be free of serious potential predators as well as direct competitors for the available food. Kenya's upland rivers fulfil all the conditions necessary to sustain thriving naturalised stocks of trout (which they still do) and, being on the equator where conditions are theoretically far removed from those in the temperate climes of the trout's native range, provide an unusual example of the impact of the introduction of trout on an indigenous fauna.

If transposed onto the East African topography, the requirements of specific water temperature and oxygen content to support a thriving population of brown trout restrict the fish's range to an average lower limit of 1,800 meters. The limit varies depending upon the formation of the river bed and its gradient, both of which influence oxygen content. The altitude at which a stream originates may also affect this lower limit, as may speed and volume of water and the extent to which riparian vegetation shields the water from the sun. The colder conditions required for breeding are generally restricted to altitudes above 2,600 meters.

It is sometimes casually suggested that there are few vacant ecological niches, most natural slots having been filled during the gradual evolution of life on earth. Yet when trout were first introduced into Kenya, no indigenous fish lived in its cold upland streams, with the obvious corollary of an absence of any specialised fish-eating predators. So these first arrivals were afforded the unnatural luxury of being able to establish themselves free from both the pressures of competition from other fish and the dangers of predation by animals higher up the food chain.

Their first spawnings were so successful that over-population pressures gradually squeezed surplus fish downstream. This usually meant their being swept over a succession of high waterfalls which drop steeply through a series of faults in the rock strata. These falls constitute a quite impenetrable barrier for any fish inclined to move upstream. Even so, there is usually sufficient volume of water to carry small trout well over the lip of the fall, and a deep enough pool to absorb the impact on their reaching the bottom. Thus downstream progress from these original high-altitude stockings was only checked by the increasing unsuitability of water conditions and to a lesser extent by competition from indigenous fish already occupying the warmer lower reaches; these included a small catfish *(Amphilius grandis)* and local members of the barbel family *(Barbus tanensis)*, colloquially known as 'yellow fish'. Catfish are bottom dwellers and competed with trout for neither food nor territory but for the yellow fish the trout's arrival was disastrous. Not only did the newcomers prey on their young but mature yellow fish were often caught by fly fishermen in pursuit of trout and now they are a rarity in much of their original range.

Spotted eels *(Anguilla labiata)* may attack trout, but birds have become their main predators, especially higher up where water is clearer and fish more visible. Now trout serve to vary the diet of several different species, some of which greatly extended their range after the fish's introduction. Fish eagles *(Haliaeetus vocifer)* and long-tailed cormorants *(Phalacrocorax africanus)* eat trout and occur at altitudes over 3,000 meters along the edges of streams where they had never ranged before. The spectacular giant kingfisher *(Ceryle maxima)* has also developed a taste for trout as an addition to its original diet of mainly crabs, while hamerkops *(Scopus umbretta)* and various storks and herons all take occasional trout if they are lucky enough to find them.

Mammals are not the threat to this piscine parvenu that they may at first seem to be. The Cape clawless otter *(Aonyx capensis)* lived along the banks of many highland streams long before trout arrived. Despite this, rather than providing unexpected bounty for resident otters there is little doubt that the introduction of trout has adversely affected otter populations; this is because both trout and otters compete for the freshwater crabs (Potamonidae) which are an important item in both their diets. This particular species of otter has a broad, flat skull and exceptionally prominent molar teeth with which it can crush the hard shells of crabs and the bones of other small animals. It also eats frogs, eggs (of birds, lizards and crocodiles) and maize cobs but as this list implies, is less aquatic than other species of otter and may have difficulty in catching trout. Bones are seldom found in otter droppings although a digestive system able to cope with crab shells may render much softer fish bones unrecognisable. The species is largely nocturnal and as each pair requires a large territory numbers are hard to assess. Nevertheless it seems that the Cape clawless otter has not been able to substitute trout for crabs in its diet either in Kenya or South Africa where it also occurs.

The marsh mongoose *(Atilax paludinosus)* is a more likely predator: it is an excellent swimmer with a diet generally similar to the otter's. Also, being nocturnal and often solitary, little is known of its range and distribution. It frequents the lower reaches of trout streams, but as trout are naturally scarcer there, this mongoose's impact on their numbers is difficult to assess.

As well as supplementing birds' and animals' diets, the introduction of trout has also brought a marked change to the eating habits of the Africans through whose farm land many trout streams flow. Up until the 1950s the Kikuyu tribe never ate fish, which they regarded as water snakes. Now their habits have changed and they willingly eat trout if they can catch them with worms or grasshoppers in rivers that in their fathers' days were fishless. The Pokot of western Kenya were slower to abandon their superstitions but they too now eat trout from the streams of Mount Elgon and the Cherangani hills.

Despite the attentions of their predators, trout continue to thrive in Kenya and their adaptability is self-evident from the success with which they have been introduced throughout the world. Trout are exclusively carnivorous, but within that fundamental parameter, they consume an extraordinarily wide variety of food: it is probably this unspecialised diet which has contributed most to their successful naturalisation throughout such a broad environmental spectrum.

The freshwater crab is not native to north-western Europe and is therefore unavailable to trout in most of their natural range; however it is a very important component of the diets of trout in eastern and southern Africa. Trout take small fish wherever they are to be found and the 1940 *East African Agricultural Journal* relates that 'the remains of frogs, trout, rats and weaver birds have all been recovered from the stomachs of big trout'. Otherwise the naturalised African trout is generally insectivorous, although it takes airborne adult insects very much less than in its native rivers, preferring them in the earlier, aquatic stages of development, when they are readily available and easily caught with minimum effort. The principal orders of Ephemeroptera (mayflies), Trichoptera (caddis or sedge flies), Plecoptera (stone-flies), and Diptera (midges and other two winged flies) are all well represented throughout Africa, and their larvae, pupae and nymphs make up the greater part of the trout's food. In addition, trout eat some terrestrial insect life and ants, grasshoppers, caterpillars, bees and wasps all contribute to their nourishment.

While the trout's adaptability owes much to its catholic appetites, the scarcity of indigenous fish in many of the rivers and lakes into which it was introduced has also helped its successful propagation. The topographical upheavals during northern Europe's emergence from the ravages of the last Ice Age around 10,000 years ago, allowed migratory fish to colonise lakes and streams which now appear remote and inaccessible. However, the geological histories of other parts of the world have never afforded any fish opportunities to reach their highland waters. These have therefore remained barren and highly receptive to the artificial introduction of exotic species.

Many rivers into which trout have been successfully introduced were not devoid of fish and unfortunately the trout's success has sometimes been achieved at the expense of native species. If there was only one species of indigenous fish which had evolved in the luxury of isolation, the competitive impact of the sudden introduction of an exotic species usually proved particularly damaging. By contrast, where several species occupied a single habitat they were better equipped to face the additional competition from introduced trout. Nevertheless, wherever they established themselves trout needed space and food, both of which could usually only be secured to the detriment of native fish.

At the extreme end of the disaster scale is the New Zealand grayling *(Prototroctes oxyrhynchus)*, last recorded in 1923 and whose probable extinction may have been largely the result of competition from introduced trout. There are now only twenty-seven species of indigenous fish in New Zealand. Nearly half of these belong to the family Galaxiidae whose members are actually quite closely related to the northern hemisphere Salmonids with which they are now forced to cohabit. Seventeen of these migrate to and from the sea to feed or breed. As such, they are easy prey for brown trout lower down the rivers but as these migratory fish encounter intense predation at sea anyway, the added attentions of trout probably have little effect on their numbers. The decline of landlocked populations of otherwise migratory koaro *(Galaxias brevipinnis)* — once so common that Maoris harvested them like whitebait — coincided undeniably with the introduction of brown trout which themselves fell off in numbers and condition once they had devoured most of their prey. At least two other Galaxiid species may be forced to compete with brown trout, the giant kokopu *(G. argentus)* for food while the non-migratory dwarf galaxias *(G. divergens)* is probably excluded from much of its former range by the activities of spawning trout or their newly hatched offspring. In general though, the smaller non-migratory species have suffered less than might have been expected due to their preference for the small, densely forested streams that trout seldom reach.

Elsewhere other native species have also been affected. In the Falkland Islands, what was once the most conspicuous indigenous freshwater fish, known colloquially as zebra trout *(Aplochiton zebra)*, has disappeared from many of the rivers now stocked with brown trout. The range of the Australian grayling *(Prototroctes maraena)* is much reduced in parts of south-east Australia where naturalised trout are established, and the continued survival in Western Australia of the Swan galaxias *(G. fontanus)* is due mainly to impassable waterfalls on the Swan river which trout cannot negotiate. In South Africa local populations of various small barbel and minnows (e.g. *Barbus treurensis* and *Oreodaimon quathlambae*) have disappeared from several trout streams, and in East Africa, trout have forced indigenous yellow fish out of the upstream limits of their range.

It is in North America that the impact on indigenous fish of introducing brown trout has received most attention. There it competes directly with all the continent's native Salmonids. At first brown trout were usually introduced into waters either devoid of native Salmonids or at least only marginally suitable for them. However, in eastern America they were found to offer better sport fishing than brook charr, and their introduction was to the certain detriment of that native fish. West of the Rocky mountains, rainbow trout being generally more tolerant of a wider temperature range, there were few troutless waters suitable for the introduction of brown trout; sportsmen therefore had little to gain from introducing them into waters with established populations of freer-feeding, faster-growing rainbows.

It is sometimes difficult to dissociate the consequences to indigenous fish of the introduction of trout and of general habitat degradation by mankind. The range of the Australian grayling was already severely reduced by 1870 when trout first began to make an impact on the local fish fauna. Increased cultivation, forest destruction, damming and human pollution may all have contributed to the demise of the New Zealand grayling and certainly continue to affect numbers of other indigenous species. The native range of brook charr in eastern North America had already contracted before brown trout arrived, due in part at least to the felling of riverine vegetation by early settlers — pines for building and hemlock for curing leather; this caused the lethal warming of waters already only marginally suitable for brook charr. Yet man's impact on the Falkland Islands rivers remains negligible and the shrinking range of the indigenous zebra trout is exclusively due to competition for food and space from introduced fish.

The potential for ecological damage of importing any animal into a foreign environment is now well appreciated and the long-term consequences given far more consideration than before. Even so, on balance, it seems that the spread of trout beyond their natural range has brought — quite by accident rather than intent — comparatively few adverse consequences for indigenous faunas. That certain species of native fish have been detrimentally affected by predation or competition from imported trout is unarguable. Nevertheless, some piscivorous birds and mammals have actually extended their range in taking advantage of this exotic bounty, and human populations have benefited from an additional source of food, as well as profiting from visiting fishermen.

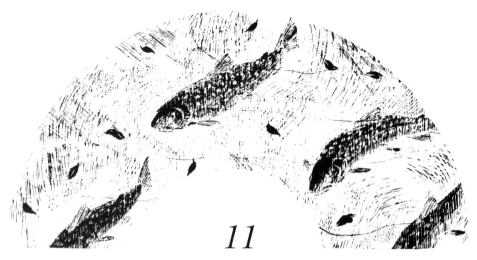

# 11
# *The Hand of Man*

The march of industrial and agricultural progress through the nineteenth and twentieth Centuries has been lamentably unmatched by strides in the development of mandatory controls over environmental abuse, and public concern has yet to emerge as a sufficiently powerful champion of Nature's welfare. It is not therefore surprising that those who fish have become the unofficial custodians of the waters where they do so. This mantle of guardianship may well be assumed unwittingly and fishermen's motives for the preservation of fresh waters are primarily selfish, but there is no interest as strong as self-interest. Conservation for its own sake is certainly becoming a more widely adopted notion throughout much of Europe; yet the concerns of vested interests continue to speak much louder than those of conservationists.

Before any altruistic sentiments took root in British minds, the fate of much virgin countryside rested in the hands of the sportsmen who hunted and shot over it. Enthusiasm for their sport was enough to ensure the effective preservation of woods, marshes, heathlands and hedges. During the last hundred years, the self-interests of many large landowners have slowly changed. Financial burdens have forced them to sell off land to farmers who cannot afford to indulge in the luxury of retaining a landscape not patterned to maximise returns from their investment. Even such landowners as retain land are compelled to increase their incomes by the use of farming techniques that often conflict directly with the welfare of a countryside that is squeezed to the point of exhaustion to yield higher returns.

Fresh waters first felt this insidious spread of commercialism and over-exploitation through a huge jump in the demand for sport fishing. Two hundred and fifty years ago, trout and salmon nourished many country people who lived close to rivers and lakes, but fishing methods were unsophisticated and there was never any real danger of exhausting fish stocks. With the advent of the Industrial Revolution, rural populations began to drift to the new towns and while fresh fish became a less important source of food, increasing numbers of wealthy industrialists began to pursue good trout fishing, especially in the Scottish highlands. A spreading network of railways, long summer holidays and the use of ponies for transport suddenly brought remote lochs and streams within reach of sportsmen to an extent that, in the context of current social organisation and dependence on motor cars, has probably lessened since. Backed by the thoughtless notion of the inexhaustability of Nature's bounty and unfettered by any concept of catch limits or other fishing restrictions, the Victorians took thousands of fish from still waters on the happy assumption that natural regeneration would almost instantly replenish depleted stocks. Only very slowly did it dawn on fishermen that the supply of trout was not boundless and could not continue indefinitely to satisfy their absurd demands. However, fishery owners were only too anxious to compensate for Nature's perceived shortcomings and lost no time in taking advantage of the concurrent development of fish farming to stock any stretches of water whose native trout stocks showed signs of becoming exhausted.

As trout fishing gained in popularity it gradually ceased to be the exclusive preserve of the wealthy. By happy coincidence the enormous demand for fishing from large urban populations has been partly satisfied by the simultaneous creation of new reservoirs to assuage the thirst of industrial and domestic Britain. But greater mobility and extra leisure time have gradually pushed increasing numbers of anglers further afield in search of their sport. Now, progressively distant waters are appeasing the demands of more and more fishermen.

Today, use of land and water is strictly regulated by central government legislation and local or water authority controls. At the same time, increasing numbers of naturalists and other caring individuals show genuine concern for the state of the countryside. But despite all this, the loudest protests over environmental abuse continue to come from those who feel their own interests threatened. Where fresh waters are concerned these are the fishermen and fishery owners who stand to lose their sport or money if, for whatever reason, fish stocks decline.

It should be no surprise that self-interest remains the strongest defender of the aquatic environment against the depredations of agricultural, industrial and domestic activities. Fishermen want to fish and for that reason are anxious to preserve their quarry. For all their adaptability, trout are highly sensitive creatures and need clean, well-oxygenated water to survive. Just as dying canaries warned miners of dangerously high methane levels in pits, so dying trout are among the first indicators of the serious pollution of their element. Trout live underwater, often unseen, and unless fished for, their well-being or that of their environment might easily pass unnoticed. So fishermen may justifiably claim a role as custodians of fresh water, no matter what their motives. And until not only governments but, more importantly, those they govern, appreciate their responsibilities fully and accept the role of environmental protectors themselves, the need for such custodians remains as critical as ever.

Because of the delicate equilibrium of the pristine natural state, any interference with Nature's order is almost inevitably harmful. Certainly trout are introduced to distant fishless lakes without upsetting natural balances, and migrating fish helped up previously impassable waterfalls by modifying the landscape. Even so, no survey of man's influences on fresh water can really read other than as a chronicle of environmental disruptions with often lethal consequences. Only after destroying or damaging are we called upon to repair, to improve, to right our wrongs, to endeavour to restore to a natural state what has become, through our influences, wholly unnatural. Until there is a dam, there is no need for a fish pass.

Throughout the second half of the twentieth century, the most insidious threat to fresh waters has come from increased acidity in the atmosphere which eventually, as acid rain, reaches the earth and thence the water. Allied to this appears to be environmental damage caused by the afforestation of much of upland Britain.

The acid deposits which ultimately contaminate fresh water are discharged during many and varied industrial and domestic activities. Sulphurous oxides from coal burning and nitrous oxide from the combustion of gas and oil pour out of chimneys and exhaust pipes, and are then sucked high up into the atmosphere. There, these pollutants may be blown hundreds of miles before climatic conditions combine to dump them on an innocent landscape, often far-removed from the scene of their creation. This deposition process may be either dry or wet. If it is dry, gas or minute particles settle on trees, buildings, water surfaces or the ground usually close to the source of emission. Wet deposition involves a further chemical change which converts oxides into nitric and sulphuric acids. These then fall with rain, hail, sleet or snow as acid rain, or less precipitously as fog or drizzle.

Once down on earth, both dry and wet depositions add to the acidity of soil and water. The extent of increased acidity is reflected in lower pH values, although other considerations may mitigate or exacerbate its otherwise harmful effects, particularly the composition of the soil and underlying rock. Limestone and chalk have a strong buffering capacity which can do much to neutralise even heavy falls of acid rain. However, if the soil is already acidic and underlaid with granite or other non-calcareous rock, heavy acid rain can be horribly dangerous. Most nitric acid is absorbed by vegetation unless it falls on bare rock and therefore quickly finds its way into a river system, but sulphuric acid rain is particularly noxious.

Trout may not be able to survive in water which is naturally highly acidic (Chapter Seven), but if they can, increased acidity affects both their ability to breed and the chances of eggs and alevins surviving. As pH levels fall still lower, the balance of trout's body fluids may become unsettled and eventually even mature fish will die. A pH of 5.0 is often considered theoretically critical, but in practice trout can tolerate much higher acidity and breed successfully in water with a pH of 4.5, adults even surviving when it falls as low as 4.0 if the water's calcium content is high. The effects of acid rain may be intensified by the action of aluminium which is often released from the soil as acidity increases. Aluminium's solubility is greatest at a pH of 5.0, and if present in any quantity its release may kill fish by clogging their gills, well before acidity falls to otherwise lethal levels. Both calcium compounds and peat in the soil can lessen the lethal effect of dissolved aluminium.

Far more harmful to all underwater life than average acidity, which may rise slowly with years of accumulating pollution, are the higher levels brought on by acid surges. Sometimes unusual weather conditions cause especially heavy falls of acid rain in a particular area. Sudden springtime thaws of several months of accumulated snow

(*Above*) Introduced brown trout thrive in this stream in Kashmir, India (*Robert Falkner*) and in New Zealand's Fiordland National Park (*below*). (*Ardea*)

(*Above*) Stake nets on the Dumfriesshire coast. (*Ardea*). (*Below*) Drainage off disturbed land. (*I.F.E.*)

(*Above*) Air pollution in the Midlands. (*Ardea*). (*Below*) Swans on the River Kennet. (*Author*)

And man will fish — sea trout fishing in Connemara, Eire. (*N. Giles*)

can be even more serious, generating spates of lethally acidic water which can seriously harm eggs or newly-hatched fry.

The acidifying effects of large-scale afforestation, particularly in northern Britain, worry both conservationists and fishermen. That coniferous forests add to the acidity in their area is now almost beyond doubt. Nevertheless, no longer are the trees thought to act as primary acidifiers through either their own natural processes or the general forestry practices associated with growing them. Over vast areas of North America, and through much of Scandinavia which has yet to be devastated by acid rain, trout thrive in streams, rivers and lakes surrounded by forests of indigenous conifers. In Scotland, many hillsides that have been newly planted with exotic conifers were once covered with Scots pines, and yet the rivers that ran down those highland glens were then almost certainly full of small trout. So the mere presence of coniferous forests does not itself seem to preclude trout from thriving in nearby streams.

Lower pH levels do certainly appear to follow large afforestation programmes but this connection is largely confined to Britain and has not been reported from other countries which are often far more densely wooded. Several different explanations have been advanced for this increased acidity, centred around the biological consequences of planting large numbers of pine trees close together on what are often very steep hillsides. Despite these, the current consensus of opinion largely exonerates the actions of trees themselves or of their dead needles, from adding acid to water. Instead it appears as if trees serve to intensify the transfer of pollution from atmosphere to soil and thence to water. Pollutants — largely sulphates — collect on leaves and branches, later to be washed off by rainstorms. Accentuating the damage is the rapid drainage from closely-planted forest with minimal undergrowth. This rushes polluting acids into burns and ditches far faster than if the rain that brought them had been able to percolate slowly through the soil of unplanted land, excess acid being gradually neutralised as it did so.

But for all their presumed innocence of the charge of direct acidification, large coniferous plantations bring other hazards to nearby waters. Trees are often planted right down to the water's edge causing banks to erode, and their broken branches dam up streams and disrupt the migrations of breeding fish. When these bankside trees mature, their canopy can darken the water below so much that plant growth and aquatic life become almost non-existent and water temperature appreciably lower. Few insects are attracted to the needles of exotic conifers, and their overhanging branches, unlike those of deciduous trees, do not act as purveyors of regular supplies of terrestrial trout food. When leaves from deciduous trees fall into the water they are quickly broken down by insect larvae and other organisms but conifer needles simply accumulate in sterile layers. Nearly all these harmful effects can be moderated by leaving a good space of open land next to all water courses running through conifer plantations, or at least planting such open spaces with a row or two of hardwood trees a short distance from the bank.

Surface water run-off is far from being an exclusive consequence of tree planting. Long before the boom in forestry, large-scale agricultural drainage of sweeping areas of upland Britain started cycles of ferocious spates followed almost immediately by drought-level lows. These precipitate rises and falls in water levels are now so familiar that they no longer seem unnatural, but assuredly they are.

In open country, the main purpose of upland drainage is to dry out the land to improve its potential for sheep farming, and in some cases to try to make marginal land more arable. That this is nothing new is well attested by the Earl of Home's writing in 1837 that falling catches of salmon in the Tweed were the result of

'the drainage of the sheep farm on the hills, the effect produced being that a little summer flood which took a fortnight to three weeks to run off previous to 1795 is now completely run out in eight hours.'

Six years after Lord Home's observations, William Scrope wrote in *Days and Nights of Salmon Fishing in the Tweed*, of the consequences of the flash floods that may be unleashed by any upland drainage system and which

'come raving down from the mountains and from the lakes, and with their united volume, raise that river to an alarming height in the space of a few hours, which then spreads over the haughs, and sometimes sweeps off corn and cattle, and levels the bridges in its irresistable course. In these awful spates, the water is too strong and turbid for fish to travel; the soil is washed away partially from the ploughed lands.'

Now, to prevent surrounding land being swamped by unnatural floods, a river is often straightened out or its bed dredged up to increase the volume of water it can carry. In this way the harmful effects of upland drainage are corrected by further damage lower down the river, bringing yet more distress to its piscine inhabitants.

Straightening and dredging rivers also increases and evens out the speed of water flow which may then scour out redds and destroy holding pools. Gone is the river's natural sequence of pools and runs, aquatic vegetation may not be able to take root and there are fewer quiet areas where trout can maintain their position without expending too much energy in doing so; even if eggs are not washed away by the current, it may be too strong for fry to hold their stations. The disappearance of water plants following the draining, straightening and dredging of rivers an Eastern England has bean blamed for the probable extinction of burbot — the only European freshwater-dwelling member of the cod family — from their last British strongholds.

Of all the repercussions on fresh waters of modern farming, the most significant is probably their enrichment through the seepage of nitrates from adjoining land. The finger of guilt has been pointed firmly at the farming community for its excessive use of nitrogenous fertilisers, but the case is still far from proven and in fact other agricultural practices are more likely to blame.

All plants require nitrogen which they convert into protein as they grow. Most cannot take nitrogen straight out of the atmosphere but instead must absorb it through their roots, growing poorly if there is a shortage in the soil, when their leaves often turn brown. Water seeping through soil leaches out nitrogen and to compensate for this farmers intersperse other crops with clover, peas or beans which can fix atmospheric nitrogen into the soil. Nitrogen is also added in the form of either natural fertilizers like farmyard manure or manufactured ones.

Nitrates can fertilise water plants as well and if allowed to seep into lakes or rivers, these may become over-enriched and choked with aquatic vegetation. The quickest plant organisms to respond to eutrophic conditions are tiny algae. Being so small, these quickly multiply until they not only discolour the water but may even form a green or blue blanket over its surface, preventing light from reaching the plants below. This rooted vegetation then gradually begins to rot and as it does so, uses up valuable oxygen and releases further nitrogen, thus setting up a vicious and potentially lethal circle, especially after long spells of hot weather. Sometimes surface concentrations of blue-green algae become so dense that they actually poison the water.

It is extremely difficult to isolate the eutrophying effects of excessive artificial fertilisation from the consequences of the release of nitrogen during general land usage. There are large natural reserves of nitrogen in the soil which can be broken down into soluble forms by bacterial activity during ploughing, harrowing and other cultivation. Some of this natural nitrogen may then be leached out by rainfall, especially from land left bare during winter, before spring corn is planted. Other crops like winter wheat are sown late in the year, giving the earth only the sparsest cover until spring, while turnips, beet and potatoes are harvested in autumn, also leaving the soil particularly vulnerable to early winter rain. Even with good plant cover, winter growth is minimal; so therefore is nitrate consumption, leaving more for release into drainage systems.

Adding nitrogen, whether as organic or artificial fertiliser, may certainly result in more escaping from the soil in the end, especially after particularly dry conditions when growing crops have failed to use up all their extra nutrition; however, research so far indicates that the actual cultivation of land rather than what is spread over it appears more likely to cause the eutrophication of rivers and lakes. If properly applied, fertilisers may be largely absolved from blame for damage to the aquatic environment. Similarly, pesticides sprayed in correct quantities and calm conditions which confine them to their proper place should not harm nearby land or water. It is only misapplications of fertilisers or pesticides that so often damage plants and animals both above and below the water's surface.

Insecticides, herbicides and fungicides must be poisonous in order to kill the insect, weed or fungus that they target. Fortunately, controls over their production are now much tighter and the chances of chemicals with such lethally far-reaching effects as DDT being cleared for general sale are greatly reduced. Even normal applications of DDT had cumulative and deadly consequences right through the animal food chain and from which fish were not exempted. Now pesticides are more selective and the dangers of incidental harm to other species are far less. They also break down much faster so reducing the chances of damage from unresearched after-effects. Farmers are called upon to produce food for those who cannot do so themselves and unless they receive incentives to stop boosting yields by applying fertilisers or pesticides to their crops, cannot possibly be expected to spare the environment at the risk of their own financial ruin. Certainly, heavy rainstorms can leach dangerous quantities of pesticides from the soil after even the most controlled applications, and sudden gusts of wind can always disperse chemicals where they were not meant to go. But where dangerous chemicals are in use it is accidents or abuses that really cause harm and not normal, carefully controlled applications in the course of considerate farming.

Never are the consequences of accidental agricultural discharge more deadly than when silage effluent is allowed to drain into a river. A fodder crop made from green grass through fermentation, silage produces an organic liquor of almost incredible potential for de-oxygenating any water it contaminates. The liquor is quite harmless when fed to animals together with the silage from which it derives but is extremely corrosive, and because containers are eroded or otherwise inadequate, its accidental discharge accounts for more agricultural pollution than any other farming practice. One litre of silage effluent can completely deoxygenate nearly 9,000 litres of well-aerated water, making it more than 200 times more powerful a deoxygenator than raw domestic sewage. Every year brings reports that entire fish populations in long stretches of river have been completely wiped out through the negligence of riparian farmers, and while dead fish are the most conspicuous consequence of drastic deoxygenation, invertebrates and other small aquatic animals are even more at risk.

Slurry is another agricultural by-product which — though less so than silage — is a horrifyingly effective deoxygenator if it leaks into fresh water. Basically livestock excrement, slurry is kept in tanks before being spread on the land in the same way as ordinary farmyard manure. When badly stored, it can seep into adjoining watercourses with catastrophic consequences and if there is rain soon after spreading, the extent of the run off can make slurry just as dangerous as silage.

Farming activities are probably responsible for well over half the fish kills in Britain and Ireland each year, although sometimes it is difficult to isolate the precise cause of any specific instance of eutrophication or deoxygenation. There is no family of fish more dependent on clear, well oxygenated water for their survival than the Salmonids. Brown trout are the most widespread of these in Europe and are therefore numerically most at risk from pollution and other environmental interferences.

Naturally, trout live in fast-flowing stretches of river which tend to be nearer the source (Chapter Seven) as well as in cool upland lakes fed by streams where they can spawn. The surrounding land is predominantly agricultural, which is one very real reason why the pollutants which kill trout so often derive from the land. By contrast, since the demise of the textile mills which depended on hydro-electric power, industrial activity in Britain is now largely confined to lowland areas where conditions in adjacent rivers are often unsuitable for trout. So not surprisingly, while the indirect results of acid emissions are alarmingly far-reaching, industrial pollutants are generally less of a direct threat to the trout's welfare.

One industrial activity which once scarred much of upland Britain was mining. Lead was extracted from the hills of Wales, northern England and southern Scotland until the end of the last century, badly affecting trout in the streams below, and even now lead and zinc may be leached from spoil heaps. Upland coal mining has largely ceased in England and Scotland but seriously polluted rivers before it did so, killing off runs of migratory fish in Dumfriesshire's river Nith — now restored to one of the best lowland fishing rivers in Scotland. Gravel is often easily excavated from the bed of a river whose strong current has exposed the small stones. Silt stirred up by its extraction, as well as during mining and quarrying, can ruin spawning redds and even choke young fish.

Industrial processing and manufacturing plants are usually sited in lower-lying areas. There, more at risk are different species of coarse fish which are relatively tolerant of polluted waters and therefore a less reliable barometer of a river's health. Yet sea trout must still run the gauntlet of the lower reaches of their natal stream as they swim out to sea or back to spawn, and eventually stop migrating if these are too contaminated. Industrial activity effectively killed runs of migratory fish in the river Wear in County Durham, but now that the river is cleaner, sea trout come up in huge numbers when there is enough water. In the neighbouring Tyne, spectacular catches of salmon have followed the clean-up of the river mouth; even the Thames, where after 1833 none was caught for 150 years, may soon boast a run of salmon again if spawning facilities prove adequate and the fish can negotiate the weirs and locks on their way up.

Effluent from such industrial activities as chemical production, textile manufacture, brewing and food processing still continues to contaminate fresh water. Often water becomes tainted in the course of cleaning or cooling plant and machinery, and the discharge of improperly treated waste can also contaminate rivers. Pollution controls are now far stricter than they were, and as the sources of direct industrial pollution are usually easy to track down, this has become a less serious problem. All the same, wherever dangerous substances are in industrial use there remains the possibility of enormous accidental damage which is sometimes sadly still fulfilled.

Domestic waste is just as potentially destructive to aquatic wildlife as industrial effluent and throughout the nineteenth century a lethal cocktail of the two poured untreated into Britain's river systems, which were then little more than open sewers. In London, Parliament met behind disinfected curtains while the River Aire at Leeds was described as

'. . . a reservoir of poison carefully kept for the purpose of breeding pestilence in the town . . . full of refuse from water closets, cesspools, privies, common drains, dung-hill drainings, infirmary refuse, waste from slaughter houses, chemical soap, gas, dye houses and manufacturers, coloured by blue and black dye, pig manure, old urine wash; there were dead animals, vegetable substances and occasionally a decomposed human body.'

Prompted more by fear for human health than by any real concern for the wellbeing of rivers, many of which were already ecologically dead, the Victorians belatedly began to treat their domestic waste. The Public Health Act of 1875 and Rivers Pollution Prevention Act of 1876 introduced inadequate statutory requirements to do so, which have since been tightened up by subsequent legislation. Now, sewerage systems theoretically exist to treat all human effluent but still sometimes combine with surface drains that channel water off streets and roads. During bad floods the combination often adds up to more than the system can cope with, causing untreated sewage to empty straight into rivers. Normally, sewage treatment works should, after a series of sedimentation processes, reduce the raw material to a combination of an innoxious liquid which can be safely discharged into fresh water, and a sludge which is equally harmless when spread on the land. Nearly all antiquated and inadequate sewerage works have been upgraded so that their effluent conforms to the higher standards of purity now demanded by both legislators and conservationists. Most domestic detergents are also broken down by sewage treatment works, so if these function as they should, effluent is unlikely to be a danger to aquatic wildlife. Despite this, there remains the possibility of accidental discharges of untreated sewage or of poisons entering a system unable to treat them. Furthermore, large urban centres impose such pressures on treatment works that effluent often accounts for over half the volume of the river into which it discharges, particularly in summer when natural flow is much reduced. Then the dangers of deoxygenation are almost inescapable if the processing plant is anything but wholly efficient.

While specific poisons act in many different ways to impair the proper functioning of organs in a fish's body, deoxygenation is much the most common biological consequence of severe pollution. Bacteria immediately start to decompose organic effluent entering the river, using up dissolved oxygen as they do so. Aeration may give some oxygen to water near the surface, but below, the river bed becomes blackened, and foul-smelling methane and hydrogen sulphide bubble up from the mud. In these conditions only bacteria and other microbes can survive, in addition to rat-tailed maggots; these are the larvae of bee-like hover flies (*Eristalis* spp.) and breathe atmospheric air through respiratory tubes pushed up through the surface, quite independently of any oxygen supply in the water.

Further downstream from the source of pollution, organic matter is more decomposed, there are less bacteria and even small amounts of dissolved oxygen in the water. More animals can tolerate such conditions and most, like bloodworms which are chironomid larvae coloured red by their haemoglobin, are specifically adapted for survival in them. Such creatures exploit this ability to the full and where they occur, are usually abundant. Alder and caddis fly larvae are also common, preying on the chironomids, and lower down the river are water slaters, snails and blackfly larvae. Roach and sticklebacks might survive here too. Often unpleasantly conspicuous below established sewage outflows are the grey fungus-like bacteria, Sphaerotilus; these cling to stones in round colonies the size of golf balls and despite their rather insalubrious look, benefit the water by breaking down organic matter.

Low water aggravates the effects of pollution in streams and rivers, concentrating pollutants in water which may already be short of oxygen because of the warmer temperatures that usually accompany reduced flow. Droughts often happen naturally, but low water levels are now an almost permanent consequence of upland drainage or of the excessive water abstraction, which is currently one of the greatest threats to the wellbeing of fresh waters in Europe. Even without dramatic rises in human populations, which in many developed countries have remained fairly static or are even declining, demand for water for industrial and domestic use continues to grow, quite unmatched by any increased awareness of its scarcity. Summer shortages sometimes force regional authorities to limit consumption by fitting meters, banning the use of hose pipes or by other temporary expedients. Still, the need for self-imposed limitations on usage seems beyond the understanding of most Europeans and so abstraction continues, flows diminish, water tables drop and streams dry up.

Abstraction of water is nothing new, but over the last 200 years demand for industrial, agricultural and domestic use has grown to such an extent that throughout much of Britain it threatens soon to exceed supply. Whether hot rainless summers prove to be a temporary diversion from the climatic norm or the lasting results of long-term changes in the earth's temperature, remains to be seen, but if the latter is the case the problem can only get worse. Even now, much London water has been several times through the treatment plants which, even if it tastes dreadful, at least speaks for their effectiveness.

When industry first began to dip into the country's aquatic resources, abstraction had no serious effect on water levels. Slowly, urban development began to sprawl out around industrial centres compounding demand for water and now, especially in summer, river levels fall dangerously low. As they do, trout are discouraged from migrating, not only by pollution but also by the reduced flows that make their upstream journey so much harder. For resident fish there is a whole complex of other dangers. When water temperatures rise, oxygen content falls, often to near lethal levels, and less water space inevitably results in overcrowding, stranded aquatic plants and depleted food supplies. If droughts last through to autumn, there may not be enough water to cover spawning redds and populations of all but the smallest species of fish will gradually decline. In extreme cases, streams dry up completely and in southern England there is well-founded concern that abstraction is plundering subterranean aquifers so seriously that the pathetic summer trickles, which run shamefully down the middle of many river beds, may have become all too permanent reminders of human profligacy.

To compensate for the reduced flow caused by excessive demands on a river's resources, its headwaters may be dammed to create a reservoir. Sometimes water is piped away from the reservoir to an area where the river's natural course could not otherwise deliver it. More often, reservoirs collect surplus water in times of plenty for release into the river in periods of drought. Intermittent discharges avert dangerously low water levels which can so seriously damage all river life, but while impounding water behind a dam fulfils certain human needs, it also creates environmental problems in the process.

Dam building cannot help but cause silting in the river below which is often serious but usually only temporary. Once the work is completed and the reservoir begins to fill, spawning grounds may be flooded as eventually what once was a stream becomes submerged by a lake. Downstream of the dam fish cannot reach redds above, although sometimes salmon and migratory trout are helped up by fish ladders. In hydro-electric schemes young fish risk being killed as they are swept through the turbines, but the mortality rate is surprisingly low and seldom justifies the cumbersome process of trapping and transporting them below the dam in trucks.

As reservoirs fill up trout usually grow unnaturally well on the rich diet of terrestrial creatures which emerge from the newly-flooded land. Gradually this bounty falls off and fish revert to more normal feeding on aquatic invertebrates which gradually colonise the new water. Acidic land, like much of northern Britain, harbours fewer worms and other small terrestrial animals. Once flooded, it also supports less aquatic vegetation than lowland reservoirs with more alkaline underlying soil which is also being continually enriched from adjacent arable farms.

The effect on the downstream fish fauna of reservoirs constructed to stabilise water flow is generally favourable. The flash floods caused by upland drainage are absorbed and summer droughts levelled off by regular releases of extra water; these are sometimes tantamount to small spates and on rivers like the Helmsdale and Beauly in Scotland are often enough to encourage salmon and sea trout up the river. Silt collects in the reservoir leaving the water that is released cleaner and clearer. For fishermen, this, like the generally more predictable flow, is a bonus; all the same, a rising river after days of cloudless skies can be confusingly disconcerting and water from a reservoir is often much cooler than it would otherwise be.

Aside from their primary function, almost all man-made expanses of water offer potential recreational opportunities not only for fishermen, but also for naturalists and water sports enthusiasts. Provided these often competing interests can be effectively balanced, reservoirs can be of great social benefit to their environs, to an extent that usually far outweighs their potential for ecological damage.

Perhaps the most direct and dramatic assault on fish and their element comes from illegal fishing. Tickling small trout in highland burns is probably a less effective way of catching fish than a hook and worm, although it may be just as much fun. Wholesale poisoning with cyanide compounds that coat fish's gills, or with other poisons that deoxygenate the water, is abhorrent, wasteful and liable to kill not only fish but all other underwater life as well. Between these two extremes are a range of other unlawful fishing activities designed to extract fish from the water, either to be eaten or sold by their poachers. Netting or spearing spawning sea trout on their redds is easy and particularly harmful in its destruction of the next unborn generation. Illegal fishing for brown trout is usually confined to occasional, harmless acts of poaching with no commercial aim in sight. Even so, they may sometimes be the unwitting victims of large-scale poisoning aimed at salmon or sea trout, whose market value encourages their illegal pursuit with considerable risk and sophistication.

Their value also makes sea trout well worth the legitimate attentions of commercial fishermen at sea. Stake nets, fixed between high and low water marks, are less used than they were but are highly effective in trapping shoals migrating close to the shore. Seine (drift) nets are used in a sweeping manner; one end remains secured to land while the rest is gradually fed out, catching up fish in the semicircle created along a length of shore, before the net is pulled out of the water. The mesh size of seine nets is usually regulated to allow small fish to escape, as it is with the long and lethal monofilament drift nets which catch fish by their gills. These drift nets are banned round much of Britain, and as the mesh is designed to catch salmon, they are possibly not as harmful to sea trout, especially the smaller, west coast fish.

That a lake or river supports a thriving stock of brown trout is the surest indication of the water's wellbeing. Only salmon and charr require purer, better oxygenated water and no-one is more concerned to ensure that trout continue to flourish in the widest possible range of habitat than those who want to catch them. If only for selfish reasons, people who fish are deeply conscious of the health of Britain's fresh waters and ring the loudest bells when these are threatened by pollution, poaching, de-oxygenation or other environmental intrusions.

The efficiency of this piscatorial early-warning system was well illustrated during the catastrophic yet localised collapses in sea trout numbers, first reported in the late 1980s although they actually began much earlier. Whether these resulted from over-fishing or food shortages at sea, seal or sea lice attacks, disease, the unforeseen consequences of estuarine salmon farming, or a combination of these factors, or even from some other unidentified cause, may never be agreed. Yet if sea trout were less highly prized as game fish, their disappearance would have passed unnoticed much longer, before alarms sounded. By then the cause of their plight could have affected not only sea trout but also other species of fish and animals within the great jigsaw of marine life. As it was, the interests of fishermen and fishery owners eventually prompted detailed research into the reasons for the sea trout's decline. So too when other environmental disasters have struck fishermen have repeatedly acted as the most effective pressure group to safeguard the network of still and running waters that gives life to a country and everything within it.

But for all their role as unofficial fresh water guardians the legitimate activities of fishermen in pursuit of their prey are far from unimpeachable. Their impact on plant and animal life round the water's edge is often harmful, and although their concern for the general health of the water is unquestioned, the actual act of removing fish from it is open to much, often justifiable, criticism. The ethics of fishing are tortuously complex and unavoidably subjective; logical criticism of fishing is equally so but there remains much concerted censure of many of its aspects.

That coarse fishing methods may prove more environmentally damaging than the more mobile practices of most trout fishermen is no moral condemnation, just a simple fact. Coarse fishing waters tend to support more fish than trout rivers and lakes, and the tradition of returning coarse fish to the water at the end of the day ensures that many of these are there to be caught again. This in itself means that rivers, canals or ponds can sustain far greater coarse fishing pressure and are therefore much more disturbed than trout waters whose fewer fish are gradually removed.

The hardest charges for coarse fishermen to answer are probably those related to litter generally and lead weights in particular. The poisoning of swans and other waterfowl which swallowed discarded lead weights to help grind up food in their gizzards, caused a national outcry before a combination of half-hearted legislation and voluntary restraint caused fishermen to abandon lead in favour of zinc alloy. Other forms of fishing-related litter, especially nylon line, bare hooks, flies, tins, polythene bags and camping rubbish are not peculiar to any one group of fishermen. Nevertheless, the static habits of coarse fishermen and their use of disposable bait containers often cause more localised concentrations of litter round specific fishing points, which may also attract scavengers that will then turn their attentions to nesting birds.

At least three times more people fish for coarse fish than for trout and salmon and, if only because of their numerical superiority, coarse fishermen are more likely to destroy or disturb bankside vegetation. Also, the very nature of coarse fishing requires good access to the water, often so that many anglers can fish close together. Well-trodden paths link specific fishing pegs creating a web of trampled plants and shrubs. However, coarse fishermen only start to go about their business on 16 June when most plants are growing strongly and are much less susceptible to serious damage than earlier in the year. Trout fishermen move up and down the banks far more, causing less severe but more widespread damage as they do so. Successful trout fishing is often dependent upon good bankside plant cover, but casting a fly needs empty space which may need creating. Also, fly fishermen often wade far into the water to increase their casting range crushing or even uprooting moss and other submerged plants as well as kicking up sediment from the bed.

Some disturbance to bird and animal life is quite unavoidable on any visit to the water's edge for whatever purpose. Fishermen spend more time there than any other group of people, so it is difficult to avoid allegations that wildlife suffers from their repeated intrusions into its habitat. Yet for many animals, disturbances by potential predators, or large animals with no malevolent intentions but which look threatening enough to provoke some form of evasive action, are daily, even hourly, events. When disturbed, birds or animals either flee away from the scene or simply take cover in the hope of avoiding detection. Unless repeated too often, most living creatures seem able to tolerate persistent interruptions to their normal daily life without suffering unduly, although if interference is so frequent as to prejudice successful feeding they may starve if they cannot move elsewhere. Except when nesting or moulting, birds can usually fly off to a less disturbed area to rest and feed. Waterfowl appear to swim away from local disturbances with little concern, but the shallow edges of still waters — where fishermen also congregate — provide them with their best feeding areas and they may be more agitated than they look. Waders and wagtails pecking along the shoreline seem quite unperturbed by having to flutter on a few yards and immediately resume feeding when they land. Still, there is clear evidence that bird populations are higher in areas from which fishermen and other humans are specifically excluded, showing that while birds can usually tolerate human presence they much prefer life without it.

Disturbance to breeding birds is potentially much more serious, especially around waters fringed with thick emergent or bankside vegetation. Waterfowl, waders and warblers, kingfishers, dippers, wagtails and many more nest along the edges of lakes and rivers, and fishermen's repeated encroachments into breeding territories can pressurise nesting birds to the point of desertion. It has even been suggested that the start of the coarse fishing season should be delayed for a month to allow fledglings time to leave their nests. A far wider variety of birds nest around eutrophic lowland waters more suited to coarse fish, where there is thick riparian vegetation and prolific invertebrate life, than along the shores of windswept highland lochs. However, the activities of fly fishermen — and the dogs that often accompany them — are in some cases even more damaging. Their season starts much earlier in the year and fishing pressure on southern chalk streams is now so intense that some beats are fished over several times each day to the obvious detriment of nesting birds. On highland loch shores the breeding privacies of red-throated divers *(Gavia stellata)*, Slavonian grebes *(Podiceps auritus)* or greenshanks *(Tringa nebularia)* may seldom be invaded, but often birds that breed far from human habitation do so precisely because they are more sensitive and easily disturbed than those species better habituated to mankind.

Mammals are less mobile than birds and more prone to avoid detection by taking refuge in thick vegetation and holes or under roots in the banks. Otters have been much researched and there is no doubt that fishing indirectly contributed to their decline towards the end of the nineteenth century. This was mostly the result of deliberately killing otters in the belief that fish numbers would then increase. During the twentieth century, their trapping and hunting has gradually stopped and the dramatic crash in the otter population in the late 1950s is now firmly attributed to poisoning and pollution. Disturbance by visiting fishermen seems to have little effect on numbers unless it repeatedly unsettles females with cubs. Otters are shy, secretive animals but seem prepared and able to coexist with humans by avoiding contact rather than escaping to a less disturbed area. They have large territories with usually several different holts in each. Dogs cause a very different reaction, but there is no reason why fishermen and otters cannot compete openly and peacefully for their common prey.

Like otters, when disturbed, water shrews and water voles take refuge in banks or beneath water plants and can tolerate all but the most repeated interference with their normal lives. Amphibians such as newts, frogs and toads, although needing to breathe through their lungs as adults, spend much of their time under water, and pollution is a far greater threat to their welfare than occasional bankside interruptions.

Sadly it must be true that at the present time, the main problem with fishermen as a group is simply that there are too many of them. Inevitably they cause involuntary disturbance to the environment in pursuit of their quarry. Such disturbance is sometimes excessive and, with greater care and a better understanding of the web of life above and below the water's surface, could be greatly reduced.

Deliberately tampering with aquatic flora and fauna in an attempt to improve fishing is often more damaging than many of the fisherman's other environmental disruptions. Now, with fewer river keepers and bailiffs, efforts to influence the composition of the fish community and enhance trout stocks by controlling predators and competitors, have surrendered to a blind reliance on regular stocking with keepable trout. Nonetheless, the piscine populations of many rivers would be very different than they presently are if mankind had not unnaturally manipulated them for his own ends. Pike are the enemy of all fisheries, and the natural balance between them and their prey would usually accommodate far more pike than survive after man's efforts to remove them. The perfect-looking waters of southern English chalk streams are by nature fit for large numbers of coarse fish, rather than the ponderous, well-fed trout that owe their untroubled existence to the artificial control of their competitors. The reputation of many lowland reservoirs as first class trout fisheries is largely maintained at the expense of native roach populations, and in some lakes and reservoirs perch are netted or trapped in the belief that they compete seriously with brown trout for food.

Man is forever attempting to alter the composition of fish populations in order to improve trout fishing, but generally the consequences are only localised. Far more significant have been the effects of deliberately importing or translocating new species, in the hope of improving sport, to areas where the forces of Nature had yet to disperse them. Brown trout already occurred naturally in nearly all British waters suitable for them. They also prefer much lower temperatures than most other European fish. Thus their introduction has seldom caused lasting damage to existing fish stocks in the way that the spread of other alien species has.

Introductions of different coarse fish have more than made up for the dearth of indigenous species in Ireland. Grayling, tench, bream and chub were probably all translocated to Scotland during the last century when enthusiasm in Britain for propagating local and exotic species almost matched that of the acclimatisation societies in Australia and New Zealand. Predatory zander have been introduced into England with tragic consequences for smaller species of native fish. Ruffe *(Gymnocephalus cernuus)* have recently been introduced into Loch Lomond where they prey upon the eggs of the rare powan (or schelly — *Coregonus lavaretus)* which also live there. The only pollan *(Coregonus autumnalis)* in western Europe occur in a few Irish loughs and may have suffered unwanted competition from the introduction of roach into Lough Neagh.

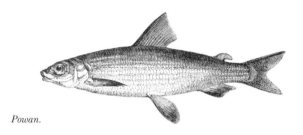

*Powan.*

The spread of brown trout overseas undoubtedly harmed some indigenous fish (Chapter Ten). However, the only introductions to have any marked effect on Britain's native brown trout stocks are of other trout, with which established populations must compete for food and space. Newly-arrived brown or rainbow trout are often larger and, having been artificially selected over many generations, their effect on the gene pool of the resident fish may be to dissipate the evolutionary benefits built up over thousands of years (Chapter Nine). Salmon farms also produce huge numbers of parr for restocking depleted rivers. These interlopers may have equally undesirable consequences for remaining local stocks, as may escapees from salmon-rearing cages in the sea.

Fish farms themselves bring problems of pollution in the course of rearing trout for stocking or eating. Nitrogenous waste, phosphorus and other suspended solids mixed with disinfectants and chemicals used for disease control discharge, usually untreated, straight from farms to rivers. Settling tanks do little more than hold back solid waste and even if mature fish are not harmed by this gruesome mixture, other aquatic animals may be.

Predator control is perhaps the aspect of fishery management which is potentially the most damaging to the fisherman's cause. Bird watching is even more popular than fishing and continues to attract new enthusiasts who are often blindly critical of any other activity which threatens the subjects of their own interest. The limelight is already focused on gamekeepers and the control of avian predators in the cause of better shooting is a highly sensitive issue. Not far removed from this is the question of controlling birds and, to a lesser extent, mammals that prey upon game fish.

The disappearance of nesting ospreys and white-tailed sea eagles *(Haliaeetus albicilla)* and the decline in otter numbers during the last century, give some idea of the action Victorian landowners were prepared to take to improve their fishing. Then, the sporting lobby carried more weight and made more noise than the small band of amateur naturalists, many of whom were anyway quite prepared to shoot large numbers of any species, rare or not, on the pretext of scientific study. Now, with the tables turned, field sports in general and hunting and shooting in particular are much in an increasingly disapproving public eye.

Less damaging predators like kingfishers, grebes and dippers flourish through the preservation of fish stocks to which they are relatively insignificant threats, and are therefore freely tolerated by fishery managers. But goosanders, red-breasted mergansers and cormorants may each eat up to half a kilogram of fish in a day, and grey herons can decimate the trout in fish farms or small shallow streams. Few fisheries can stand such sustained predation of expensive fish stocks but shooting, while not necessarily illegal, is a conspicuous and often ineffective means of control, likely to attract bad publicity for all fishermen. Discouraging birds from breeding or roosting near the water's edge is more likely to reduce their numbers and is also far less objectionable.

For all their potential for environmental damage, it remains essentially true that fishermen only have trout to catch if the aquatic ecosystem that supports those trout is in good health. So while mankind may attempt to maintain an unnatural balance, for instance by controlling predators in an effort to increase natural stocks of their prey, it is nevertheless a balance of a kind. And its maintenance depends upon nurturing the complex web of interdependent relationships of which the underwater community is composed.

Many attempts at fishery improvement involve changing the physical habitat. Because these are designed to help fish they usually benefit other underwater life, often by encouraging healthy vegetation which in turn supports more invertebrates. Sometimes plants need controlling but this is usually to prevent night-time oxygen levels falling dangerously low or to ease the flow of water. The importance of healthy aquatic vegetation is not lost on fishermen and if this is best nurtured by cutting rather than planting, the intention still remains the same — to provide the best shelter and most food for the maximum number of trout.

Building stone buttresses (groynes) or a succession of small dams or weirs can form quieter pools which help plant life take root and create easier lies for all fish. Banks are shored up by planting riparian vegetation or using stakes and boards to contain them; in either case this restricts further erosion and reduces the concentration of silt in the water. Fish passes help migratory trout up past man-made obstructions or previously impassable waterfalls, where they then confer the benefit of their presence not only on fishermen but also on other predators that depend upon fish for their food.

The most dramatic way of modifying the environment is to create new still waters on what was once dry land. The demand for fishing usually makes damming old gravel pits and other excavations well worth the expense. As well as creating new fisheries, these become valuable refuges for wildlife, for water and its immediate surroundings support a far greater mass and diversity of plants and animals than any equivalent area of dry land.

Fishermen's influences on the aquatic environment are complex and conflicting. Removing any more than minimal numbers of fish inevitably modifies the whole aquatic community which nurtured them. To counter this, more fish can be added, or the natural balance may be altered in other ways, perhaps either by killing predators or tampering with the habitat in the hope that it will then support more fish. Yet, it cannot be denied that the fisherman's main object is to catch fish, whether or not these are then put back where they came from. This is his greatest interference with Nature, and it is this act — the very *raison d'etre* of fishing — that is hardest to justify, most open to criticism and most disturbing to underwater life.

A discussion of the ethics of fishing is beyond the scope of this book. Every fisherman must live with his conscience and none but the most insensitive is able to fish in the face of its dictates. Whatever individual set of values each fisherman adopts will guide his actions in pursuit of trout. However, allegations of cruelty are so often directed at the act of catching fish that they cannot be ignored in any review of man's impressions on the environment in the course of his sport.

Inherent in any act of cruelty is an element of pitilessness or indifference, overlaid on a voluntary act of inflicting unnecessary pain or suffering. Almost certainly fish feel pain when hooked, and continue to do so until they are either killed or released. Yet one particularly effective way of catching fish is with rod and line. Man's dentition testifies to Nature's intentions for an omnivorous diet. Killing fish or other animals to eat, cannot of itself therefore be considered cruel — every carnivorous creature must do so to stay alive. That enjoyment may be gained in the course of fishing, whether from the natural surroundings or the actual act of casting a fly or bait into the water, is no reason to condemn the practice, nor is the use of hook, line and rod in the process. So much seems simple. But the ice to support these piscatorial arguments becomes distinctly thinner where most coarse fishing is concerned and also in the increasingly popular 'catch and release' policies which many trout fisheries are being forced to adopt. In both cases fish are caught only to be returned to the water, either immediately or at the end of a day spent in the confines of a keep net.

Killing fish that are never to be eaten is usually indefensible but once caught, actually killing fish to eat is not cruel. It may seem perverse to suggest that catching fish with the intention simply of returning them to the water is crueller than catching them to kill — certainly if fish could indicate a preference they would disagree, but so too would every potential meal for every potential predator. Yet catching fish only to release them is an act devoid of concern for the plight of the fish upon which unnecessary pain is voluntarily inflicted and is therefore, by most accepted definitions, cruel. It is quite simply an act of gaining pleasure at the expense of another creature's suffering and this must be cruel. Even so, the capture and release may be accomplished quickly and the use of barbless hooks may lessen actual pain, even if not reducing the trauma of the whole event. If fish are quickly brought to the net and the greatest care taken to ensure that when returned to the water they suffer the minimum of injury in the process, cruelty would be minimised and man's pleasure can only be enhanced through his effort to minimise the lesser creature's pain.

Perhaps it may even be argued that if fish are returned unharmed to their element, the simple pleasure gained by human beings at one end of the line justifies the pain and trauma they inflict on the creature at the other. If measured on some strange gauge able to calibrate one creature's pain against another's pleasure, perhaps the ends would be found to justify the means. Yet if pleasure is to be justified at the expense of even limited suffering inflicted on a fellow creature it is a justification with frightening implications.

Few fishermen have deliberately opted to fish for trout or salmon on the grounds that these fish can be kept and eaten while other species are less palatable, and generally, participation in what may be the least cruel form of fishing owes nothing to any sense of morality. Instead, fishermen probably continue to catch those species common in the lakes or rivers where they learned to fish or in which some inner motivation provokes a particular interest. Yet trout fishermen cannot afford complacency just because their branch of fishing may better escape allegations of cruelty, and it is hard to argue in support of certain aspects of their sport. The use of light tackle which can only prolong the fish's struggles is one practice which all thinking fishermen should abominate unless stronger, thicker line would be so visible as to put off the fish. Stocking trout simply to catch and kill them, whether they are put in as small fingerlings or as takeable fish, also raises a whole tangle of other moral questions which have obvious parallels in the rearing of game birds to shoot. The effective preservation of many stocks of trout requires the destruction of piscine or avian predators or the removal of unwanted fish, all of which may involve acts of cruelty.

So, in his pursuit of trout, man not only intrudes upon the lives of the plants, birds and animals along the edge or on the surface of the water but also disrupts the lives of the fish that live in it. Some of these fish will be removed from the water permanently and others returned, either because they are too small, or to preserve them so that other fishermen may repeat the act. Every time man catches a fish he inflicts pain but such infliction need not be cruel. Animals have nerves so they can feel pain which acts as a warning of disorder. For all of them, life contains peaks of tranquillity and satisfaction and troughs of pain and distress on either side of a calm of normal, everyday existence. In the natural world, pain is frequently the forerunner of death, as it may be in the act of catching a fish. If it is not, returning fish to the water after causing them pain is something which the conscience of most fishermen can condone, however contorted, illogical or self-deceiving the reasoning by which they reach this decision — otherwise they would not fish.

Only man has the ability to understand and anticipate pain, its causes and effects. This faculty for comprehension is a privilege and there is no privilege without responsibility and duty. It is his ability to comprehend and to reason that sets man apart from all other creatures and, by so doing, entrusts him with the responsibility for their destiny and the duty to care for his and their environment. This trust is a heavy burden to bear but its bearing is the price of superiority and it must be shouldered by mankind with compassion for his fellow creatures and consideration for his descendants.

## CONVERSION TABLE

*Weight*

| | | |
|---|---|---|
| 28.4g | = | 1oz |
| 454g | = | 1lb |
| 1kg (1000g) | = | 2.2lb (35.27oz) |

*Length*

| | | |
|---|---|---|
| 1cm | = | 0.39 inch |
| 25.4mm (2.54cm) | = | 1 inch |
| 30.48cm | = | 1 foot |
| 0.914m | = | 1 yard |
| 1 metre | = | 39.37 inches |

*Temperature*

To convert centigrade (°C) to Farenheit (°F) use the formula:

$$°F = \left(°C \times \frac{9}{5}\right) + 32$$

*Pressure*

| | | |
|---|---|---|
| 1kg p.s.cm | = | 14.22lbs p.s.i. |

# Bibliography

Set out below, after a general list of useful reference material, are details of selected books, articles and papers which are particularly relevant to the contents of each chapter. Inevitably, many of these sources were drawn upon in the course of writing more than one chapter, but in most cases their titles adequately indicate their contents. The inclusion of any particular work in this bibliography serves not only to acknowledge the help I have received from other people's earlier efforts in writing this book or preparing its illustrations, but also to direct the researches of those who may wish for more detailed information on any particular aspect of the trout's natural history.

## GENERAL

ADE, R. (1989) The Trout and Salmon Handbook: a guide to the wild fish — Christopher Helm, London.

BERNERS, Dame J. (1496) Treetyse of Fysshynge wyth an Angle.

ELLIOTT, J.M., editor (1989) Wild Brown Trout: The scientific basis for their conservation and management — *Freshwater Biology* Vol.21, No.1 — Blackwell Scientific Publications, Oxford.

FROST, W.E. and BROWN, M.E. (1967) The Trout — Collins, London.

JONES, J.W. (1959) The Salmon — Collins, London.

LONSDALE LIBRARY. Vol.2. Trout Fishing from All Angles — Vol.24. River Management — Vol. 34. Anglers' Fishes and their Natural History — Seely Service & Co. London.

MAITLAND, P.S. and CAMPBELL, R.N. (1992) Freshwater Fishes of the British Isles — Harper Collins, London.

MUUS, B.J. (1967) Freshwater Fish of Britain and Europe — Collins, London.

NORMAN, J.R. and GREENWOOD, P.H. (1963) A History of Fishes, second edition — Ernest Benn Limited, London.

PHILLIPS, R. and RIX, M. (1985) Freshwater Fish of Britain, Ireland and Europe — Pan Books, London.

PINCHER, C. (1947) A Study of Fishes — Herbert Jenkins Limited, London.

PRATT, M.M. (1975) Better Angling with Simple Science — Fishing News Books, Surrey.

REGAN, C.T. (1911) The Freshwater Fishes of the British Isles — Methuen, London.

SEDGWICK, S.D. (1982) The Salmon Handbook — Andre Deutsch, London.

SUTTERBY, R. and GREENHALGH, M. (1989) The Wild Trout: the natural history of an endangered fish — George Philip, London.

WALTON, IZAAK (1653) The Compleat Angler.

WILLERS, W.B. (1981) Trout Biology — University of Wisconsin Press, Wisconsin.

CHAPTER 1 — WHAT, WHERE AND WHY?

CACUTT, L. (1979) British Freshwater Fishes: the story of their evolution — Croom Helm, London.
DARWIN, C. (1859) The Origin of Species — John Murray, London.
DAY, F. (1887) British and Irish Salmonidae — Williams and Norgate, London.
GUNTHER, A. (1866) Catalogue of Fishes in the British Museum — Printed by order of the Trustees.
MAXWELL, Sir H. (1904) British Freshwater Fishes — Hutchinson & Co. London.
SMITH, G.R. and STEARLEY, R.F. (1989) The Classification and Scientific Names of Rainbow and Cutthroat Trout — *Fisheries*, Vol. 14, No. 1.
YARRELL, W. (1836) A History of British Fishes — John Van Voorst, London.

CHAPTER 2 — FORM AND PHYSIOLOGY

CLARK, B. and GODDARD, J. (1980) The Trout and the Fly — Nick Lyons Books, New York.
MAITLAND, P.S. (1972) Key to the Freshwater Fishes of the British Isles — Freshwater Biological Association, Ambleside.
RONALDS, A. (1836) The Fly Fisher's Entomology — Longman, Rees, Orme, Brown, Green and Longman, London.
WHITEHEAD, P. (1977) How Fishes Live — Galley Press, Leicester.

CHAPTER 3 — BREEDING AND HEREDITY

CRISP, D.T. (1990) Water temperature in a stream gravel bed and implications for Salmonid incubation — *Freshwater Biology*, Vol. 23.
CRISP, D.T., MANN, R.N.K. and McCORMACK, J.C. (1975) The populations of fish in the river Tees system on the Moor House National Nature Reserve, Westmorland — *Journal of Fish Biology*, Vol. 7.
FERGUSON, A. (1985) Lough Melvin: a unique fish community — Royal Dublin Society, Ireland.
JONES, J.W. and BALL, J.N. (1954) The spawning behaviour of brown trout and salmon — *British Journal of Animal Behaviour*, Vol.2, No.3.
SMITH, M.H. and CHESSER, R.K. (1981) Rationale for conserving genetic variation of fish gene pools — *Ecological Bulletin of Stockholm*, Vol.34.
STEPHEN, A.B. and McANDREW, B.J. (1990) Distribution of genetic variation in brown trout in Scotland — *Aquaculture and Fisheries Management*, Vol. 21.

CHAPTER 4 — LIFE AND GROWTH

CAMPBELL, R.N. (1979) Ferox trout and charr in Scottish lochs — *Journal of Fish Biology*, Vol.14.
CAMPBELL, R.N. (1971) The growth of brown trout in northern Scottish lochs with special reference to the improvement of fisheries — *Journal of Fish Biology*, Vol.3.
CAMPBELL, R.N. (1961) The growth of brown trout in acid and alkaline waters — *Salmon and Trout Magazine*, Vol.161.
EDWARDS, R.W., DENSEM, J.W. and RUSSELL, P.A. (1979) An assessment of the

importance of temperature as a factor controlling the growth rate of brown trout in streams — *Journal of Animal Ecology*, Vol.48.

HORTON, P.A. (1961) The Bionomics of brown trout in a Dartmoor stream — *Journal of Animal Ecology*, Vol.30.

SOLOMON, D.J. and TEMPLETON R.G. (1976) Movements of brown trout in a chalk stream — *Journal of Fish Biology*, Vol.9.

SOUTHERN, R. (1932) The food and growth of brown trout — *Salmon and Trout Magazine*, Vols. 67,68 and 69.

SVALSTOG, D. (1991) A Note on maximum age of Brown Trout — *Journal of Fish Biology*, Vol.38.


## CHAPTER 5 — COMPETITION, PREDATION, DISEASE AND DEATH

MAITLAND, P.S. (1965) The feeding relationships of salmon, trout, minnows, stone loach and three-spined sticklebacks in the river Endrick, Scotland. — *Journal of Animal Ecology*, Vol.34.

MANN, R.K.H. and ORR, D.R.O. (1969) A preliminary study of the feeding relationships of fish in a hard-water and soft-water stream in southern England — *Journal of Fish Biology*, Vol.1.

SAWYER, F. (1952) Keeper of the Stream — A & C Black, London.


## CHAPTER 6 — FOOD AND FEEDING

GODDARD, J. (1988) Waterside Guide — Unwin Hyman.

HARRIS, J.R. (1952) An Angler's Entomology — Collins, London.

HILLS, J.W. (1934) River Keeper: The Life of W.J. Lunn — Geoffrey Bles, London.

HOLMES, P.F. (1960) The brown trout of Malham Tarn, Yorkshire — *Salmon and Trout Magazine*, Vol.159

KELLY-QUINN, M. and BRACKEN, J.J. (1990) Seasonal analysis of the diet and feeding dynamics of brown trout in a small nursery stream —*Aquaculture and Fisheries Management*, Vol.21.

KENNEDY, M. and FITZMAURICE P. (1971) Growth and food of brown trout — *Proceedings of the Royal Irish Academy*, Vol.71.

KIMMINS, D.E. (1972) A revised key to the adults of the British species of Ephemeroptera — Freshwater Biological Association, Ambleside.


## CHAPTER 7 — THE FRESHWATER ENVIRONMENT

BROWN, A.L. (1987) Freshwater Ecology — Heinemann Educational Books, London.

FITTER, R. and MANUEL, R. (1986) Field Guide to the Freshwater Life of Britain and North West Europe — Collins, London.

MACAN, T.T. and WORTHINGTON, E.B. (1951) Life in Lakes and Rivers — Collins, London.

PEART, L. (1956) Trout and Trout Waters — George Allen & Unwin, London.

PRICE, M. (1991) Water from the ground — *New Scientist*, 16 February.

SOLBE, J. (1988) Water Quality for Salmon and Trout — The Atlantic Salmon Trust, Pitlochry.

## CHAPTER 8 — THE URGE TO MIGRATE

BERG, O.K. and BERG, M. (1987) Migrations of sea trout from the Vardnes river in northern Norway — *Journal of Fish Biology*, Vol.31.

ELLIOTT, J.M. (1985) Growth, size, biomass and production for different life stages of migratory trout in a Lake District stream, 1966-83 — *Journal of Animal Ecology*, Vol.54

FAHY, E. (1985) Child of the Tides: a sea trout handbook — Glendale Press, Ireland.

FALKUS, H. (1962) Sea Trout Fishing — H.F. & G. Witherby, London.

LE CREN, E.D., editor (1984) The Biology of the Sea Trout — The Atlantic Salmon Trust, Pitlochry.

McDOWALL, R.M. (1988) Diadromy in Fishes: migration between freshwater and marine environments — Croom Helm, London.

PEMBERTON, R. (1976) Sea Trout in north Argyll sea lochs, population, distribution, movements and diet — *Journal of Fish Biology*, Vol.9.

SCOTT, D. (1964) The migratory trout in New Zealand — *Transactions of the Royal Society of New Zealand*, Vol.4, No.17.

SKAALA, O. and NAEVDAL, G. (1989) Genetic differentiation between freshwater resident and anadromous brown trout within watercourses —*Journal of Fish Biology*, Vol. 34.

## CHAPTER 9 — FARMING AND STOCKING

BUCKLAND, F.T. (1863) Fish Hatching — Tinsley Brothers, London.

CRESSWELL, R.C. (1981) Post-stocking movements and recapture of hatchery-reared trout released into flowing waters: a review — *Journal of Fish Biology*, Vol.18.

GREENHALGH, M. (1990) Angling and the cultivated trout — *Salmon, Trout and Sea-trout Magazine*, June

CROSS, T.F. (1989) Genetics and the Management of the Atlantic Salmon —The Atlantic Salmon Trust, Pitlochry.

PAWSON, M.G. (1989 & 1990) Stock management of put-and-take trout fisheries — *Trout News*, Nos. 9 & 10.

PAWSON, M.G. (1991) Comparison of the performance of brown trout and rainbow trout in a put-and-take fishery — *Aquaculture and Fisheries Management*, Vol.22.

SEDGWICK, S.D. (1985) Trout Farming Handbook, fourth edition — Fishing News Books, Surrey.

STEVENSON, J.P. (1987) Trout Farming Manual, second edition — Fishing News Books, Surrey.

TAYLOR, A.H. (1978) An analysis of trout fishing at Eye Brook, a eutrophic reservoir — *Journal of Animal Ecology*, Vol.47.

The Story of Howietoun — Institute of Aquaculture, Stirling.

CHAPTER 10 — BEYOND THEIR NATIVE RANGE

CLEMENTS, J. (1988) Salmon at the Antipodes — Eels pty. Australia.
COPLEY, H. (1940) Trout in Kenya Colony — *The East African Agricultural Journal.*
CRASS, B. (1986) Trout in South Africa — Macmillan, South Africa.
INGRAM, B.A. et.al. (1990) Threatened native freshwater fishes in Australia: some case histories — *Journal of Fish Biology*, Vol.37.
MACRIMMON, H.R. and MARSHALL, T.L. (1968) World distribution of brown trout — *Journal of the Fisheries Research Board of Canada*, Vol.25.
MACRIMMON, H.R. (1970) World distribution of brown trout: further observations — *Journal of the Fisheries Research Board of Canada*, Vol.27.
MACRIMMON, H.R. (1971) World distribution of rainbow trout — *Journal of the Fisheries Research Board of Canada*, Vol.28.
McDOWALL, R.M. (1990) When Galaxiid and Salmonid fishes meet: a family reunion in New Zealand — *Journal of Fish Biology*, Vol.37.
PAWSON, T. (1987) Flyfishing Around the World — Unwin Hyman, London.
RITCHIE, J. (1988) The Australian Trout — Victorian Fly-fisher's Association, Melbourne.
SKELTON, P.M. and DAVIES, M.T.T., editors (1986) Trout in South Africa — Ichthos newsletter.
STEWART, L. (1990) Why no Southern Hemisphere salmon? The gyre theory — *Salmon and Trout Magazine*, No. 213.
VAN SOMEREN, V.D. (1952) The Biology of trout in Kenya Colony — Government Printer, Nairobi.


CHAPTER 11 — THE HAND OF MAN

GRIBBIN, J. and KELLY, M. (1989) Winds of Change — Hodder & Stoughton, London.
MAITLAND, P.S. and TURNER, A.K. (1987) Angling and Wildlife in Fresh Waters — Institute of Terrestial Ecology.
MAITLAND, P.S. (1990) Threats to Britain's native salmon, trout and charr — *British Wildlife*, No.1.
MANN, R.H.K. (1988) Fish and fisheries of regulated rivers in the U.K. — *Regulated Rivers: Research and Management*, Vol.2.
MILLS, D., editor (1989) Tweed Towards 2000 — The Tweed Foundation.
NISBET, T.R. (1990) Forests and Surface Water Acidification — Forestry Commission bulletin 86, HMSO.
PAGE, R. (1987) The Fox and the Orchid — Quiller Press, London.
SAULL, M. (1990) Nitrates in soil and water — *New Scientist*, 15 September.
SCROPE, W. (1843) Days and Nights of Salmon Fishing in the Tweed — John Murray.

# Index